Do South Africans Exist?

Do South Africans Exist?

NATIONALISM, DEMOCRACY AND THE IDENTITY OF 'THE PEOPLE'

Ivor Chipkin

WITS UNIVERSITY PRESS

Wits University Press
1 Jan Smuts Avenue
Johannesburg
South Africa
www.witspress.co.za

Text © Ivor Chipkin, 2007
Cover artwork © William Kentridge, 'Casspirs Full of Love',
1988-1989, charcoal and pastel, Collection: Johannesburg Art Gallery
Citations © archives and institutes from which sourced, as indicated

First published 2007

978-1-86814-445-7 (Paperback)
978-1-77614-377-1 (Web PDF)
978-1-77614-378-8 (EPUB)
978-1-77614-379-5 (Mobi)

All rights reserved. No part of this publication may be reproduced, stored in a retrieval system, or transmitted in any form or by any means, electronic, mechanical, photocopying, recording or otherwise, without the express permission, in writing, of both the copyright holder and the publishers.

Cover design and layout by Hybridesign

To Ingrid, Eamonn and Liat

Table of Contents

Acknowledgements

This book began its life as a PhD thesis at the Ecole Normale Superieure. Phillipe Gervais-Lambony made my French adventure possible and I want to thank him for his faith and friendship during this time and since then. My gratitude also goes out to Marie-Anne and Isis. I think too of Afifah Barkallah and Justus Njagu.

The text has also benefited from discussions with Debbie Posel and Achille Mbembe and other former colleagues at the Wits Institute for Social Economic Research. Vyjayanthi Rao has been an inspired friend in Johannesburg, Mumbai, New Haven and cyberspace. I am especially grateful to William Beinart and also to St-Antony's college for the chance to spend some time at Oxford, where several chapters of this book were written. Peter Hudson has always been a generous reader of my work and given me invaluable support and assistance.

I was able to complete this manuscript while working for the Human Sciences Research Council. I am grateful to Adam Habib and my other colleagues in the Democracy and Governance Programme for their collegiality and friendship.

In preparing this book for publication, I was fortunate to have the excellent services of Hilary Wilson as proofreader, Margie Ramsay as indexer and Karen Lilje as book and cover designer. If this book is a little easier to read it is because of the editing and the advice of Alex Potter. Estelle Jobson managed to bring this whole project together. I am very grateful to her.

The publishers and I wish to thank Jeannine Howse of the Johannesburg Art Gallery and Byron Kozakiewiez of Beith Digital for assistance with locating and scanning the cover artwork. We gratefully acknowledge the permission granted by William Kentridge to reproduce his art on the cover of this book. We wish too to acknowledge the following institutions, from whom extracts in their archives or publications have been reproduced and credited accordingly: Grove/Atlantic, New York; Image, Doubleday, Random House, New York; The *South African Labour Bulletin*, Johannesburg; and Verso, London.

List of Acronyms

ACT	Area Co-ordinating Team (Manenberg)
ANC	African National Congress
Comintern	Communist International
Cosatu	Congress of South African Trade Unions
CPSA	Communist Party of South Africa
Devcon	Department of Community Development
Fosatu	Federation of South African Trade Unions
GWU	General Workers' Union
Mawu	Metal and Allied Workers' Union
MK	Mkhonto we Sizwe
NDR	national democratic revolution
NGO	non-governmental organisation
Numsa	National Union of Metalworkers of South Africa
PAC	Pan-Africanist Congress
RDP	Reconstruction and Development Programme
SACP	South African Communist Party
Sactu	South African Congress of Trade Unions
SALB	*South African Labour Bulletin*
Saso	South African Students' Organisation
TRC	Truth and Reconciliation Commission
UDF	United Democratic Front

Introduction:
The Sublime Object of Nationalism

This book sets out to address a gap in contemporary studies of nationalism and the nation. Despite the extraordinary growth of articles and books about nationalism and nations over the last 20 years, critical studies of African nationalism are not reflected in this literature. This is surprising for two reasons. In the first place, resistance to European colonialism usually happened in the name of nationalism and in pursuit of independent African nation states. In the second place, the pursuit of independent African nation states was not the only form that resistance to colonialism took.

Opposition to French colonialism, in particular, sought not so much the dissolution of empire as its democratisation. Before his conversion to nationalism, Leopold Senghor, the first president of independent Senegal, was a deputy in the French National Assembly. He only reluctantly sought independence for his country (Meredith, 2005). Closer to home, we will find in the figure of Sol Plaatje an ambivalence towards the British Empire. On the one hand, he railed against its injustices; on the other hand, he thought of himself as a loyal subject of the British crown (Willan, 2001).

What this means is that it is necessary to account for the rise of nationalism – and African nationalism in particular – as the pre-eminent form of resistance to colonialism and apartheid. This vision of what freedom from colonialism might look like has itself been a victim of nationalist mythologies, which narrate the story of an African people oppressed and exploited by foreign ones. Here, 'the people' are taken as something that preceded the period of nationalist struggle. What this conceals, however, is how an African people came into being in the first place. This book addresses itself to this question in the South African context.

The book will argue that African peoples emerged primarily in and though the process of nationalist resistance to colonialism. Here we must distinguish between the people as datum and the people as political subject. In the first case, the term 'the people' refers to an empirical collection of individuals in a given geography; in the second, it refers to a collectivity organised in pursuit of a political end. I am interested in this second sense of the term. The argument here is that the South African people came to be defined and produced in and through the politics and culture of nationalist struggle. Even if there are traces of other notions of what the term 'the people' means (clannic, for example), the image of the South African nation looms large in the political imaginary.

This view helps us recover the specificity of the nation, not simply as a cultural artefact, but as a political one. I will say more about this in the course of the book, which will argue that the nation is a political community whose form is given in relation to the pursuit of democracy and freedom. If democratic authority is lodged in 'the people', what matters is the way that the concept is defined, delimited and produced. In this sense, the nation precedes the state, not because it has always already existed, but because it emerges in and through the nationalist struggle for state power. The history of the postcolony[1] is, in this sense, the history of 'the people' *qua* production.

From this perspective, we have to re-evaluate knee-jerk judgements about the failure of modernity in Africa. If the mark of modern power – as opposed to tribal, monarchical or dynastic authority – is that it vests sovereignty in 'the people' themselves, African nationalism too 'locates the source of individual identity within a "people", which is seen to be the bearer of sovereignty, the central object of loyalty, and the basis of collective solidarity' (Greenfeld, 1992: 3). What matters is: (a) the limit and character of 'the people' in whom power is supposed to repose; and (b) the political forms through which 'the people' are represented. Simply put, the democratic project firmly places the identity of 'the people' on the agenda. We should not be surprised, therefore, to observe that the ongoing democratisation of African states has been accompanied by a renewed preoccupation with authenticity (Geschiere, 2005). Yet, if the democratic project poses the question of 'the people', we will see that an answer can take one of two forms. The first is that 'the people' constitute a nation; alternatively, that 'the people' constitute a democracy.

As a way of prefacing this argument, I want to consider an advertisement that appeared in the *Sunday Times*, a major South African weekend newspaper, in 2001. In 'The media vs President T. M. Mbeki', Ashley Mabogoane, Jabu Mabuza, Pearl Mashabela, Prof. Sam Mokgokong, Kgomotso Moroka, Don Ncube, Ndaba Ntsele, Christine Qunta, Mfundi Vundla, Peter Vundla and Sindiwe Zilwa accused the media of providing a platform for a right-wing plot to subvert South African democracy (Mabogoane *et al.*, 2001). They caution the president not to 'be distracted by the current campaign against [him]', and add that 'under [Mbeki's] leadership we have the best government this country has ever had'. Finally, they advise the president to 'go ahead and govern: govern fairly; govern with compassion but govern decisively'. Let us note the terms of the argument in this advertisement.

On the one hand, a right-wing conspiracy is posited. It is supposedly spearheaded by white, so-called liberals from the apartheid era, certain so-called independent research organisations (it is not clear which ones) run by whites, and a 'few' members of the white business community. They are aided by black commentators 'who unwittingly contribute to this campaign' (Mabogoane *et al.*, 2001). These forces are acting in concert, spreading vicious, underhanded 'disinformation' about the president. Their intentions are malicious: to discredit him personally, and by way of him, the competence of black people generally. Even more sinister is their sabotage of the country's economy (by portraying South Africa as a place not to do business in), and their attempt to subvert the will of the people (by questioning the fitness of a democratically elected president). In doing all this, the whites involved want to obstruct the dismantling of the apartheid system in order to secure the benefits they gain from its workings.

On the other hand, there are blacks who deeply love their country, who balance criticism with constructive mention of the government's landmark achievements, and who see in the attacks on the president a hateful, contemptuous assault on democracy. Blacks are presented as having faith in the potential of the country to be a well-managed, technologically advanced and truly egalitarian society. Moreover, whereas racist whites see in the 'errors' of the president the necessary failures of a black man, the blacks observe such errors as all-too-human weaknesses. Whereas whites question the very competence of Mbeki's leadership, and by association the leadership of all blacks, blacks propose guidance to a leader whose only weakness is that he is human.

Let us not worry about the truthfulness of this claim – that there is a conspiracy – other than to note how commonplace such claims have become in South Africa. Let us note rather that the advertisement makes certain epistemological claims that will help us determine its political genealogy. In particular, what is at stake is the nature of certain facts. Do they consist of independent and mostly unrelated actions or events? Or are they merely moments in a larger drama that is unfolding? Take, for example, the question of the media 'campaign'. Here a number of articles, appearing in different newspapers and at different times, and written by various journalists are seen as evidence of an underlying unity, one that exceeds their literality (as newspaper articles), to reveal the secret and underhand work of (racist) conspirators. Of course, many journalists and newspaper editors, in countering this claim, assert precisely the opposite. Abbey Makoe writes in the *Saturday Star*, for example, that '[t]he era of white-owned media dominating public opinion in South Africa can no longer be used as an excuse for lazy black professionals who hardly ever make an effort to participate in matters of public debate' (Makoe, 2001). Rather than being symptomatic of a conspiracy, these 'awful' claims against Mbeki are the work of 'individuals', the article claims. More importantly, their predominance is less a sign of a white conspiracy than it was of something else: the 'quietude of silence' into which black commentators had fallen. Unlike the 1960s and 1970s, which buzzed with the eloquence of writers like Steve Biko, Barney Pityana, Nchaupe Mokoape, Mamphela Ramphele and many others, the new elite ('self-styled struggle heroes') do not read, they do not write and they fail, therefore, to participate in the processes of national agenda-setting. Instead of whining privately, whingeing among themselves, and then dangling fat chequebooks in front of editors, writes Makoe (2001), they should state their views in public debate. Unfounded perceptions about Mbeki, he implies, are prevalent in the media because they have not been shown up as the 'horrible' views that they are by literate and articulate black writers. If Makoe, nonetheless, sympathises with Mabogoane *et al.*'s frustration that Mbeki is the subject of offensive articles, John Matshikiza is more dismissive. In the *Mail and Guardian* he calls it 'nonsense': 'So, where are these whites?' he asked. 'And where are the forums that are endemically racist and reactionary?' (Matshikiza, 2001). What both authors criticise are the so-called facts of the advertisement: that there is a white right-wing media campaign. What neither raise, however, is the logic of the argument itself. It is composed of the following premises:

- Blacks want to dismantle the legacy of apartheid.
- President Mbeki is black.
- He is head of a democratic black government.
- Since 1994 a million houses have been built, 1.3 million housing subsidies approved, 400,000 homes electrified and 120 clinics completed.

- Mbeki as the successful leader of a black government redressing the legacy of apartheid is helping black people regain their dignity.
- To criticise President Mbeki is to want to preserve the legacy of apartheid, undermine black rule, threaten democracy and insult the dignity of blacks.

The syllogisms above rest on three argumentative devices. The first is what we might call logical, the second empirical and the third is a rhetorical device. The least interesting part of this argument is its circularity: turning back the legacy of apartheid is included in the very definition of being black. This makes it *logically* indifferent to any empirical proof. Blacks are, by definition, reversing the apartheid inheritance. Yet the advertisement is not content with such an argumentative fiat; rather, it invites us to measure the truthfulness of its claims by a 'factual' measure: the number of houses built, and so on. It begs the question: What if the president cannot be shown empirically to be reversing the legacy of apartheid? For the most part, this is the level at which the debate happens.

This line of reasoning, whatever its merits and demerits, obscures another more worrying argumentative device. The advertisement employs a rhetorical claim that appeals to a different standard of evidence than that of the record in fact of President Mbeki and his government. On the advertisement's terms, the argument can still be true even if the 'facts' are wrong. Or even: the 'bad' facts are enrolled as further support of why the president is so good. What is at stake are the criteria of good and bad, true and false. Discussing when people have the 'right to criticise', the advertisement makes the following claims:

> The White rightwing forces do not realise that the right to criticise is accompanied by a responsibility to be fair and to recognise the landmarks and the achievements of the government and Black people in the way Black journalists and commentators do. In the absence of such balance,

> no amount of self-righteous claims of the public interest, transparency and press freedom will conceal their real motives (Mabogoane *et al.*, 2001).

Valid criticism is here premised on love for the country and its people, and predicated on loyalty to the government. This is what authentic blacks do: they caution when the president 'errs', they lift him when he 'stumbles', they know that he is human and sometimes behaves as such, and they know too that his government is the best South Africa has ever had. This is the standard of authentic criticism, and to act differently is evidence of, at least, a lack of patriotism and, at worst, racism and treason. This is why black writers and journalists balance their criticism with praise. But there is an anomaly here: certain blacks, it would seem, do not. In discussing the identities of the plotters, the advertisement makes the following startling claim: 'Separately from them (the White right-wingers), there are a few Black commentators who unwittingly contribute to this campaign' (Mabogoane *et al.*, 2001). What these unspecified blacks lack is authenticity, presumably because they find fault without praise. It is precisely this rhetorical device that Xolela Mangcu rebuts:

> [T]he advertisement raises an important point about the moral autonomy of black people. The ad relies on a logic of black authenticity that urges them to put solidarity with their leaders or heroes above everything else. In this case the history of racial oppression is used as racial blackmail, or what Mothubi Mutloatse describes as 'the liberation handcuffs that have given us Mugabe, Nujoma and now Chiluba' (Mangcu, 2001).

Mangcu is troubled that the appeal to black solidarity is elevated above what he calls 'moral reasoning': the autonomy to make ethical judgements about what is right or wrong. In other words, he refuses to condone the line that the president should be supported simply because he is black.

Mangcu is defending a notion of blackness that balances solidarity with what he calls 'moral reasoning', in contrast to the terms of the advertisement: blackness/loyalty to the president and government. His remarks go to the core of what is novel in the way blackness is sometimes (and more and more) discussed. Authentic blacks support the president and the government, not on the basis of their record in advancing a certain project, but simply because they are black. Herein lies the fundamental rupture with Black Consciousness[2] and the politics of national democratic revolution (NDR)[3], two key views of what it means to be a South African that will be discussed in detail in later chapters.

Blackness no longer denotes a social position (in the racial capitalist relations of production) or a psychological condition. It designates an authentic national subject that is loyal to the state simply because that state is controlled by other blacks like it. The facts are irrelevant to the proof. Or rather, the argument appeals to other 'facts'. But what are these facts? Or rather, what is the new mark of authenticity? Who is 'Black' and not merely black? If the measure of 'Blackness' is not given by the degree to which the legacy of apartheid is reversed, then nor is it simply a question of complexion. We recall that there are 'Blacks' (more correctly, blacks) in the service of the plotters. So, to what does 'Blackness' refer?

Let us approach this displacement in the following way. In terms of Black Consciousness and NDR, a black was 'Black' to the extent that he/she undertook certain concrete, particular actions: resisted racial oppression, struggled against exploitation, and asserted the value of black culture and history. In the same way, and following this logic, a government was 'Black', i.e. *libératoire*, to the extent that it took certain actions to reverse the legacy of apartheid: ended racial discrimination, redressed the material inequality between blacks and whites, and so on. Authenticity had a measure that was evidenced by particular facts. What matters here is a certain epistemology: that belief *follows* from evidence: 'I support the government because, through a process of reasoning and verification, I have come to the conclusion that it is truly reversing the legacy of apartheid.' We recall, however, that this is not the standard of truth suggested by the advertisement. Valid criticism, criticism in other words that is true, is by definition balanced by praise. And how do we know this? Precisely because, according to the advertisement, blacks that reproach the African National Congress (ANC) government without complimenting it lose their claim to authenticity. Certainly, President Mbeki makes mistakes, but in essence, the advertisement holds, he is turning back the apartheid tide. Or, rather: President Mbeki is an excellent 'Black' leader, over and above the details of his actual political record.

What is the condition of truth in such a claim? What is at stake is a certain ontology: belief (that the government is authentically 'Black') does not derive from evidence (data collected, sorted and interrogated by reason). Rather, *the facts are revealed through belief* – a mysterious inversion. Only through loyalty to the government (patriotism) is it apparent how President Mbeki and his government are addressing the vestiges of apartheid. Knowledge follows from belief, or access to the truth is only attained through faith. This last term is precise here. For the analogy is Christian religious conviction: 'to believe in Christ because we consider him wise and good is a dreadful blasphemy – it is, on the contrary, only the act of belief itself which can give us insight into his goodness and wisdom' (Kierkegaard, cited in Zizek, 1992: 37).

We might therefore say: to gauge the excellence of President Mbeki on the basis of his record is unpatriotic. On the contrary, belief in his excellence itself will reveal just how the legacy of apartheid is being redressed. The 'facts' by which we measure the merit of President Mbeki (as a 'Black') are those of a mysterious and sublime quality. 'Blackness' here is attached to a spiritual knowing: a knowing through faith, where turning back the vestiges of apartheid refers to some spiritual, metaphysical redress. And this knowledge is accessible only to authentic 'Blacks' because they alone are true believers. What this kind of nation-building does is transform the presidency and the government into quasi-religious objects that endure all torments and survive with immaculate beauty.

Unless we recognise that there is a profoundly new articulation of blackness today, we will not be in a position properly to evaluate its politics. The measure of blackness is today that of national sovereignty. By this term I do not mean state sovereignty. If the latter refers to the ability, in Agamben's (2005) terms, to define the state of exception, national sovereignty refers to the control of state institutions by authentic representatives of the nation. An authentic national community is merely that group deemed to be the veritable bearer of the national mission – whatever it may be. It is that community of true believers. A distinction must be made between a citizen as such and an authentic national subject. So, even if citizenship is founded on principles of universal human rights, for example, nation-building would have us say that some citizens are more authentically members of the nation than others. At stake is the measure of freedom. Nationalism associates being free – the ability to see the world as it really is and act accordingly – with determinate marks of population. By this I mean a schema of physical marks and social-psychological characteristics: being of a certain race, practising a particular religion, preferring certain kinds of sexual partners, and so on. Conversely, the absence of these marks of population is associated with a state of unfreedom. We might say that citizens who are not national subjects are not equal because they are not free and they are not free because they are not national subjects.[4] What we are discussing here, essentially, is the nature of legitimate authority. Who, in other words is a legitimate bearer of state power in society?

In these terms, the current struggle within the ANC over the identity of President Thabo Mbeki's successor is a national conflict *par excellence*. At stake is less an ideological struggle between, say, (neo-)liberalism and socialism, than a conflict about the measure of national authenticity. Who is more authentically a representative of the nation, Jacob Zuma or some other (as yet unnamed) contender?

During the apartheid period, the nation was delimited by virtue of a measure of population. In considering the major constitutional changes that have accompanied, and to some extent inaugurated, the democratic dispensation, we will see that they have sought to overcome these particular measures by outlawing discrimination, including on the basis of race, religion and sexual orientation. In so doing, however, we have to ask: is the South African demos without a measure of population at all?

The book will open (Chapter 1), with a survey of the literature on African nationalism, to argue that contemporary writing on Africa and South Africa pays very little attention to this phenomenon. Indeed, the subject has almost escaped serious academic treatment for 20 years or so, despite its overwhelming relevance. In South Africa, at least, the post-apartheid period has been fraught with debates about the 'national question'. When the subject is broached, studies tend to be ambivalent about nationalism's character. Following Thomas Hodgkin's well-known definition of the phenomenon, there is a tendency to understand African nationalism, including African nationalism in South Africa, simply as resistance to colonial authority, irrespective of its form. Yet reading carefully, many of these same studies effectively treat it as a modernist form of anti-colonialism: urban, post-tribal/non-racial, secular and interested in an industrialised post-colonial system.

In Chapter 2, I will try to overcome this ambivalence by directly confronting the nature of African nationalism. I will do so by reading the phenomenon against a selected literature. I am especially interested in nationalism as a specific kind of democratic imaginary. Whereas this relationship is easily obscured by authors more interested in it as a cultural artefact, we will see that democracy was until recently believed to lodge naturally in nations. By the eighteenth century, for example, this view was axiomatic for as diverse a group as Johan Gottfied Herder, John Stuart Mill and the French revolutionaries. In the South African context, African nationalism opposed apartheid in the name of national democracy.

In Chapter 3, I will seek the form of the South African nation in the struggle against apartheid and for national democracy. In this regard, I will pay particular attention to the development of the theory of national democratic revolution (NDR). Although Pan-Africanism and Negritude were important discourses informing the terrain of struggle, resistance to apartheid was pre-eminently framed by the politics and theory of NDR. In this chapter I will try to generate the identity of the authentic national subject from the repertoire of images, figures and practices of the theory of NDR. In particular, I will ask: Who, according to this theory, is free?

The theory of NDR may have been the pre-eminent expression of nationalist resistance and organisation in South Africa, but apart from its name, what was nationalist about its discourse? In Chapter 4, I take up this question with regard to the politics of NDR and also that of Black Consciousness. What, if anything, made their respective politics a truly nationalist politics? By carefully reading their respective discourses, I will suggest that both discourses appealed to gendered subjects embedded in particular cultures and languages. Hence, despite appearances, we will see that both posited the citizen as a bearer of marks of population.[5]

Chapter 5 will argue that the history and practice of the theory of NDR helps us understand the terms of a violent conflict that overcame three townships east of Johannesburg between 1990 and 1994.

Chapter 6 will consider the conditions of a public domain that does not conflate the citizen with an authentic national subject. It will argue that citizens are interpolated into democratic ideology through the practice of democratic institutions. In this way I want to argue for a theory of democracy that locates its conditions in its very practice; instead of seeking them, that is, in either a culture or civilisation ('Western' values, for example) that precedes them. Here the conditions of democracy refer to: (a) the circumstances around which formal democratic institutions are established (their production), and (b) the situation that needs to prevail for them to function effectively over the long term (their reproduction).

Chapter 7 will pursue the conditions of a non-national imaginary by considering the work of the South African Truth and Reconciliation Commission. We will see that one of the key tasks of the commission was to identify and establish the basis for national unity. At stake was the principle of identity or commonality among South Africans as a 'nation-people'. In the commission's very failure we will identify another principle of political community – a principle that is not national.

The concluding chapter will pose further the conditions of democracy as a society by asking how such a demos might generate its own limit. A meaningful discussion about the *democratic* limit or boundary is only now beginning. Chantal Mouffe, for example, has recently argued that democracy always entails relations of inclusion–exclusion that speak to a notion of the political frontier. One of the key problems of democratic theory, she suggests, has been its inability to conceptualise such a limit (Mouffe, 2000: 43). This has not, until recently, seemed an urgent task. The reason, I imagine, is largely political: the figure of the citizen has, historically, been deemed either a resident of a nation or of the world. Nation–world are the two poles that have exhausted the democratic imaginary. Yet over the last two decades, both identities have become increasingly unsettled. In the first place, the collapse of 'really existing'[6] socialist states (primarily the Soviet Union) and the associated crisis of Marxism have disturbed the prospect of internationalism. In the second place, feminist and multicultural critiques of the nation have inspired thinking about new forms of political community. More and more, writers have been drawn together around the notion of cosmopolitanism. It is in this context that there is a growing interest in a principle of political demarcation, a principle of the frontier, that can simultaneously (a) discriminate between citizens and non-citizens, and that is (b) congruent with a definition of citizenship that is universal. The problem in contemporary terms is of a particular demos, *not constituted on any measure of population*, be it of race, culture, religion, ethnicity or any combination of these. The concluding chapter will attempt to propose a solution to this problem.

Before continuing, I want to discuss some of the concepts and vocabulary of this analysis. I have used a range of familiar terms in an unfamiliar way and also made up some new ones. Most important among these are 'citizen' and 'authentic national subject' (discussed throughout the text, for the sake of brevity, as a 'national subject'). I have opposed these two terms in order to capture the difference between two kinds of political community. The first is a democracy conceived not simply as a mode of government, but as a *form of society*. The second is a nation, also understood as a particular kind of society. The first is composed of citizens, and the second of national subjects. I have invoked this last term, 'national subject', in order to avoid confusion.

We will see, for reasons associated with the historical origins of democracy, that the term democracy is seldom opposed to that of nation. In other words, the two terms are hardly thought to be contradictory, except when nationalism goes 'bad' – when it is associated with fascism and racism. This is hardly surprising. Nationalism was an important vehicle of democracy, especially in relation to colonialism, monarchies and empires. It has also played an important role in equalising members of society, at least at the level of political rights. Historically, democracies were lodged in nations, such that citizenship implied closure in a particular state. 'The citizen', moreover, is a pre-democratic appellation. Enlightened monarchs often referred to themselves as citizens of the realm.[7] In this regard, in conversational and some academic writing, it makes sense to talk and write of 'citizens of the nation'. Here the two terms are reconciled by an appeal to distinct levels. The nation refers to the political community (demos) in which citizens are entitled to exercise their rights and responsibilities. We might say that the nation belongs to the ontology of the political, whereas the citizen belongs to the ontic (see Chapter 7). In other words, the term 'citizen' is simply the name for the subject of the nation. We will see later that this is the way that Jurgen Habermas (2001) conceptualises the relationship between them.

The purpose of this book is to argue that there is a heavy price to pay for this seemingly benign formulation. It comes at the expense of a certain idea and practice of democracy. The citizen is the subject *par excellence* of democracy, not of the nation.

The historical contiguity of nations and citizens obscures their political-theoretical distance. Even though they are both products of the democratic imaginary, the citizen and the national subject are the effects of answering the question of democracy differently: Who are 'the people' in the rallying cry 'Power to the people'?

When we discuss democracy simply as a kind of politics, as a way of exercising power, it becomes akin to, say, dictatorship or oligarchy or republicanism or liberalism. What such a notion foregrounds is democracy *qua* system of institutions, practices of decision-making, rules and regulations, rights, and obligations. As a form of society, what comes into view, in contrast, are the very persons that inhabit the political community. What are the customs and codes that govern how they relate to one another? From such a perspective, we are able to undertake a political anthropology of the demos. This is where the difference between the citizen and the national subject becomes most apparent. The citizen is hailed through democratic institutions and acts according to democratic norms – what I will call 'ethical values'. The national subject is produced in and through the nationalist movement, supplemented by state bodies if it comes to power.

1
The Nature of African Nationalism

In 1991 the historian Saul Dubow declared that 'in recent years our historical understanding of Afrikaner nationalism [in South Africa] has been transformed' (Dubow, 1991: 1). 'We now have', he continues, 'a much deeper understanding of the ways in which Afrikaner identity was forged from the late nineteenth century, and the means by which Afrikaner ethnicity was mobilised in order to capture state power in the twentieth century' (p. 1). What remained, he suggests, were certain gaps in the historical record. These omissions were a result of a general amnesia about the place of racist ideas in Christian thought. They also reflected, he suggests, the pre-eminence of a Marxist scholarship fearful of 'idealism'. Marxist scholars were not interested in questions of ideology and culture on their own terms. 'The ideology of race', Dubow observes, 'has therefore tended to be discussed in terms of its functional utility: ... the extent to which racist ideas can be said to express underlying class interests' (p. 1). Dubow had in mind the tradition of radical political economy that announced itself so boldly in the mid-1970s.

In September 1976, just three months after the beginning of a massive student revolt in Soweto, the *Review of African Political Economy* published a special edition on South Africa. It contained several essays that would partly define the terms of South African studies for at least the next ten years. Of especial importance was an article on the state by Robert Davies, David Kaplan, Mike Morris and Dan O'Meara. Applying theoretical developments within French Marxism to a periodisation of the form of the state in South Africa, the authors explored what they called the secondary contradictions of the social formation. They argued that the form of the state was given, in addition to the primary contradiction between workers and capitalists, by struggles for hegemony between different fractions of capital itself (Davies *et. al.*, 1976). Between 1920 and 1948, they argued, the critical division within the capitalist class was between imperialist/foreign capital(s) on the one hand and national capital(s) on the other (p. 29). At stake was whether 'South Africa was to remain an economic chattel of imperialism or to generate its own national capitalist development' (p. 29). The 'unique' feature of South Africa, they concluded, was the early hegemony that national capital exercised in the state. The displacement of imperial capital from this position after World War II saw the transformation of the economy away from reliance on primary production (mining) towards relatively high levels of industrialisation (p. 29). What is important to notice is how Davies *et al.* treated phenomena like Afrikaner nationalism. On their terms, political/ideological criteria reflected the latter's base in different sectors of production (p. 5). '[It] is here', Davies *et al.* continue, 'that the English/Afrikaner *traditions* are to be located' (original emphasis) (p. 6). English traditions in South Africa reflected the interests of foreign capital; Afrikaner nationalism was an ideological effect of national capital.

These were the terms of analysis that Dubow protested. John Lonsdale too had complained, at about the same time, that 'Marxists were not much interested in the historical study of ... nationalism' (Lonsdale, 1992: 301). Both noted how, in the hands of such scholars, notions of race, *volk*[1] and nation were reduced to mere effects of class positions. So too was racism. On these terms, there was little place for studies of ideology, politics and culture *on their own terms*. What Dubow was, in effect, celebrating when he toasted the growth of research on Afrikaner nationalism was the emergence of an environment more conducive to the study of nationalism, race and politics generally.

At least since the early 1980s, in South Africa and Britain, so-called French structuralist historiography was being taken on by a school of historians that claimed sympathy with the Marxist project, often self-identified as radical, and yet refused the idea that history was a process without a subject. Instead of privileging the role of anonymous structural processes, they emphasised the agency of historical actors and the contingency of beliefs and practices. In South Africa, these scholars often rallied behind the banner of social history, citing E. P. Thompson's *The Poverty of Theory* (1978) in their disputes with those sympathetic to Althusser and Poulantzas. By the early 1990s, this dispute had ostensibly been won: Althusser had disappeared from the academic scene and Poulantzas was dead. Moreover, social history was on the ascendancy.

We might reasonably suppose that in this environment, Dubow looked forward to new studies of nationalism, including African nationalism. He had reason to be optimistic: in 1987 Shula Marks and Stanley Trapido had edited a collection of essays that were published together as *The Politics of Race, Class and Nationalism in Twentieth Century South Africa*. In their introduction, Marks and Trapido offered a continuous historical narrative as a first step towards accounting for nationalism and ethnicity in a synthesis of twentieth-century South African history. The book was an invitation to further research.

With the hindsight of more than a decade, we are obliged, unfortunately, to conclude that Dubow's optimism was nothing more than that. It is true that around about the time of his article a few new studies emerged on Zulu nationalism.[2] These were exceptions, however. Apart from a few journal articles, most of them published as part of the Marks and Trapido collection mentioned above, the last major studies of African nationalism in South Africa were published in the 1970s: *Black Nationalism in South Africa* by Peter Walshe came out in 1973; the most recent edition of *Black Power in South Africa* by Gail Gerhart was published in 1979; and Eddie Roux's *Time Longer than Rope* was even older, first appearing in 1964. Roux's text is typical of the way that African nationalism has been construed in South Africa, even in the later Marks and Trapido study, and its sub-title is instructive: *A History of the Black Man's Struggle for Freedom in South Africa.* African nationalism has been defined in terms of resistance to colonialism, racial segregation and apartheid. Scholars, moreover, have been ready to accept a person's or an organisation's own designation as nationalist on their own terms: if they identified themselves as nationalists, that is what they were taken to be. What, however, was nationalist as such about the form of their resistance? This question has never been addressed in South Africa. It is a question, moreover, to which there are only disparate answers when it comes to African nationalism more generally.

The vast majority of studies of African nationalism date from the period of decolonisation, between the 1950s and 1970s. Among the earliest and still the most important of these texts is Thomas Hodgkin's *Nationalism in Colonial Africa.* It first appeared in 1958, and was already in its sixth edition ten years later. When it appeared, readers were familiar with political revolts – Hodgkin (1968: 10) calls them 'explosions', to give a sense of their sudden violence – in Nigeria, the Gold Coast (today Ghana), the Sudan, French West Africa (especially the Ivory Coast) and South Africa (presumably, the Defiance Campaign). Even more 'tranquil' territories like Northern Rhodesia (today Zambia), Nyasaland (Malawi), French Equatorial Africa and the Cameroons were in an 'eruptive state' (p. 11). Readers had also witnessed new self-governing, if not fully sovereign, states emerge in Africa. In 1956 the Sudan declared its independence, refusing a constitutional link with Egypt. Formerly Italian Eritrea had since 1952 become an autonomous territory within the federal Ethiopian Empire. The Gold Coast was on the verge of independence; so too were parts of Nigeria. The year 1956, Hodgkin wrote, 'has been noted in the diaries of British West African politicians as the year of decision' (p. 11). In 1957 the independent state of Ghana came into being. Then, in 1960, Cameroon, Togo, Mali,

Senegal, Malagasy, the Congo Republic (Belgian), Somalia (Italian and British), Dahomey, Niger, Upper Volta, Ivory Coast, Chad, the Central African Republic, the Congo Republic (French), Gabon, Nigeria and Mauretania became independent. In total, 17 new countries appeared within months of each other. The following year, Sierra Leone was declared independent, as was Tanganyika. In 1962 Ruanda (Rwanda) and Burundi became independent; so too did Algeria and Uganda. In 1963 Nigeria became a republic and Kenya a sovereign state. Malawi followed in 1964; Northern Rhodesia became independent Zambia. And 1964 also saw the emergence of Tanzania from the union of Tanganyika and Zanzibar.

In this context, studies of African nationalism usually documented resistance to colonial rule. The term 'African nationalism' was used interchangeably with several other expressions: anti-colonialism, anti-imperialism, 'Black Protest' and 'National Liberation'. Such studies showed a fundamental preoccupation with *struggle*; and struggle against colonialism in particular. They read two terms together: nationalism and independence.

'My own inclination', writes Hodgkin,

> is to use the term 'nationalist' in a broad sense, to describe any
> organisation or group that explicitly asserts the rights, claims
> and aspirations of a given African society … in opposition to
> European authority, *whatever its institutional form and objectives*
> (emphasis added) (Hodgkin, 1968: 23).

Hodgkin defended his methodology against those who wanted to be more circumspect in their use of the term. There are those, he observes, who 'describe only those types of organisation which are essentially political, not religious, economic or educational, in character, and which have as their object the realisation of self-government or independence for a recognisable African nation, or nation-to-be'. Yet, he continues, to restrict the use of the term in this way seems to raise two difficulties.

Firstly, it tends to conceal the 'mixed-up' character of African political movements. 'In a single African territory', he continues,

> it is possible to find coexisting a diversity of organisations, of different types, with different objectives, operating at different levels, each in its own way expressing opposition to European control and a demand for new liberties; and to discover a network of relationships between these organisations (Hodgkin, 1968: 24).

Some might be political organisations seeking independence for the 'nation'; others, messianic movements; still others, church groupings; tribal associations; or trade unions. These diverse organisations, Hodgkin insists, were only intelligible in relation to 'a single historical process, of nationalist awakening, to which they all belonged' (Hodgkin, 1968: 25). If one did not see them as 'variations on a single theme' then one was bound to conclude that nationalism was non-existent in places where 'nationalist aspirations have not yet begun to express themselves in the language of separatism' (p. 25). Hodgkin was thinking here of the Belgian Congo, which he describes as being in a state of 'incipient nationalism' (p. 25). Two years later, he seems to have been proven right: in June 1960 Patrice Lumumba addressed dignitaries at the ceremony marking the independence of the Congo. He juxtaposed nationalism and independence in the very way that Hodgkin suggested was meaningful:

> Your Majesty, Excellencies, Ladies and Gentleman, Congolese men and women, Fighters for independence who today are victorious, I salute you in the name of the Congolese government. ... The Republic of Congo has been proclaimed, and our beloved country is now in the hands of its own children. ... Homage to the Champions of National Sovereignty! Long Live Independent and Sovereign Congo! (cited in Kohn & Sokolsky, 1965: 118–21).

Yet Hodgkin himself gave reason to be more discerning about what was and what was not a nationalist movement. *Nationalism in Colonial Africa* is, in part, a study of new forms of urban association. Part II of the books considers the 'new towns' of Africa – 'great, amorphous, squalid *agglomération urbaine*' (Hodgkin, 1968: 64) – where, Hodgkin tells us, a new 'indigenous civilisation' is being created (p. 83). It is there that he locates the rise of African nationalism, in some of the 'characteristic institutions of this new civilisation' (p. 83). What is novel about this civilisation, according to Hodgkin, is its peculiar urban form: 'By mixing men from a variety of social backgrounds', he explains,

> [the new towns] make possible the discovery of new points of contact and interest. Around these interests there develops a network of new associations, through which for the first time men come to think of their problems as social rather than personal; as *capable of solution by human action rather than part of the natural order* (p. 63; emphasis added).

Hence, he argues,

> African towns have this two-fold aspect: seen from one standpoint, they lead to a degradation of African civilisation and ethic; seen from another, they contain the germs of a new, more interesting and diversified civilisation, with the possibilities of greater liberty (p. 63).

African nationalism, according to this account, intends a new African civilisation, one that transcends kinship and ethnicity, where freedom heralds social mixing and ethnic diversity. Its culture is urban and secular, permitting a view of the world unmediated by supernatural cosmologies. African nationalism construed in this way fits uncomfortably with a definition that reduces it to the search for independence. It is not indifferent to the form of society after independence. Indeed, in this account, nationalist movements become so when they struggle for a particular version of the postcolony.

This ambivalence regarding the definition of African nationalism produces very different appraisals of historical phenomena. Take, for example, the Mau Mau revolt in Kenya. According to the first definition of African nationalism (whereby nationalism = anti-colonialism), it is easily construed as an African nationalist movement. This is how, for example, Bruce Berman characterised it. It was not an atavistic Kikuyu tribal rebellion, he said, but a modern national movement against colonial rule (Berman, 1991). Kofi Opoku, in a similar way, suggests that Mau Mau attained 'national consciousness' and 'cultural awareness' because it struggled for independence (Opoku, 1986). More circumspect, however, is John Lonsdale's analysis in a book he jointly edited with Bruce Berman: even if Mau Mau was a nationalist movement, it mobilised on the basis of Kikuyu tribalism. Lonsdale is interested in the relationship between nationalism and ethnicity and concludes with the notion of ethnic nationalism: Mau Mau was an ethnic nationalist revolt, he suggests (Lonsdale, 1992: 268). He introduces this qualification – ethnic nationalism – because he knows that the history of Mau Mau sits uncomfortably with the implicit normative register of most views of nationalism (Lonsdale, 1992: 275). Firstly, it organised on tribal (ethnic) lines. It was not multiracial, nor did it imagine the time after colonialism as the time of black Kenyans. It appealed to a quasi-mysticism. It was not urban-based, nor did it attach special value to technological and economic progress. Hodgkin himself thought that there were more constructive methods of channelling African political energies than Mau Mau, which represented for him an example of a blighted ambition 'wasted in messianic and puritanical religious movements, or … attracted to terrorism as a violent means of breaking the bonds of the plural society' (Hodgkin cited in Lonsdale, 1992: 282). The 'undecidability' of the phenomenon *qua* nationalist centres precisely on this question of definition. At stake, ostensibly, is a historiographical problem: What facts counted as proof of national phenomena?

THE NATURE OF AFRICAN NATIONALISM

The temptation to treat African nationalism as the name for resistance to colonialism is, nonetheless, widespread. So pervasive has been its influence, writes Anthony Smith in the early 1980s, 'that to this day one of the most popular views on nationalism in the "Third World" regards itself as a movement for national liberation and a reaction to European colonialism' (Smith, 1983: 37). Smith worries, in effect, that if African nationalism were construed simply in terms of what it opposed, the impact of territorial division and bureaucratic homogenisation, key to the force and shape of nationalism, would be overlooked. Such an appraisal was also mute about the cultural features of nationalism: 'But this is to miss much of the point behind a nationalist movement,' he objects, 'its ability to attract diverse groups, to renew itself after attaining independence, and to provide a basis and rationale for new social and political units and institutions' (p. 38). In response, Smith proposes a typology and a periodisation of African nationalism. There was a phase of 'primary resistance' to European incursion, a period of 'millennial protest', a phase of 'gestation' and 'adaptation', a period of nationalist agitation for self-rule and, finally, the adoption of social programmes (p. 39).

Smith is certainly correct about the dangers of construing nationalism simply in terms of resistance. Yet we must sometimes distinguish between what the literature says it is doing and what it does in fact do. Literature from this period often goes in two directions simultaneously. It discusses African nationalism in relation to struggle, yet it also discusses it as a particular form of struggle. However, it is the view of the present book that it is better characterised in terms of an ambivalence about nationalism's form.

For example, Ndabaningi Sithole's 1959 history of the subject under discussion, entitled *African Nationalism*, documents how the 'spirit of independence' after World War II spread to Africa. It discusses African nationalism largely in the terms that Hodgkin defined, as 'a move against European domination which tends to devalue the African people' (Sithole, 1959: 24). Sithole's text is clearly addressed to European readers, and is at pains to assure them that African nationalism is not anti-white (nor Communist), but that it merely represents the 'fierce hunger' of African peoples to be 'recognized by the people of the world as their fellows and equals' (p. 50). '[A]n African nationalist movement', he states, 'is an honest effort on the part of the African people to reassert their human dignity which the foreign powers have denied them. It is an honest effort to overthrow foreign rule that relegates them to an inferior position' (p. 136). Yet Sithole's text cannot be reduced to this anti-colonialism standpoint. In his account, African nationalism does not bear a simply negative relation to colonialism; it also represents the soul of a 'new African'. Whereas it is true that the majority of Africans have not emerged from a 'primitive state' (p. 162), he explains, the

> modern African lives in an environment in many instances totally different from that in which his forefathers lived. He is not only conscious of the country in which he lives, but also of Africa as a whole, and of the whole world .... Unlike his forefathers' environment that hummed with bees, and that was livened with singing birds, disturbed by wild animals, and moved at nature's pace, the modern African now lives in an environment where the mechanical bird has superseded the bird, where automobiles, trains, and tractors have pushed the ox, the donkey, and the horse into the background. ... If the African forefathers should come back to life and behold their descendants on the modern scene, it is not far-fetched to say they would mistake their own children for the gods (p. 159).

Here African nationalism does not simply resist foreign domination: it is the harbinger of modernity. Even more than that, it constitutes those in Africa as African subjects *per se*.

The content of African nationalism became a major preoccupation, especially during the 1960s and 1970s. For example, Amilcar Cabral, founder of the Partido Africano da Independencia da Guiné e Cabo Verde, which sought independence from Portuguese rule in Guinea, during his address to the first Tricontinental Conference held in Havana in 1966, worried about the 'ideological deficiency' if not the 'total lack of ideology' in the national liberation movements (Cabral, 1969: 75). Without such theory, he stated, national liberation movements would not correctly appraise the 'foundations and objectives of national liberation in relation to the social structure' (Cabral, 1969: 75). Cabral wanted such movements to pay greater attention to the form of society after independence – independence *per se* was not liberation. African nationalists needed to be able to distinguish between genuine national liberation and what he called neo-colonialism: 'To retain the power which national liberation puts into its hands,' he argued, 'the petty bourgeoisie has only one path: to give free rein to its natural tendencies to become more bourgeois ... that is to negate the revolution and necessarily ally itself with imperialist capital' (Cabral, 1969: 89). Such a situation, Cabral continued, was a neo-colonial one (Cabral, 1969: 89).

Hence, a genuine African nationalism was one that allied with the working class to overcome imperial capitalism. At stake was the prospect of industrialised African societies not beholden to foreigners or a parasitic comprador class. Cabral was echoing concerns raised by Kwame Nkrumah the year before, in particular, that new African nations were vulnerable to the 'extended tentacles of the Wall Street octopus' (Nkrumah, 1965: 240). Trepidation about the form of society after independence, and hence the character of the movements calling themselves nationalist, reflected a temporal change. The task of African nationalism was no longer simply to resist and overcome colonialism. As the discourse of new governments and state officials, African nationalism looked to to a new horizon, the future, and was asking some important questions: What was a nation? How did a society become one? What was the path to national sovereignty?

Cabral posited an African nation as a socialist, industrial society, reflecting the growing Marxist-Leninist influence on African nationalism. What mattered, for him and many like him, was the particular class character of the new society and the appropriate path to development: socialism or capitalism? Hans Kohn and Wallace Sokolsky describe the situation in 1965:

> In the minds of African leaders, [nationalism] is no longer thought of in anti-imperialist terms, its original motivation. Nationalism is now conceived of as the necessary framework for and propelling force behind catapulting Africa into a complex, industrial world (Kohn & Sokolsky, 1965: 9).

This is how the term was used in Robert Rotberg and Ali Mazrui's collection, *Protest and Power in Black Africa*, which appeared in 1970. The title of the book was already significant. It substituted 'protest' for 'nationalism' as the generic name of African resistance, implying that nationalism was only one form of protest. Typically, James Fernandez, a contributor to the Rotberg and Mazrui collection, wanted the adjective 'nationalist' only to apply to a movement if it contributed to what he called 'modernisation'. For this reason, he reserved judgement about the nationalist credentials of the Bwiti movement in central and northern Gabon (Fernandez, 1970). (As an aside, we can note that he worried about the correctness of its application to Mau Mau fighters too [Fernandez, 1970: 454].)

This attention to the relationship between nation and modernisation was accompanied by interest in another couplet: tribe and nation. In *From Tribe to Nation in Africa*, published in 1970, Ronald Cohen and John Middleton sought to debunk the notion of tribe. They call it a 'clear-cut racist stereotype', preferring the term 'ethnicity' (Cohen & Middleton, 1970: 2). The notion of 'tribe', over and above its growing pejorative connotations, exaggerated the fixity of African social groups, their clear-cut demarcation as separate social units, and the stability of their cultures and customs (Cohen & Middleton, 1970: 2–3). Cohen and Middleton suspected that profound social changes were happening in Africa, but the problem was that they could not be described in the existing academic and popular lexicon. This was especially true of the notion of 'detribalisation'. The term only made sense, they suggest, '[i]f there is a clear-cut, empirically real and, therefore, identifiable entity called a tribe or if there is a real person whom we can label the "tribal" African.' '[T]hen of course', they continue, 'there must be a sharp change or loss when the African man or woman does not manifest tribal qualities – hence "detribalization" became a problem for research in social policy' (Cohen & Middleton, 1970: 2). Yet such characters were more products of colonial fiction than of serious observation of Africans and African societies. Cohen and Middleton witness and also welcome a new form of society in Africa. They call it 'plural', and seek a new analytical vocabulary to describe it, which they find in the notion of 'incorporation'. At stake was the emergence of 'plural' societies 'in which people from differing ethnic backgrounds are interacting to a greater or lesser degree' (Cohen & Middleton, 1970: 9). 'The more each group changes toward reduction of boundary maintenance with respect to the other,' they explain, 'the greater is the degree of incorporation' (Cohen & Middleton, 1970: 9). The collection considers this process among the Tonga in Zambia, the Lugbara in Uganda, the Alur in southern Sudan and the non-Nyamwezi in Tanzania. It investigates marriage policy and incorporation in Ghana; in Bornu, among the Mossi; in Rwanda; in the former Transkei; and in Nigeria. What was of especial importance is the effect of independence on the incorporation process (Maquet, 1970: 201), and in particular, the phenomenon of urbanisation. On these terms, 'a nation' referred to a plural society.

There are two noteworthy features of this literature. In the first place, it posited the African nation as a particular *type of society*. Secondly, African nationalism was not treated as a question of identity: it did not matter if its members identified with state institutions or state symbols. This is a recent concern, about which more will be said shortly.

The degree to which a society was plural or industrialised was not a question of subjectivity or opinion. Note, for example, D. F. Malherbe's *Stamregister van die Suid-Afrikaanse Volk* (*Genealogical Register of the South African People*), published in South Africa in 1966. Like the anthropologies of incorporation described above, it researched the limits of the South African nation in terms of intermarriage and genealogy. There are two things to observe. Firstly, it draws a *white* limit, a racial boundary, despite the apparently all-inclusive term 'South African people'. There is palpable relief in South African Prime Minister Hendrik Verwoerd's preface to the book: 'That the people remained white', he marvels, 'in spite of exceptional circumstances, is ... remarkable' (Verwoerd, 1966: v).[3] In the second place, the book defines a *family* limit: it is a chronicle of marriages and intermarriages, of forebears and descendants that sketches the lines of common descent of white South Africans. Therein lies its importance: it is a family tree that establishes the ancestral origins of the people. To Malherbe, membership of the South African nation is not a question of identification; it is one of genealogy. Nor was this a peculiarity of Afrikaner nationalism: if we cast our view wider than Africa, we will hear the nation discussed in similar terms.

Note this extract from the utopian history of Bhudeb Mukhopadhyay. Partha Chatterjee discusses it in the context of an Indian nationalism that defined 'the people' as Hindu:

> Although India is the true motherland only of those who belong to the Hindu jāti and although only they have been born from her womb, the Musalmans [*sic*] are not unrelated to her any longer. She has held them at her breast and reared them. Musalmans are therefore her adopted children. Can there be no bonds of fraternity between two children of the same mother, one a natural child and the other adopted? There certainly can, the laws of every religion admit this. There has now been born a bond of brotherhood between Hindus and Musalmans living in India (Chatterjee, 1993: 111 & 222).[4]

What mattered was the limit of the polis. Yet the metaphor above does not only speak of those whom the nation excludes; more importantly, it describes the character of those whom it takes in as well: they are all family, bonded by relations of fraternal love.

What counts is the character of the state. Three broad themes emerged in this regard. Anthony Smith calls them territorialism, democracy and Pan-Africanism. He means by territorialism a concern, not so much with the limits of the nation's territory as with who controlled the state (Smith, 1983: 54). European colonisers, he argues, were highly successful in imposing the territorial aspect of the Western state on the African demographic and political map. They were able, not only to map the African political and economic reality, but also to imprint these boundaries in the 'psychic identity and cultural vision of the new elites' (p. 54). As a result, the 'shape' and 'face' of the state, its bureaucratic-territorial form, was already given by the time of independence. On these terms, the African nation is discussed in relation to the form of the state as a bureaucratic-institutional constellation and the particular character of its politics (clientelist, centralised-bureaucratic, 'spoils politics'[5]). Smith himself defends this state-centric approach against others. As much as Pan-Africanism (and/or Negritude) informed the nationalist imaginary, furnishing it with the metaphors and images for a vision of the postcolony, giving to it a specific culture, African nationalism was, argues Smith, 'more firmly grounded' and 'prosaic', lacking the florid poetic fancy of, say, Eastern European nationalisms (p. 57). Over and above their distinctive culture or the specific content of their programmes, African nationalisms, continues Smith, were firstly and foremostly 'territorial nationalisms' (p. 55). He states:

> It was the colonial state that became the mould as well as the target of African nationalisms, and on them it stamped its special character and aims. It has been the special features of the colonial State – gubernatorial, territorial, bureaucratic, paternalist-educational, caste-like – that have given them its peculiar impetus and shape (p. 56).

The form of the African state has been a subject of continuous interest. The nation is considered an effect of the state itself. The state in Africa or the African state, to recall Bayart's (1993) own ambivalence, remains one of the key prisms through which Africa is apprehended.[6] It has given rise to an extensive literature on the African political economy, exemplified by journals such as the *Review of African Political Economy*. What matters for this literature today is the relationship between the form of the state (failed, weak, in crisis) and the features of post-independence politics: limited sovereignty; corruption; and ethnic competition for state resources, governance, and so on (Comaroff & Comaroff, 2001).[7] Exemplary in this regard is the widely cited article by Chris Allen, to which we shall return shortly. For the moment, we can note that in his article 'Understanding African politics', Allen seeks to relate the variability of politics in Africa to several 'entwined and sequential patterns of political development' (Allen, 1995: 316). More recently, we can note the report by the Commission for Africa, which was chaired by British Prime Minister Tony Blair. The report was issued in 2005 to coincide with the G8 meeting in Gleneagles in Scotland, where leaders of the world's wealthiest countries planned to discuss increasing aid and debt relief to African countries. In a section on the 'lost decades', the report outlines Africa's predicament by comparing the state of the continent with that of another, Asia. 'For 30 years', it observes,

> the average income in sub-Saharan Africa was twice that of both South and East Asia. In the intervening decades an astonishing turn-around has taken place. The average income in Africa is now well below half of that in East Asia. The story is similar in South Asia, Latin America and the Middle East. Africa is the only continent in the world which is stagnating (Commission for Africa, 2005: 16).

'Why has Africa fallen so behind?' the commissioners ask. The answer comes shortly afterwards: 'One thing underlies all the difficulties caused by the interactions of Africa's history over the past 40 years. It is the weakness of governance and the absence of an effective state' (Commission for Africa, 2005: 23–24).

Jean and John Comaroff periodise this discourse as characteristic of what they call the first of 'two epochal phases' (Comaroff & Comaroff, 2001: 632). They associate it with the period of decolonisation, though its terms, as witnessed above, are still pervasive. Here 'postcoloniality' is thought of in terms of 'the international order of sovereign nations within the industrial capitalist world system' (p. 632). According to this narrative, 'Africa found the promise of autonomy and growth sundered by the realities of neocolonialism, which freighted [African countries] with an impossible toll of debt and dependency' (p. 632). Under such conditions, African regimes became more and more authoritarian, evidencing deteriorating standards of governance and respect for human rights.

The Comaroffs observe a 'second epoch', beginning in 1989, in the genealogy of independent African states. Associated with the coming of age of 'neoliberal global capitalism', sub-Saharan African countries began to experience unprecedented demands for democracy (Comaroff & Comaroff, 2001: 632–33). Yet this movement has seen a lot more than democratisation. According to this discourse, it has

> metamorphosed the old international order into a more fluid, market-driven, electronically articulated universe: a universe in which supranational institutions burgeon; … in which transnational identities, diasporic connections, ecological disasters, and the mobility of human populations challenge both the nature of sovereignty and the sovereignty of 'nature'; in which … liberty is distilled to its postmodern essence, the right to choose subjectivities, commodities, sexualities, localities, identities, and other forms of collective representation (p. 633).

In Africa, the coming of post-modernity, however, is said to bring with it growing appeals to difference and diversity. The very existence of society itself is called into question. The state is said to be in perpetual crisis, its power chaotically dispersed (pp. 633–34).

The difference between these two moments, pre- or post-1989, on the Comaroffs' terms, hinges on the characterisation of the state: singular and unified, as opposed to polymorphous and pluralistic. Even if, according to the Comaroffs, the sense of crisis evoked by these discourses is exaggerated, they nonetheless speak to a real condition: the predicament of the African nation state (Comaroff & Comaroff, 2001: 632). At stake is the increasingly hyphenated relationship between state and nation: the former is unable to fulfil its task as progenitor of the latter.

The sense of crisis – hyphenation – of the relationship between state and nation in Africa has been associated with renewed interest in the (dis)organisation of African societies. As the African state haemorrhages into a multiplicity of fragmented organisations and authorities, as it loses its ability to manage urbanisation, poverty relief, service delivery or economic growth, what new powers have occupied this space? How are they organised? What is the form of society that emerges in and through their activities? These are the questions that are increasingly being taken up by Africanist scholars. Abdou-Maliq Simone, for example, situates Johannesburg in a larger African context of what he terms 'ruined urbanization' (Simone, 2004: 407). '[T]he truncated process of economic modernization at work in African cities', he argues, 'has never fully consolidated apparatuses of definition capable of enforcing specific and consistent territorial organizations of the city' (p. 409). By this he means that state administrations and civil institutions have been unable to order and control activities taking place in the city (buying, selling, residing, etc.) (p. 409).

This renewed interest in the state of African society (or societies in Africa), its cultural practices and its cosmological organisation (witchcraft, religion, etc.) is not simply a corrective to at least 20 years of attention to the state as a political-institutional configuration.The current interest in the inscrutability of the African scene and the elusive[8] and elliptical character of African societies follows from the sense that Africa has witnessed 50 years of ruined modernism. At stake is the supposedly hyphenated relation between state and nation in the continent. We can summarise the conclusions of this scholarship as such: African nationalism has not given rise to African nations. There is now a substantial literature, both journalistic and academic, dealing with this apparent failure. It seeks its reasons on a continuum from avaricious African elites (Meredith, 2005), bad governance (European Union, 2005; Commission for Africa, 2005), the position of Africa in the world capitalist system (Wallerstein, 1991) to the form of the African state (Bayart, 1993; Mamdani, 1996).

In his new book on the state of Africa 50 years after independence, Martin Meredith, for example, asks 'why, after the euphoria of the independence era, so many hopes and ambitions faded and why the future of Africa came to be spoken of only in pessimistic terms' (Meredith, 2005: 13–14). What is striking, he suggests, is that despite the variability and diversity of African states, they have all 'suffered so many of the same misfortunes' (p. 14). 'Time and time again', he concludes, '[Africa's] potential for economic development has been disrupted by the predatory politics of ruling elites seeking personal gain, often precipitating violence for their own ends' (p. 14). 'The problem is not so much that development has failed,' he states, citing the Nigerian academic Claude Ake, 'as that it was never really on the agenda in the first place' (p. 688). At stake is an African state used for purposes other than nation-building. If Meredith *et al.*, including the Commission for Africa publication mentioned earlier, lay the blame for the state of contemporary African states at the door of African leadership (but it is also where they find reason for hope), more academically oriented scholarship stresses the form of the African state.

A case in point is Mahmood Mamdani's *Citizen and Subject* (1996), which relates the corrupt and authoritarian character of contemporary African regimes to the form of the colonial state that preceded them. His argument, somewhat telescoped, is that the colonial state was a double-sided affair. In the cities it governed directly through civic institutions that, though they refused citizenship to Africans, nonetheless established a public domain constituted on the basis of individuated rights and contract. In the rural areas, however, the colonial state ruled indirectly through tribal authorities. These fused in the authority of the chief, judicial, legislative, executive and administrative powers, interpolating those under its 'clenched fist' as tribal subjects. Post-colonial regimes usually set out to 'deracialise' civil society, neglecting to 'detribalise' the 'Native Authority'. As a result, argues Mamdani, 'the unreformed Native Authority came to contaminate civil society, so that the more civil society was deracialized, the more it took on a tribalized form' (Mamdani, 1996: 21). In his terms, clientism, ethnic mobilisation and corruption are all effects of the 'bifurcated' form of the African state. What is important to note is the consequence of this argument. We might infer that the failure of such states to realise the nation in Africa had less to do with the *ad hominem* qualities of their elites than with the very form of the state itself. The 'bifurcated state' was an inappropriate instrument for nation-building.

Achille Mbembe too locates the form of the contemporary African state in the character of colonial sovereignty. Yet unlike others before him, Mbembe is not content to analyse corruption and violence as symptoms of failure or crisis. Rather, the gothic form of power in Africa – corruption, vulgarity and violence – speaks both to the specificity of sovereignty in Africa and its creativity. The peculiarity of colonial sovereignty, Mbembe suggests, is that relations between the coloniser and the colonised are homologous to those between the master and the slave (Mbembe, 2001: 31). Here Mbembe is drawing on Hegel to define a form of authority 'where power [is] reduced to the right to demand, to force, to ban, to compel, to authorize, to punish, to reward, to be obeyed, in short, to enjoin and direct' (Mbembe, 2001: 32). Instead of subverting this form of power, decolonisation reproduced it, substituting for the colonial master a new potentate. What gives to the postcolony its particular character – its monstrousness and its vulgarity – is the way that this form of sovereignty is reproduced under new conditions – chiefly that of International Monetary Fund (IMF)-imposed strictures.

The 'regimentation of privileges and immunities,' (Mbembe, 2001: 29) the disregard for the common law and the arbitrary granting of concessions to individuals and corporations are legitimised through a logic of 'conviviality' (Mbembe, 2001: 110). The argument is well summarised by Adeleke Adeeko:

> The official parades, the cultural festivals, the shining plaques and medals of honor, the crimson language of official newspapers, the festival style execution of armed robbers, the public humiliation of those who deviate from the glaringly arbitrary official path, and other official and non-official absurd rituals of everyday life, together institutionalise the potentate as 'a fetish to which the subject is bound' (Adeeko, 2002: 7).

Everyone wallows in the obscene vulgarity of the ruler – his arbitrariness, his buffoonery, his self-importance. In the absence of real state power, sovereignty is reproduced through vulgar performance.

It is necessary to draw attention to the epistemological underpinnings of these arguments, especially as they pertain to the state–nation relationship. What counts is a certain conception of the relationship coloniality–post-coloniality. It is especially evident in the work of Mbembe (2001)[9]. *On the Postcolony* pays almost no attention to the form of colonial resistance, the social and political character of the parties that came to power after independence or the avowed aims of the new administrations. This is a very full absence. By omitting these factors from the analysis, Mbembe implies that the form of the postcolony is unmarked by their enterprise. Despite his plea for a mode of writing that acknowledges or respects African agency, rather surprisingly, such agency dissolves before the terms of colonial power. New regimes and leaders can only mimic colonial sovereignty. They are unable to transform the very form of this power itself. Independence thus marks a point of both absolute rupture and continuity. From the perspective of anti-colonial resistance, it marks a moment of radical breach: the very identity of the resistance is erased, and its attributes and form dissolved in the character of colonial power. From the perspective of the state there is continuity in its form, though not necessarily of its empirical existence. Even if, under the strictures of IMF structural adjustment, the post-colonial state is individualised and privatised into a myriad of agencies and organisations, and it therefore lacks coherence in a hierarchical unity. Like the colonial state, it nonetheless produces homologous relations of power, those between master and slave.

We saw at the beginning of this chapter that these were precisely the terms that Dubow suggested obscured the study of nationalism. Marxist essentialism reduces nationalism to a mere epiphenomenon of economic class interests, thereby devaluing studies of nationalism in Africa on their own terms. Post-colonial essentialism treats the postcolony as a mere phenomenon of colonial power. Crawford Young examined the latter point in an address to the Centre for African Studies at the University of Copenhagen in 2001. The purpose of his intervention was to consider the merit of such a view, both on analytical and political grounds. He concluded that it lacked any, because despite the fact that

> the lexical habit of post-colonial usage to label the African
> political world persists, ... in many countries little remains of
> the hegemonic apparatus which African rulers inherited and
> initially sought to reinforce and expand as an instrument of
> rapid development (Young, 2004: 24).

From the perspective of such studies, however, the colonial state is treated as a Sadeian corpse. It remains immaculate and pristine, even when it is ostensibly overthrown, toppled or when its power is dispersed and privatised. Is this not the form of a simple essence? Colonial power is deemed determinant, but is never itself overdetermined. The social totality (in this case the postcolony) is the development of a simple unity, of a simple principle (the colonial state); so strictly speaking, it is the phenomenon, the self-manifestation of this simple principle, that persists in all its manifestations.[10] On these terms, nationalist politics *qua* nationalist politics is deemed irrelevant to the form of the independent state. What becomes invisible – indeed, unthinkable – on these terms is that African nationalism has, indeed, transformed the colonial state. At stake is the emergence of African nations.

The emergence of nations in Africa, furthermore, is doubly obscured by a sometimes uncritical reflection on the claims of African nationalists themselves. Scholars take the nationalist vision of the postcolony on its own terms, and then judge African nationalism lacking when independent states do not resemble the imaginary. Again, what is at fault is a certain epistemology. We saw that for the Comaroffs, the problem was the hyphenated relation between state and nation. Yet such an appraisal assumes that the state is the subject and the nation is its object. The object remains elusive because the agent is not up to the task. Yet the measure of the nation is not the degree to which the state realises the nation, but the degree to which the nation controls the state.

2

The Democratic Origin of Nations

It has been suggested that the nationalist imaginary must be understood as a particular democratic imaginary. More precisely, nationalism is a response to the question of democracy *par excellence*: Who are 'the people' in whom sovereignty is vested? This relationship between the nation and the democratic imaginary is easily overlooked if the nation is conceived of as, above all, a cultural artefact; worse, if culture is opposed to the political. This is what happens in *The Nation and Its Fragments*, Partha Chatterjee's (1993) discussion of post-colonial nationalism in Asia. His argument is that anti-colonial nationalism is unlike European nationalism, precisely because it does not imagine the space of the nation as a political domain. This is an important claim that needs to be addressed.

Chatterjee starts by acknowledging the importance of Benedict Anderson's influential book, *Imagined Communities* (1991) for animating fresh discussion about nationalism. 'I have one central objection to Anderson's argument,' Chatterjee writes. 'If nationalisms in the rest of the world have to choose their imagined community from certain "modular" forms already made available to them by Europe and the Americas, what do they have left to imagine?' (Chatterjee, 1993: 5). He is worried that Anderson, in a long tradition of European orientalism, denies agency to non-Europeans and/or non-Americans. 'History, it would seem,' he writes sarcastically, has decreed that we in the postcolonial world shall only be perpetual consumers of modernity. Europe and the Americas, the only true subjects of history, have thought out on our behalf not only the script of colonial enlightenment and exploitation, but also that of our anticolonial resistance and postcolonial misery. Even our imaginations must remain forever colonized (Chatterjee, 1993: 5).

Might Michel Foucault not have, in all seriousness, replied, 'Yes, as a postcolonial subject, you are indeed a perpetual consumer of modernity'? Let us recall Foucault's argument about disciplinary apparatuses, at least in *Discipline and Punish* (1979) and the first volume of the *History of Sexuality* (1998): that the very things such apparatuses seek to discipline and control are already their effects. We are told over and over again, for example, that during the nineteenth century, efforts to control and discipline sexuality resulted in its proliferation. Slavoj Zizek extends the logic of this argument to the field of colonialism. Somewhat playfully, he writes: 'One is tempted to say that the will to gain political independence from the colonizer in the guise of a new independent nation-state is the ultimate proof that the colonized ethnic group is thoroughly integrated into the ideological universe of the colonizer' (Zizek, 2000: 255). Why? Because it is precisely colonialist oppression that 'brings about the … eminently modern will to assert one's … identity in the form of a nation-state' (Zizek, 2000: 255).[1] Zizek is being playful, precisely because he wants to disagree with such arguments for foreclosing on the possibility of real resistance: a resistance, that is, that exceeds the terms of the coloniser. In this regard, we might anticipate Zizek's possible critique of Achille Mbembe's *On the Postcolony*.

In the postcolony, Mbembe writes, the 'commandement' (the term he uses to refer to an authoritarian mode of power) institutionalises itself, and achieves legitimation and hegemony by inventing signs officially invested with a surplus of meanings that are not negotiable, and that one is officially forbidden to depart from or challenge (Mbembe, 2001: 103):

To ensure that no such challenge takes place the champions of state power invent entire constellations of ideas; they adopt a distinct set of cultural repertoires and powerfully evocative concepts; but they also resort, if necessary, to the systematic application of pain (p. 103).

Turning Bakhtin on his head, Mbembe finds two of these ideas in that of the 'grotesque' and the 'obscene'. No longer strategies of ordinary people to parody officials, they become the characteristics of occasions that 'state power organizes for dramatizing its own magnificence' (p. 103). The state is necessarily extravagant, needing to 'furnish proof of its prestige and glory by a sumptuous (yet burdensome) presentation of its symbols of status, displaying the heights of luxury in dress and lifestyle, turning acts of generosity into grand theatre' (p. 109). Yet the 'ordinary people' do not resist these grotesque spectacles. Rather, 'the popular world borrows the ideological repertoire of officialdom, along with its idioms and forms; conversely, the official world mimics popular vulgarity, inserting it at the core of the procedures by which it takes on grandeur' (p. 110). This leads Mbembe to his conclusion:

> It is unnecessary, then, to insist ... on oppositions or, as does conventional analysis, on the purported logic of resistance, disengagement, or disjunction. Instead, the emphasis should be on the logic of 'conviviality', on the dynamics of domesticity and familiarity, *inscribing the dominant and the dominated within the same episteme* (p. 110; emphasis added).

Has Mbembe not slipped into a type of theoretical formalism, positing a society that is hermetically closed in on itself? There is no (radical) outside (to borrow a term from Ernesto Laclau), no possibility of resistance that can break the terms of post-colonial power. Dominant and dominated merely mimic each other, producing what Mbembe calls a mutual 'zombification' that robs each of their vitality and leaves them both impotent (p. 104).[2] Is this not another way of saying that the post-colonial subject's imagination has indeed been colonised?

What Chatterjee finds in post-colonial nationalism is precisely a 'difference' with the colonial discourse: 'The most powerful as well as creative results of the nationalist imagination in Asia and Africa', he writes, 'are posited not on an identity but rather on a *difference* with the "modular" forms of the national society propagated by the modern West' (Chatterjee, 1993: 5; original emphasis). 'By my reading,' he continues,

> anticolonial nationalism creates its own domain of sovereignty within colonial society well before it begins its political battle with Imperial power. It does this by dividing the world of social institutions and practices into two domains – the material and the spiritual. ... [N]ationalism declares the domain of the spiritual its sovereign territory and refuses to allow the colonial power to intervene in that domain (p. 6).

Hence, if Western nationalism is a state project, anti-colonial nationalism is a cultural one. It seeks to 'fashion a "modern" national culture that is nevertheless not Western' (p. 6).

One wonders, however, if Chatterjee has not moved too quickly. We get a sense of this from his style of writing. In the passage referred to above, he invokes a 'we' (post-colonial subjects) and a 'them' (the West): 'History, it would seem, has decreed that *we in the postcolonial world* shall only be perpetual consumers of modernity. Europe and the Americas, [are] the only true subjects of history' (Chatterjee, 1993: 5; emphasis added). The argument of this book is that the proper domain of nationalism is in the emergence of this 'we'. The individual that refers to himself or herself in the name of a people – *this* nation – is already a national subject, whether this naming takes place in the field of art, culture, theatre or political battle. What has to be explained, in other words, is the emergence of such a collective pronoun in the first place.

The problem with Anderson's account is not that he locates the origins of the nationalist imagination in Europe – the fact that something originates somewhere tells us virtually nothing about how it is appropriated, developed, elaborated and transformed. The trouble is that his account of nationalism is not political enough: he does not sufficiently explore its origins in the democratic imagination of the eighteenth century. Let us dwell for a moment on his argument.

Political communities, Anderson suggests, are to be distinguished 'by the style in which they are imagined' (Anderson, 1991: 6). In contrast to dynastic and religious communities that conceived their unities, not in terms of causality or dependence, but, rather, of prefiguring and fulfilment – what Walter Benjamin described as 'messianic' time – the nation was imagined in *homogenous time*. The conditions of the nation idea, Anderson tells us, were prepared when certain cultural conceptions lost their axiomatic grip. 'The first of these was the idea that a particular script-language offered privileged access to ontological truth' (Hebrew or Latin, for example) (p. 36). The second was

> the belief that society was naturally organized around and under high centers – monarchs who were persons apart from other human beings and who ruled by some form of cosmological (divine) dispensation. Human loyalties were necessarily hierarchical and centripetal because the rule, like the sacred script, was a node of access to being and inherent in it (p. 36).

The third was a 'conception of temporality in which cosmology and history were indistinguishable, the origins of the world and of men essentially identical' (p. 36).

How do these cultural axioms combine to give the form of religious and dynastic communities? On their own terms, Anderson explains, religious communities have no history other than the schema of God: their events, trials and happenings are merely moments of some otherworldly logic. The time of society is the time of God, since the social totality, being merely an epiphenomenon of the divine will, develops according to His plan. The rise and fall of civilisations, the elliptical circuit of the moon, the setting of the sun, war, poverty, peace and abundance all happen according to some great design. Hence the radical distance between these communities and modern ones: the meaning of things was given uniquely by their place in the scheme of God, revealed through certain privileged texts or miracles. The limits of the community are fixed by divine, symbolic referents that are either announced or revealed. Hence the empirical boundaries of the Christian, Islamic and Buddhist communities, for example, were given by the limits of their sacred languages (Latin, Arabic, Mandarin Chinese) – which were solely capable of expressing divine intentions – so that literate priesthoods were the privileged savants of Godly purpose.

Dynastic communities, on the other hand, Anderson continues, produced and reproduced their unities through marriage and intermarriage – the community, given corporality in the body of the sovereign (as the site of God on earth), expanded or contracted according to his/her marital liaisons. Hence the form of dynastic and religious communities: they encompassed diverse linguistic and cultural groups, and they were not territorially fixed. The community did not receive its coherence or its consistency from the subjects that belonged to it, but merely from the monarchical figure that embodied it. Therefore, its reproduction coincided exactly with *his/her* fortune: expanding or contracting through war (displacement of or by another monarch) or through marriage (the joining of communities).

What replaced this mode of apprehension, we are told, was an 'idea' of homogenous time. Anderson approaches a description of this idea through the example of the modern novel. Characters that never meet and whose existence is unknown to each other are nonetheless connected in the story through a double movement: (1) they are 'embedded' in particular 'societies' (Hardyesque landscapes of the mind such as Wessex, Lübeck, Los Angeles); and (2) they are 'embedded' in the reader's mind, so that despite their simultaneous and parallel actions, they nonetheless constitute a community of characters in the book.

To give to Anderson's analysis the full force of homogenous time as intended by Walter Benjamin, we should add that the parallel and simultaneous lives of all the characters are embedded in a single movement evolving towards a climax. Past, present and future are stages in an evolving teleology. This, Anderson tells us, is analogous to the idea of the nation: a community of individuals mostly anonymous to each other (we do not have personal relations with all our compatriots) who steadily and simultaneously go about their affairs in a common space, content in the belief that they share with each other something or other in common.

This leads Anderson to his well-known definition of the nation: 'it is an imagined political community – and imagined as inherently limited and sovereign' (Anderson, 1991: 6). It is 'limited' because it always has finite boundaries beyond which lie other nations. It is 'sovereign' because it emerges at a time when the 'gage and emblem of … freedom is the sovereign state' (p. 7). It is a 'community' because whatever real inequalities and exploitation prevail, it is imagined as a 'deep, horizontal comradeship' (p. 7).

Our first problem arises when we ask: Why did the weakening of religious and dynastic cultures produce the 'idea' of the nation? It is worth dwelling on Anderson's answer.

Faced with the arbitrary character of 'man's' (*sic*) mortality, the ineluctability of his particular genetic heritage, gender, 'life-era', physical capabilities and so on, he seeks meaning for his life. 'The great merit of traditional religious world-views', Anderson argues, has been their ability to give sense to the 'overwhelming burden of human suffering – disease, mutilation, grief, age, and death' (Anderson, 1991: 9). With the ebbing of religious belief, Anderson continues, death and deliverance seemed arbitrary and ridiculous. The 'disintegration of paradise' and the 'absurdity of salvation' required, in their place, a new 'style of continuity': a secular transformation of fatality into continuity and contingency into meaning. 'Few things', he continues, 'were better placed to achieve this than an idea of the nation', since nations always loom out of an immemorial past and glide into a limitless future (pp. 12–13). Anderson is saying that the nation 'idea' is an Enlightenment response to the 'death of God'. Apparently, we all seek meaning and continuity where this takes the form of a will to immortality. The nation fulfils such needs because it is seemingly eternal.

Yet Anderson's explanation begs more questions than it answers. Is the will to immortality not itself a religious idea, rather than a state of 'man's' nature? If nations emerge from the eclipse of the religious imagination, then Anderson cannot account for them. Why are they imagined as quasi-religious objects? If they do not, then he also cannot account for them. If nations are consubstantial with religion, then, on their own terms, they cannot be products of a radically new style of imagining.[3] This is the substance of Adrian Hastings' critique of what he calls the 'modernist school', including Benedict Anderson, Eric Hobsbawm, Ernest Gellner and John Breuilly. They have, he suggests, understated the importance of religious thinking to nationalism. He argues: 'The Bible provided, for the Christian world at least, the original model of the nation. Without it and its Christian interpretation and implementation, it is arguable that nations and nationalism, as we know them, *could never have existed*' (Hasting, 1997: 4; emphasis added).

What is at stake in this disagreement is before the periodisation of the origins of nations. Unlike the modernist school, for whom the nation does not exist prior to the 1780s – that is before the American and French Revolutions – Hastings is sure that 'the sense of "nation" was already found in the fourteenth century' (Hastings, 1997: 18). Starting with the English Bible, Hastings finds the term 'nacion' – a translation of the Vulgate text, which used the Latin 'natio' – employed as early as the mid-1340s. Thus Psalm 107.4 is translated by Richard Rolle of Hampole, who died in 1349, as 'I sall singe til the in nacyuns' (cited in Hastings, 1997: 16). This is not simply a coincidence of a term: 'What is clear', claims Hastings, 'is that there has been a surprisingly firm continuity in usage across more than six hundred years' (Hastings, 1997: 18). He is suggesting that the medieval term 'nacyun' or 'nacion', like the contemporary term 'nation', referred to a historico-cultural community with a territory it regards as its own and over which it claims some sort of sovereignty so that the cultural community sees itself with a measure of self-awareness as also a territorial and political community, held together horizontally by its shared character rather than vertically by reason of the authority of the state (Hastings, 1997: 25).

Hastings is, ironically, drawing on Anderson's own definition of a nation as a 'deep horizontal comradeship'. Hastings' point is that both the word and concept, 'nation', were already at the heart of the English linguistic, cultural and religious tradition from the Middle Ages, though they became more widespread with the Reformation and the diffusion of knowledge of the Bible achieved by Protestantism (Hastings, 1997: 18). What Hastings does is make clear a contradiction at the heart of *Imagined Communities*. If the nation is chiefly a cultural artefact, then its form precedes the Enlightenment.

Anthony Smith, for his part, finds the origin of national communities in pre-modern ethnic sentiments (Smith, 1986: 5), even finding an analogue for modern systems of nation states in the fourteenth century BC (Smith, 1986: 11). In this view, the nation as defined by Anderson and Hastings resembles what Smith calls an ethnic community (*'ethnie'*) in that it is a community with 'shared ancestry myths, histories and cultures, having an association with a specific territory and a sense of solidarity' (Smith, 2003: 27). Yet if this is how we construe the nation, then, according to Smith, 'such communities have been widespread in all eras of history, at least since the onset of the Bronze Age in the Middle East and Aegean' (Smith, 2003: 27). Seyoum Hameso, for example, in his study of *Ethnicity and Nationalism in Africa*, simply substitutes for Smith's term *ethnie* the word nation. Hence, where Smith suggests that *ethnie* is the basic force and process of the modern as well the pre-modern epochs (Smith, 1995: 57), Hameso simply renders this as: nations are the basic units of the modern and pre-modern periods (Hameso, 1997: 33).

What all these accounts have in common is that they elevate the cultural dimensions of the nation – its basic anthropology – and reduce its significance as a political community. In this regard, there is no sharp division between the modernist and pre-modernist accounts of the nation.

Ernest Gellner, someone for whom the nation is a modern phenomenon, for example, sees in it a functional response to the 'Great Transformation' – the emergence of industrial societies from agrarian ones. Accompanying this movement, he suggests, was a radical change in the nature of work. Physical labour (the 'application of human muscle to matter' [Gellner, 1999: 106]) was replaced by 'controlling, managing and maintaining a machine' and more usually by the 'rapid manipulation of meanings and people through computers ... telephones and typewriters and faxes ... and so on' (p. 106). Industrial production presupposed that the system of symbols in use were immediately legible: that meaning, as Gellner puts it, 'was carried by the message alone' (p. 107). Rapid communication between sometimes-distant interlocutors, who were selected more and more on the basis of merit rather than rank (and, therefore, of different ranks), required an orderly, standardised system of ideas and rules for formulating and decoding messages (p. 107). This is what Gellner calls a 'high culture' (p. 107). With industrialisation, Gellner concludes, 'the entire society must be pervaded by one standardised high culture, if it is to work at all' (p. 107), i.e.

> Society can no longer tolerate a wild proliferation of internal subcultures, all of them context-bound and severely inhibited in their mutual inter-communication. Access to the appropriate high culture, and acceptability within it, is a person's most important and valued possession: it institutes a pre-condition of access not merely to employment, but to legal and moral citizenship, to all kinds of social participation. So a person identifies with his or her high culture, and is eager that he or she inhabits a political unit where various bureaucracies function in that same cultural idiom. ... In other words, he or she is a nationalist (Gellner, 1999: 107–8).

Why does it follow, however, that a high culture is necessarily a national culture? This is the gist of the question that Miroslav Hroch addresses to Gellner. Hroch observes that most national movements had, for the most part, already acquired a mass character by 1800 (Hroch, 1985) – prior, that is, to the industrial epoch. In other words, someone with a national consciousness was not necessarily a member of a high culture.

Gellner's treatment of the nation is subject to an even more important critique. On his terms, an agro-literate society is necessarily a heterogeneous culture – it 'secretes, engenders, elaborates cultural differentiations within itself' (Gellner, 1999: 103) – whereas industrial societies are attendant on *cultural homogenisation*. Gellner adduces this from the technical requirements of an advanced industrial economy: (a) the need for communication among people irrespective of social position or rank, and (b) the decomposition of stable, ascribed roles in favour of occupational effectiveness and hence social mobility.

One of the key features of South Africa, however, was that apartheid society engendered, elaborated, produced and reproduced social heterogeneity *as a condition* of industrialisation. This was the centrepiece, for example, of the theory of 'Colonialism of a Special Type'. It suggested that, on the one hand, 'white South Africa' resembled an advanced capitalist state and industrial society; while on the other hand, 'non-white South Africa' had all the features of a colony. Famously, it concluded that 'non-white South Africa is the colony of white South Africa itself' (SACP [1962], cited in Wolpe, 1989: 62). Relying on an analysis of migrant labour and its centrality to the profitability of the gold-mining sector, Marxist historians and sociologists argued that industrialisation happened by tying black South Africans to an oppressive and poverty-stricken agricultural society. Rather than create a homogenous culture, industrialisation in South Africa reproduced an agro-tribal society in its midst.

Immanuel Wallerstein, for his part, goes so far as to suggest that this is the normal state of affairs for capitalist industrialisation. Capitalists, he proposes, benefit by having the cost level of labour subsidised by an income or subsistence from agricultural production. Capitalism does not necessarily presuppose the dissolution of extended or clan societies and hence the homogenisation of culture (Wallerstein, 1991: 109; 130–31). Hence, the nation *qua* homogenous high culture cannot be read from the logic of (capitalist) industrialisation.

The age of revolution

There is an important intuition behind the periodisation of the nation to the late eighteenth century. Something happens to the nation *qua* cultural community during this period. At stake is the advent of democracy as a principle of government and political community. For the first time, the political community refers to 'the people', in whom political sovereignty resides. If the people are the nation and democracy refers to a system of government of and by 'the people', then the nation is the logical home for democratic government.

Jurgen Habermas, for example, sees in the nation a revolutionary attempt at democratisation. Where democracies on the Western model appeared, he argues, they did so in the form of the nation state (Habermas, 2001: 62). This is because the nation state fulfilled the preconditions for democratic self-control: self-governance, the demos, consent, representation and popular sovereignty (p. 61). The sovereign will was taken to be the will of the nation.

Benedict Anderson hints obliquely at this rupture, though he does not integrate it into his own analysis. Hence, he situates his discussion of nations in accounts of either popular movements for democracy (in France, America, Hungary and Spain) or dynastic responses to them. He defines the nation as a political community, and generates one of its key features – that it is sovereign – from a time when the 'gage and emblem of ... freedom is the sovereign state' (Anderson, 1991: 7). Yet, for all that, Anderson does not reflect on the idea of the nation in relation to the idea of democracy – this despite their historical contemporaneity. Eric Hobsbawm (1999), in contrast, wants the modern concept of the nation to be understood in relation to the 'Age of Revolution' – to the period, that is, of revolutionary democrats. Hobsbawm's analysis is curious, however, for not drawing its own logical conclusions.

He traces the genealogy of the term nation and concludes that in its peculiarly modern sense three elements were related: people, territory and state. These terms were articulated quite differently by nationalists, on the one hand, and by revolutionary democrats, on the other. The results were distinct concepts of the nation. In the first case, nationalists appealed to a pre-existing community seeking sovereignty in its own state. This community spoke the same language and/or shared the same customs, but was generally endowed with certain moral qualities that distinguished it from other groups. In the other case, revolutionary democrats conceived the sovereign people simply as comprising those citizens who governed themselves. Therefore, relative to the state, 'the people' were nothing more than a congress of citizens, but relative to humanity they constituted a specific demos, i.e. a nation. Hobsbawm discusses the nation of nationalists as an 'ethnic' community, and that of revolutionary democratics as a 'body of citizens'. 'There was *no logical connection*', he argues, however, 'between the body of citizens of a territorial state on the one hand, and the identification of a "nation" on ethnic, linguistic or other grounds or of other characteristics which allowed collective recognition of group membership' (Hobsbawm, 1999: 19; emphasis added).

In other words, Hobsbawm argues that the nation, defined as an ethnic community, was logically unrelated to the nation *qua* body of citizens (bearers of political rights). In this respect, Hobsbawm echoes a distinction that has become commonplace today between ethnic and civic nationalism. Yet even on his own terms, Hobsbawm cannot really account for the tenacity of the ethnic variable in the constitution of the body of citizens. If the nation of revolutionary democrats had anything in common with that of their nationalist counterparts, he suggests, it was not the element of ethnicity or language. What characterised the nation was that it was a community of common interest rather than being linguistically or otherwise homogenous. He notes, for example, that the French Republic had no difficulty electing an Anglo-American, Thomas Paine, to its National Convention. Moreover, the revolutionary and Napoleonic wars added to the French nation territories and peoples that could not on any ethnic criteria be deemed French. 'We cannot, therefore, read into the revolutionary "nation"', he tells us, 'anything like the later nationalist programme of establishing nation states for bodies defined in terms of ... ethnicity, common language, religion, territory and common historical memories' (Hobsbawm, 1999: 20).

Yet Hobsbawm concedes that for most Jacobins 'a Frenchman who did not speak French was suspect' and, moreover, that the 'ethno-linguistic criterion of nationality was often accepted' (Hobsbawm, 1999: 21). He states in this regard – and the remark is important – that:

> it was not the native use of the French language that made a person French – how could it be when the Revolution itself spent so much of its time proving how few people in France actually used it? – but the willingness to acquire this, among the other liberties, laws and common characteristics of the *free people* of France (p. 21; emphasis added).

We can leave Hobsbawm here. He has, ironically, given us all the elements needed to continue with our argument. In particular, he introduces a new variable that completes the logical relation between nationalism and democracy. What he says above is that willingness to acquire French was deemed a condition of being 'free'. Or, rather, free citizens were those that spoke French. Now, if the body of citizens is the nation, and those citizens that are free are French, then the nation is free when it is French. Even more simply: if freedom is included in the definition of being a citizen, and speaking French is a condition of freedom, then the body of citizens is also the body of the French nation. Here the linguistic/ethnic criterion is not logically unrelated to citizenship: it is the logical condition of it.

When we consider the nation *qua* imagined community in the light of the age of democracy, then its peculiarly modern features become apparent. Firstly and most importantly, the nation is a democratic community, which is its abstract form. As such, it refers to a community of citizens. Modern political theorists understand by this term a political subject having civic rights (equality before the law; personal liberty; freedom of speech, belief and opinion; the right to property; and the right to contract with another), political rights (the right to elect and to be elected, and the right to participate in government), and even socio-economic rights (equal access to health care and the regulation of work), where these rights are deemed to announce themselves from human nature (Gaille, 1998: 21–22).[4] At first glance, therefore, to qualify for citizenship, one need only be human. Our first difficulty arises when we ask: On what basis are these fundamental human rights recognised in this or that particular demos? The moment the *Citizen* (the universal bearer of rights) becomes a *citizen* (the bearer of rights in a specific community), he/she is necessarily distinguished from other citizens. In other words, something happens to make his/her rights admissible in this or that community and not in others. Our second difficulty arises when we ask if these rights apply to the mad and the mentally handicapped. Living apart and judged incapable of autonomously expressing their opinions, such people are said only to have partial political rights. Combined, we might conclude with Marie Gaille that: 'This makes one suspect that citizenship is not granted to this or that individual on the basis of the rights of man, but, rather, as a status, conferred according to relative criteria' (p. 23; my translation).

To take this point further, we can firstly say that if citizenship is a status and not a right, then it implies that duties and obligations issue not from nature, but from the political community itself. Even when judged a feature of birth, citizenship only reveals itself in relations between people and the state. Rights only appear in the light of the sovereign law; hence the disassociation possible between the 'natural rights of Man' and the civic and especially political rights of the citizen. To the extent, therefore, that rights are conferred by the law, they can be granted in degrees, and they are susceptible to political claims by those who do not enjoy them. Citizenship is thus produced in the relations between individuals or collectivities and the state. What is at stake in defining the limits of the political community, therefore, is the measure according to which rights are conferred and distributed in the polis. This brings us to the *particular form of the nation.*

Secondly, citizenship is contingent on a particular culture – what can be called a quality of population – which distinguishes one community of citizens from another. In other words, *a nation is a community of citizens with a common imagined culture.*

Understood in this way, the question is not whether the nation is modern or not. More apt is to ask: When does modernity start? Does it begin with the American and French Revolutions? For those historians for whom the first nation is that of England, modernity starts two hundred years earlier. Leah Greenfeld, for example, argues that in England as early as the sixteenth century, the term 'nation' became synonymous with 'the people' to mean the bearer of sovereignty (Greenfeld, 1992: 7). This is what was at stake in the civil wars of the mid-seventeenth century. By the time of the accession of Charles I in 1625, the principle that political sovereignty resided with Parliament, as representative of the nation, had long been established. Charles reasserted the divine right of kings in a context where this right was long deemed to have passed to the nation. The documents of Parliament, states Greenfeld, 'are characterized by an unequivocally nationalist position in the interpretation of the polity, which was this time unambiguously defined as a nation' (p. 40). This language was most clear in the documents of 1649 that abolished the House of Lords, abolished kingship, established a republic (which was called a Commonwealth) and established a court to try Charles I. The law providing for the prosecution of the king claimed that he,

> not content with those many encroachments which his
> predecessors had made upon the people in their rights and
> freedoms, has had a wicked design totally to subvert the ancient

and fundamental laws and liberties of this nation ... [and] levied and maintained a cruel war in the land against Parliament and Kingdom (cited in Greenfeld, 1992: 41).

Hence, 'for prevention [of any further attempt] to imagine or contrive the enslaving or destroying of the English nation' it was ordained that the king be brought to trial (cited in Greenfeld, 1992: 41). The law abolishing kingship did so in the name of the sovereignty of the people: 'it has been found by experience that the office of a King in this nation ... is unnecessary, burdensome, and dangerous to the liberty, safety and public interest of the people' (cited in Greenfeld, 1992: 41). The act thus abolished the office of king so that 'a most happy way is made for this nation ... to return to its just and ancient right of being governed by its own representatives' (cited in Greenfeld, 1992: 41).

For 150 years before the mid-seventeenth-century civil wars in England, suggests Greenfeld, sovereignty was already deemed to lodge in nation states, power and authority thought to derive from the nation-people (Greenfeld, 1992: 8). By the eighteenth century, this view was axiomatic for as diverse a group as Johan Gottfied Herder, John Stuart Mill and the French revolutionaries. The Committee of Public Safety, for example, opposed the cosmopolitan character of monarchical society precisely on these grounds: 'The monarchy,' it pronounced in 1794, 'had good reason to resemble the Tower of Babel .... In a free society language must be the same for one and all' (cited in Wimmer, 2002: 60). Herder addressed a similar criticism to the Prussia of Frederick the Great: 'nothing was more manifestly contrary to the purposes of political government than the unnatural enlargement of states, the wild mixing of different human species and nations under one scepter' (cited in Wimmer, 2002: 59). Mill too was sceptical about the prospects of democratic government in anything less than the nation: 'Free institutions are next to impossible in a country made up of different nationalities [because] the boundaries of governments should coincide in the main with those of nationalities' (cited in Wimmer, 2002: 60).

This intuition – that democracy is necessarily lodged in nations – has remained more or less undisturbed until recently. Its tenacity is most evident in the ambivalence of Marx and, after him, Marxist theorists, politicians and activists towards the concept of nation. Despite socialism's international ambitions, socialism *qua* democracy was to be lodged in nation states. Hence, socialism as an international order referred to a commonwealth of socialist nation states. It is only recently that the nation-democracy dyad has come under some criticism.

Starting in the 1980s, there has been renewed academic interest in the notion of citizenship. In America and Western Europe, the challenge to established notions and practices of social democracy, which was the hallmark of the Reagan and Thatcher administrations, reanimated discussion about the rights and the role of the state. Monetarist economics combined with what came to be known as the New Public Management[5] faced down the post-war consensus that associated citizenship with three categories of rights: civil (equality before the law), political (the right to choose political representatives and run for political office) and social (public education, health care, employment, insurance, housing). At stake was the relevance of T. H. Marshall's influential post-war text *Citizenship and Social Class*, which associated full citizenship with a liberal, democratic welfare state (Marshall, 1965). In Eastern Europe, the collapse of the Soviet Union and the Communist bloc further problematised established conceptions of citizenship. What mattered in this instance was not so much the content of citizenship – the rights to which it referred – as its limits. The dissolution of Czechoslovakia and the violent break-up of the former Yugoslavia, for example, revived painful questions about the political frontier or border: Who would have what rights in which political community? If the revival of nationalism in Eastern Europe shattered the prospect of cosmopolitanism[6] there, the 'cultural' aspect of citizenship was similarly raised in the wealthy liberal democracies – this time from the other direction.

As new Eastern European nations sought to tie citizenship to religion, language and culture, Western notions of citizenship were being subjected to feminist, multicultural and/or post-colonial critiques. At stake were the *internal limits of citizenship*. After Anderson's *Imagined Communities* (1991), what occupied central stage was the nation and citizenship therein. Nira Yuval-Davis (1997) and Ruth Lister (1997) demonstrated the exclusionary effects of national citizenship, especially for women. Many looked forward to a citizenship washed of racist and other exclusionary instruments. In the early 1990s, these questions received a boost from the democratic transition in South Africa. The vision of a 'rainbow nation' inspired thinking about a form of citizenship freed of the baggage of the nation. Yet at the very moment that cosmopolitan notions of citizenship seemed to be making headway against the nationalist consensus, concerns were being raised about the limits of tolerance and cultural diversity.

The year of the democratic election in South Africa, 1994, was simultaneously the year of the Rwandan genocide. Bryan Turner, for example, wondered aloud if citizenship did not presuppose a common culture. He asked whether 'postmodernisation', a term he used to describe the fragmentation and differentiation of culture, was not undermining its conditions (Turner, 1994: 165–66). In 1993 Samuel Huntington warned that:

> the fundamental source of conflict in this new world will not be primarily ideological or primarily economic. The great divisions among humankind and the dominating source of conflict will be cultural. Nation states will remain the most powerful actors in world affairs, but the principal conflicts of global politics will occur between nations and groups of different civilizations (Huntington, 1993: 22).

In *The Clash of Civilizations and the Remaking of the World Order* (1996), which followed shortly after, Huntington suggested that democratic citizenship did not only presuppose a common culture, but that it was antagonised by those that had not developed a sense of individualism and a tradition of individual rights and liberties (Huntington, 1996: 71).

Then came the attacks on New York and Washington on 11 September 2001, which seemed to put paid to a tradition of politics interested in overcoming the exclusionary effects of national citizenship. Reviewing the current state of things, Paul Gilroy remarks:

> Multicultural society seems to have been abandoned at birth. ... The resurgent imperial power of the United States has made multiculturalism an aspect of the clash of integral and incompatible civilizations, thereby transmitting an additional negative energy into this delicate postcolonial process (Gilroy, 2004: 1).

What is at stake in the rejection of cosmopolitanism is the revival of an older term: cultural *homogeneity* as the condition of citizenship. What matters is that democratic citizenship is deemed best to lodge in nations. In this context, it is hardly surprising that the ghost of Carl Schmitt has returned to haunt the political scene.[7] Schmitt rejected liberal democracy precisely because he believed that the project of social diversity and political pluralism was a non-starter.

What matters for our purposes is the way that the figure of the citizen is transformed when located in the nation. He or she is necessarily endowed with qualities of population (a racial, cultural or linguistic trait; even a mark of history) that mark his or her membership in this or that political community. The measure of citizenship, therefore, is not, primarily the degree and/or vigour of those mechanisms, processes or institutions intended to give voice to popular sentiments, opinions or interests. Rather, the measure of citizenship in the nation is the degree to which one is a bearer of this or that mark of national belonging. It means too that democratic sovereignty undergoes a peculiar transformation in the nation. It no longer refers to the degree to which citizens control the state. Rather, democratic sovereignty refers to the degree to which citizens *qua* nation *qua* bearers of the traits of population control the state. In short, in the hands of nationalists, democratic sovereignty refers to the sovereignty of the nation over the state.

3

African Nationalism in South Africa

National democratic discourse since the mid-1950s has been the pre-eminent expression of anti-colonial nationalism in South Africa. The year 1955 is, schematically, a moment of rupture. At least until the end of the 1940s, opposition to racial segregation and apartheid was framed in the terms of Cape liberalism and Christianity. More radical expressions of dissent found expression, not so much in and through the politics of Pan-Africanism, than in terms of Garveyism (Walshe, 1973: 24).[1] Within the African National Congress (ANC), Garveyite ideas were especially influential in the organisation's Youth League. As late as 1948, for example, the 'Basic Policy of the Congress Youth League' included the Garveyite slogan 'Africa for the Africans', though other more-militant slogans proved to be unpopular.

A mere seven years later, there had been a sea change in the trajectory and form of nationalist struggle. We can get a sense of it by comparing the Youth League slogan above with the key statement of the Freedom Charter, adopted at the Congress of the People in June 1955. 'South Africa belongs to all those who live in it, white and black,' it proclaimed. Yet ambivalence regarding Garveyism within the ANC could already be detected as early as 1943. In that year, the ANC issued 'Africans'

Claims', the organisation's reaction to the Atlantic Charter signed in 1941. 'Africans' Claims' called for the granting to Africans of 'full citizenship rights such as are enjoyed by all Europeans in South Africa' (ANC, 1943). It envisaged a cosmopolitan community composed of Africans and Europeans, and in this sense anticipated the Freedom Charter by more than a decade. Yet there is an important difference between the Freedom Charter and 'Africans' Claims'. If the latter reflected a brief (and perhaps expedient) engagement with liberalism, the Freedom Charter suggested the growing influence of Communists in the alliance, the rising importance of Marxist-Leninist concepts and terms and, most importantly, the emergence of the theory of national democratic revolution (NDR; see below) as the pre-eminent expression of African nationalism in South Africa. Today, although its concepts and practices are increasingly giving way to others, NDR's vocabulary continues to inform ANC policy statements and its lexicon, i.e. the day-to-day language of politicians and senior government officials.

This chapter will offer a schematic narrative of the anti-apartheid struggle *qua* national democratic struggle. It will focus, that is, on the development and elaboration of the theory of NDR, both as a concept and as a practice. For the moment, the chapter will simply accept at face value that when national democrats called themselves nationalists, this is what they were. It will postpone the question 'What was nationalist about the discourse of NDR?' until the following chapter. Before we are in a position to answer this all-important question, however, we need to understand it on its own terms.

The purpose here is not a conventional history of resistance to apartheid or even of the theory of NDR. The chapter will deal with this history only insofar as it later helps define the specificity of the theory of NDR *qua* nationalist struggle. In other words, this is less a history than a genealogy of national democratic struggle. As such, the chapter is less concerned with NDR's historical impact or role in the anti-apartheid struggle *per se* – that is taken as a given – than in its elaboration as a concept and practice. There are several features of NDR that are interesting to a historian that the chapter will, consequently, mainly pass over. It will not discuss forms of nationalist resistance, either prior to NDR or that happened simultaneously. There is no discussion here of the Garvey movement in South Africa, despite its importance as a general national movement between 1920 and 1940 (Hill & Pirio, 1987), nor does the chapter describe its antecedents in the phenomenon of Ethiopianism. There is also little mention of the influence of Pan-Africanism and Negritude on the development of NDR, nor of various brands of anarchism and syndicalism. The question that the chapter is asking of the discourse of NDR is equally valid for them: What was *nationalist* about their nationalism?

Having said this, the next chapter will discuss Black Consciousness at length. It will do this because Black Consciousness, more than Garveyism or other nationalist strains apart from NDR, became a major political and cultural force from the 1970s. Even if Black Consciousness as a movement was weak, as a discourse it strongly informed the nationalist imaginary.

There is also a methodological reason for taking some time to discuss Black Consciousness. Despite its very different genealogy to NDR – the first arising in and through debates within Marxism-Leninism, and the second emerging from a South African dialogue with Negritude – as nationalisms, they were homologous. They both conceived of freedom in relation to a sovereign people with determinate marks of population.

The Freedom Charter

The Congress of the People was the culmination of the Freedom Charter Campaign, launched by the ANC in 1954 to prepare a constitution for a democratic, non-racial and unified South Africa (Bernstein, 1999). The Freedom Charter called upon a radically new political vocabulary, and evoked a new sense of the political imaginary. From then on, the struggle against capitalism and apartheid would be discussed and contested in new terms: that of nation, race and class.

The idea for the Freedom Charter had come from Z. K. Mathews, principal of Fort Hare University, and author of the 1943 'Africans' Claims' document. Mathews was not known for his radicalism, and he was – like many of the stalwarts of the then ANC leadership – deeply distrustful of mass action or popular revolt. Like Chief Albert Luthuli and others, the path to political freedom was considered to be essentially a question of moral example and of ethical persuasion. Access to the political community, to the franchise and other civil liberties was regarded as a matter of hearts and minds, of convincing a collective white conscience that the exclusion of blacks was unjust and immoral. It was only after the victory of the Nationalist Party in the 1948 elections and the hardening and extension of racial exclusion that a younger generation in the Youth League began to make themselves heard. Rusty Bernstein, tried for treason alongside Nelson Mandela and the others at the infamous Rivonia Trial, recalls that at this time Walter Sisulu (jailed on Robben Island for 26 years with Nelson Mandela), Oliver Tambo (later president of the ANC in exile) and Mandela himself 'were still up-and-coming leaders, men to watch but as yet without the national and international recognition they would have in later years' (Bernstein, 1999: 146).

It was in the planning and execution of the Freedom Charter Campaign that two new political currents found expression and an organisational place. The first was that of African nationalism as it was being articulated through the ANC Youth League; the other was that of NDR, which was beginning to make itself felt within the Congress of Democrats. If the new African nationalism was disheartened by the reformist politics of moral persuasion and more persuaded of the need for revolution, it was still ideologically unclear about its objectives. Indeed, prior to the Freedom Charter, the shift in the ANC was more about means than ends: more about strategies as opposed to social and political goals (Lodge, 1983: 69). Until then, the major complaint of the ANC against successive white regimes was that they excluded and discriminated against the vast black majority. In this regard, the solution was deemed the granting to blacks of equal rights in a single political community: the vision was essentially of a liberal polity. At stake for the ANC was the figure of the black as an equal human being and as a citizen. What was at stake for an up-and-coming generation of ANC activists was the method of reaching such a goal: reform or revolution? It was through the rising influence of Communists and leftists in the Congress of Democrats that freedom was articulated in terms of a concrete new political horizon.

In principle, the Freedom Charter was supposed to be the product of a countrywide process of consultation, undertaken by 'Freedom Volunteers', to collect demands for the charter. In the final stage, delegates elected at countless village, workplace and township meetings would meet to draft the document. Very soon after its launch, critics condemned the process as being deeply flawed. In the first case, not all parts of the country were equally represented. But this did not reflect any inherent prejudice or bias. Instead it reflected the political environment under which the campaign unfolded – one of severe political harassment under the Suppression of Communism Act – and the degree to which the ANC and its allies were organised on the ground. Indeed, despite these shortcomings, the campaign elicited a significant popular response.

On Saturday 26 June 1955, the Freedom Charter was presented to a mass gathering at Kliptown, today part of Soweto. The site was one of the few remaining parcels of land not owned or controlled by a white authority and on which it was therefore possible to host a 'mixed' event. Removed from its context, observes Tom Lodge, the charter was bland enough: a list of basic rights and freedoms affirming the 'multiracial' character of South African society (Lodge, 1983: 79). It declared that 'The People Shall Govern', that 'All Shall be Equal Before the Law', that 'All Shall Enjoy Human Rights', and so on (Freedom Charter, 1955). But over and above a list of basic civil rights, principles were included that until then had no precedence in the politics of the ANC. In particular, the charter declared: 'The People Shall Share in the Country's Wealth':

> The national wealth of our country, the heritage of all South Africans, shall be restored to the people;

The mineral wealth beneath the soil, the banks and monopoly
industry shall be transferred to the ownership of the people as
a whole;
All other industries and trades shall be controlled to assist the
well-being of the people;
All people shall have equal right to trade where they choose,
to manufacture and to enter all trades, crafts, professions
(Freedom Charter, 1955).

What should we make of these statements? Were they spontaneous demands
from 'the people'? Or, rather, was the document thoroughly mediated by
second-hand interpreters? Raymond Suttner and Jeremy Cronin (both
members of the South African Communist Party) suggest that:

[t]he Freedom Charter has a unique authority because of the
mode of its creation. Never before, or since, have the people of
South Africa themselves put down their own vision of the type
of society in which they would like to live (Suttner & Cronin,
1986: 7).

In this account, the Freedom Charter is a transparent measure of the
popular will. We shall see shortly why it was so important for Suttner and
Cronin to insist on the indigenous, spontaneous nature of the document.
Today, however, there is another version of the document's genesis. It
has long been rumoured, but, writes Anthony Sampson, '[T]he demands
of the commitment, whether to oppose tyranny in South Africa or to
maintain ideological positions during the cold war, inhibited many
participants from writing frankly or humorously about their difficulties
or doubts' (Sampson, 1999: ix).[2] Only in 1999 (45 years later) do we
get a first-hand account of the precise circumstances under which the
document was actually drafted. It comes from the memoirs of Rusty
Bernstein. At the time this member of the South African Congress of
Democrats (of which more later) and Communist activist was on the

Working Committee responsible for the Freedom Charter Campaign. It was to him, ultimately, that the task of writing the text fell. He recalls:

> With a team of volunteers, we sorted thousands of the individual written demands into topics, until an entire living-room floor had been covered with mounds of paper, each labelled Labour, Land, Civil Rights, Votes, Education, Living Standards, and so on. ... I started to outline a skeleton Charter. It was impossible to accommodate all the topics and sub-topics. The range was too wide. Instead of a skeleton I was juggling with a museum's warehouse of unsorted bones. ... I almost abandoned the whole exercise before I realized that it was quite irrelevant how many pieces could be fitted in. This was not a straw poll where each demand counted equally with every other. ... There was nothing for it but to trim, shorten or stretch the limbs to fit together into a rough approximation of a workable skeleton.[3]

Bernstein's memoirs are self-effacing and unprepossessing. We must certainly believe him when he writes that the most difficult part of the exercise was keeping his own opinions from determining the draft. And yet he admits that '[t]here was no point in making a count; the Freedom Charter required that a compromise or a consensus be read from – or read into – what was on the paper' (Bernstein, 1999: 155). So what was the nature of the 'consensus' read from, or read into, the multitude of papers, envelopes and scraps laid out on the floor of Bernstein's flat? In other words, what sort of document was the Freedom Charter? At the time, Cape members of the Liberal Party complained that the document was the product of manipulation and conspiracy: an attempt to give to something that had already been prearranged a popular veneer. They complained, in this regard, that it reflected the influence of the Congress of Democrats, in their view merely a front for the Soviet Union (Lodge, 1983: 72); hence the document was more the voice of the Communist Party than anything else. Bernstein himself poses the same question:

Whose charter was it? This is not simply an esoteric question for the historians: it cuts to the heart of the matter. Did the Freedom Charter simply reflect Bernstein's politics? Did it reflect the politics of the Working Committee, the Congress of Democrats, the ANC or the alliance[4] as a whole? The question is important in order to trace the charter's genealogy further. Bernstein tells us that:

> On many of the topics covered by 'demands' I had strong views of my own. I am strongly biased towards a socialist economy, in which the main productive resources are held in common for the common good.
>
> There was little in the demands which could justify that proposition's inclusion in the Charter. But also little to justify inclusion of either an alternative free market or private model economy (Bernstein, 1999: 155).

Elsewhere, in a footnote, he admits that he wrote much of the material for the Congress of the People, including even the guidance circulars for campaign workers (Bernstein, 1999: 150 fn). We know too that some demands were deemed inappropriate and simply ignored. One of these was for polygamy. Another concerned the restoration of the legitimate principle of chieftainship, following rights of primogeniture rather than by appointment of the government. This too was judged atavistic.

But if it is no longer possible to conclude that the Freedom Charter was a transparent, or, more accurately, a translucent expression of the people's will (or a sincere interpretation of thousands of diverse demands), may we legitimately conclude that it simply reflected Bernstein's personal views? Bernstein recalls that after he finished it, the charter was shown to the Working Committee, who duly approved it. After that there are different accounts about what happened. Did the Joint Executive[5] meet and amend the draft? Bernstein is deeply sceptical that this happened: 'If there was any such meeting,' he writes, 'my bans would have kept me from it.' But even if this meeting did take place, the 'Charter was already printed and ready for distribution; we had no facilities for an overnight reprint. It had to be issued as it was, with or without formal approval from the Congresses.' Bernstein adds:

> I believe the Charter had drifted out of the Congress's control
> – and for all lack of foresight had taken on a free-floating life
> of its own. For all practical purposes it was – temporarily – the
> creature of the Working Committee and no one else – not even
> the ANC (Bernstein, 1999: 156).

But even this statement is only formally true – the charter was produced in and through the activities of the Working Committee. But we know too that the committee played no role in the intellectual formation of the document; it merely supervised and co-ordinated the logistics of the Freedom Charter Campaign. Indeed, Bernstein recalls that he was given the task of drafting the Freedom Charter because it was deemed 'just a writing job' (Bernstein, 1999: 153). Moreover, he remained a somewhat furtive member of the committee, taking no part in its public functions (p. 153). Surely the simplest proof would be to compare the draft written by him and what was (a) presented at Kliptown on 26 June, and (b) the document that has since been circulated. Bernstein never says anything about this, but implies very strongly that they were the same. So, was the political content of the Freedom Charter simply that of Bernstein? Should we say that despite his efforts, the charter bore his ideological signature? Such a conclusion would be too simple, for there are terms and expressions in the Charter that betray another lineage.

What is noticeably absent from the Freedom Charter is any reference to class struggle. Even in the section dealing with the wealth of the country, mention of the working class is wholly missing. Instead there are references to 'the people' and to the 'people as a whole'. Indeed, it is on behalf of the people that the document claims to speak, and it is they who are deemed the veritable bearers of the democratic mission. Some effort even seems to have been made not to refer to the term at all. This might be thought surprising in a document written by a socialist. What should we make of the following declaration: 'That only a democratic state, based on the will of the people, can secure to all their birthright without distinction of colour, race, sex or belief'? What about discrimination on the basis of property? There is another curiosity: the charter declares: 'All National Groups Shall Have Equal Rights':

> There shall be equal status in the bodies of the state, in the courts and in the schools for all national groups and races;
> All national groups shall be protected by law against insults to their race and national pride;
> All people shall have equal rights to use their own language and to develop their own folk culture and customs (Freedom Charter, 1955).

Who were 'the people' that the charter constantly invoked? In the first place, they were 'national groups'; in the second place, they were different races; in the third, they were workers; and in the fourth, they were peasants. There are also numerous references to families, to the aged, to the disabled, to women. What is interesting, moreover, is that nowhere does the charter suggest a hierarchy among these 'persons'. They are all invoked simply as empirical signifiers to denote 'the people' in all this concept's diverse aspects. In other words, nowhere does it suggest that some among the people are either more authentic bearers of the democratic mission than others or numerically constitute more of 'the people' than others. Taken together, the charter's references to 'the people' and to 'national groups' do not simply betray the personal formulations of the document's principal author: they signal the entry into South African politics of a Leninist vocabulary whose source is the Communist International. In particular, they indicate the legacy of the 'independent native republic' thesis issued by the Executive Committee of the Communist International in 1928. Indeed, even the terms and phrases of the ANC documents discussed above reflect this influence, for there is certainly no precedence for them in other documents prior to this period. The Freedom Charter, however, is not simply a transposition of Moscow politics into a local vernacular. Let us examine this issue more closely.

The 'independent native republic'

After its formation in 1921, the Communist Party of South Africa (CPSA) was mainly concerned with the identity of the authentic South African working class and the identity, therefore, of the revolutionary subject. During the early part of the decade and prior to that, through the International Socialist League, South African Communists had confined their activities to the white working class, to the neglect of blacks. This did not simply reflect racial prejudice (although it did in part). Rather, many senior members of the party doubted the revolutionary potential of migrant black workers who were still beholden to tribal structures and kinship groups. To them, the working class referred to those who that were organised and capable of strikes, i.e. white workers.

It was only when Sidney Bunting rose to prominence in the CPSA after 1923 that serious attempts were made to recruit blacks to the organisation. Bunting was no theoretician, but took seriously the maxim 'Workers of the World Unite'. It seemed clear to him that revolutionary politics would inevitably be stalled as long as capital could play white workers off against their black counterparts. He thus defined the task of the party as the recruitment of black workers to their historical mission. In addition, he intended to fight 'racialism' in the ranks of white workers. The argument was controversial, and was only won after appeal to the Young Communist League in Berlin, and once racial nationalism was seen to make inroads among white workers.[6] By the end of 1924, the Bunting faction had won out. After the December conference, to be a Communist in South Africa meant openly to identify oneself with the movement for the emancipation of blacks. While this argument paved the way for the entry of black members into the leadership of the organisation and for alliances with 'bourgeois democratic' movements (i.e. the ANC), the conditions of emancipation were held to be the organisation of both blacks and whites as workers. Indeed, there was profound mistrust of other political organisations mobilising on the basis of civil rights. Ivan Jones, then member of the International Socialist League, had once referred disparagingly to the ANC as a 'small coterie of educated natives ... satisfied with the agitation for civil equality and political rights' (cited in Bunting, 1975: 20). Now these initiatives were overtaken by events at the Sixth Congress of the Communist International (Comintern).

Prior to 1927, the Communist Party of the Soviet Union had paid little attention to political circumstances in the colonial territories. This began to change when Moscow felt increasingly threatened by British attempts to isolate it diplomatically. Poland, the Baltic States and Rumania were seen to be within the British sphere of influence: an embryonic 'White wall' around 'Red Russia' (Roux, 1964). The Soviet Union was now attempting to subvert these efforts by organising liberation movements throughout the British Empire, including South Africa. Eddie Roux recalls, therefore, that until then the Comintern had taken very little notice of the CPSA. In turn, South African Communists had made do with very little Comintern theory. Indeed, apart from a copy of the *Communist Manifesto*, there were very few of Marx's writings available in the country. Certainly, South African Communists were profoundly out of touch with the theoretical and political developments taking place in Russia and elsewhere in Europe. However, in Moscow, keener interest in the colonial territories was associated with a keener interest in the 'national question', and in particular, its relationship to class struggle.

Already at the Second Congress of the Comintern of 1923, struggles against colonialism were being cast in a Leninist vocabulary. The Sixth Congress of the Comintern declared in this regard that:

> the actual significance of the colonies and semi-colonies, as factors of crisis in the imperialist world system, has vastly increased ... the vast colonial and semi-colonial world has become an unquenchable blazing furnace of the revolutionary mass movement.

The establishment of a fighting front between the active forces of the socialist world revolution (the Soviet Union and the revolutionary movement in the capitalist countries) on the one side, and the forces of imperialism on the other side, is of fundamental importance in the present epoch of world history. The toiling masses of the colonies struggling against imperialist slavery represent a most powerful auxiliary force of the socialist world revolution (*Report of the Sixth World Congress of the Comintern*, cited in Bunting, 1975: 31).

Not only were these struggles deemed an immediate challenge to the world capitalist system, but they were, in their local expressions, national, i.e. struggles of the colonised for self-determination and freedom from imperial rule in their own territories. Hence, national struggles, even if bourgeois in their specifically local form, when seen from the perspective of world capitalism, were revolutionary. The Comintern insisted, in this regard, on a terminological shift. National struggles in the colonies were no longer to be construed as 'bourgeois-democratic' but as 'national revolutionary' (Bunting, 1975: 23). Apart from this generic formulation, the Sixth Congress also proposed specific 'appropriate' actions for Communist Parties in their respective countries. In that section dealing with South Africa – a single paragraph in a 63-page report – the report read as follows:

In the Union of South Africa, the Negro masses, which constitute the majority of the population, are being expropriated from the land by the white colonists and by the State, are deprived of political rights and of the right to freedom of movement, are subjected to most brutal forms of racial and class oppression, and suffer simultaneously from pre-capitalist and capitalist methods of exploitation and oppression. The Communist Party, which has already achieved definite successes among the Negro proletariat, has the duty of continuing still more energetically

the struggle for complete equality of rights for the Negroes, for
the abolition of all special regulations and laws directed against
Negroes, and for the confiscation of the land of the landlords. In
drawing into its organization non-Negro workers, organizing
them in trade unions, and in carrying on a struggle for the
acceptance of Negroes by the trade unions of white workers, the
Communist Party has the obligation to struggle by all methods
against every racial prejudice in the ranks of the white workers
and to eradicate such prejudices from its own ranks. The Party
must determinedly and consistently put forward the slogan for
the creation of an *independent native republic* , with simultaneous
guarantees for the rights of the white minority, and struggle in
deeds for its realization (*Report of the Sixth World Congress of the
Comintern*, cited in Bunting, 1975: 32; emphasis added).

In South Africa, the call for an 'independent native republic' provoked
turmoil in the Communist Party.[7] In the immediate short term, Bunting
worried that campaigns launched under the auspices of this slogan would
alienate white workers, and, indeed, further drive them into the hands
of 'reformists' and racial nationalists. More importantly, what did the
slogan say about the driving force for socialism? Who, in other words,
were the bearers of the democratic mission: the working class organised
in and through the Communist Party, or blacks through their 'national'
movement(s)? At stake was the political horizon: capitalism in general
or capitalism in South Africa? If national oppression was a necessary
condition of capitalism in its 'highest stages', then national revolution
was a condition of socialism at the centre of the capitalist system, i.e. in
the 'highly-developed' capitalist states. It was not necessarily a condition
for socialism on the periphery, i.e. in the colonised territory. If, however,
national oppression was a condition of South African capitalism,
then the route to socialism in that country necessarily passed through
a 'stage' of national revolution. The *Report of the Sixth Congress of the
Comintern* was profoundly ambiguous on this point, but it is likely that

the native republic was intended as a stage of the world revolution. There is nothing in the statement that links racial oppression in South Africa to class exploitation as necessary functions of each other. Even the special resolution on South Africa issued by the Comintern Executive Committee on 15 March 1928 did little to resolve the tension, and yet it offered a tantalising reformulation of the native republic slogan:

> While developing and strengthening the fight against all the customs, laws and regulations which discriminate against the native and coloured population in favour of the white population, the Communist Party of South Africa must combine the fight against all anti-native laws with the general political slogan in the fight against British domination, the slogan of an independent native South African republic *as a stage towards a workers' and peasants' republic* (Special Resolution on South Africa issued by the Executive Committee of the Communist International, 15 March 1928, cited in Bunting, 1975: 32; emphasis added).

What should we make of this statement? Did it imply that South African capitalism was premised on racial (i.e. national) oppression, such that an independent native republic was necessarily a first step towards a workers' and peasants' republic? It seems unlikely. Again, there was no suggestion that racial oppression was a condition of class exploitation, other than at the level of the world capitalist economy. Instead, the slogan in the special resolution on South Africa was simply a more explicit statement of the one contained in the *Report of the Sixth Congress of the Comintern*. And the reference point was not a reading of the South African political economy, but of the world political geography. The Comintern had placed special emphasis on a report by Lenin to the Commission on the National and Colonial Question in 1920. In it he argued that, with the rise of the Soviet Union, it was no longer correct to assume that every revolution had to pass through a bourgeois phase. Instead, with the assistance of the proletariat of 'advanced nations' and with the model of the Soviet Union, 'backward' nations could pass directly to Communism (*Report of the Commission on the National and Colonial Question*, cited in Bunting, 1975: 23).[8] Within the CPSA, this formulation triggered a long and conflict-ridden discussion about the nature of the 'national' forces in South Africa. The pedigree of the 'national revolution' was at stake: was it conducive to socialism?

In terms of this formulation, the term 'the people' took on a new meaning. In the first place, it did not simply signify the working class exploited by capitalists. In the second, it had a new sociological referent: a multiplicity of social classes commonly oppressed by a colonial regime. In the third place, it was referenced to a new political destination: not, in the first place, socialism, but national liberation. In the fourth place, the relationship between national revolution and socialism was ambiguous. Was the one a (logically) necessary condition of the other, because, that is, 'national oppression' was a condition of class exploitation? Or was socialism merely contingent on national liberation, because it gave to the working and peasant classes a chance to hone their political and strategic skills for the next 'stage' of struggle (the Leninist thesis)? All this uncertainty is present in the Freedom Charter; ironically, it was precisely this imprecision that gave to the document its force, since various political organisations could find something in it that resonated with their own politics. For example, Mandela remarked in 1956 that:

> It is true that in demanding the nationalization of the banks,
> the gold mines and the land the Charter strikes a fatal blow at
> the financial and gold-mining monopolies and farming interests
> .... But such a step is absolutely imperative and necessary
> because the realization of the Charter is inconceivable ... until
> the monopolies are first smashed up and the national wealth of
> the country turned over to the people. The breaking up ... of
> these monopolies will open up fresh fields for the development
> of a non-European bourgeois class. For the first time in the

history of this country the non-European bourgeoisie will have
the opportunity to own in their own name and right mills and
factories and trade and private enterprise will boom and flourish
as never before (cited in Lodge, 1983: 73).

But can we ever be satisfied that the correspondence between the
ambiguities in the Freedom Charter, including its very language, and the
native republic thesis is merely coincidental? We need to remember that
the Congress of Democrats was formed mainly by Communists after the
CPSA was finally banned in 1950. In other words, the charter was written
by someone who entered the party by the time it was reconciled to 'national
liberation'; i.e. after a bloody period of strife precisely over the formulations
of the 1928 slogan. Rather than simply a reflection of popular demands
and political aspirations, the Freedom Charter was edited and produced
according to the political and theoretical *zeitgeist* of the 1950s.

What is important for our purposes is the hard-won principle that the
charter celebrated: that a national struggle – a struggle waged by a 'united
front' of classes against colonialism – was not necessarily in contradiction
with the struggle for socialism. It is only later that the relationship
between the two was more clearly defined. We have seen that according to
the Leninist thesis, national revolutions in the colonies would advance the
crisis of metropolitan capitalism. But was South Africa simply a colony?
In other words, was racial oppression there in the service of an exclusively
foreign, i.e. colonial, capitalist class? In *The Road to South African Freedom*,
the 1962 programme of the South African Communist Party (SACP),[9] a
host of new analytical terms were introduced. They were not simply old
ideas rehashed in smart new words; rather, they designated new concepts.
One of these was 'Colonialism of a Special Type'; another was national
democratic revolution. In summing up, the document declared:

South Africa is not a colony but an independent state. Yet
masses of our people enjoy neither independence nor freedom.
The conceding of independence to South Africa by Britain

in 1910, was not a victory over the forces of colonialism and imperialism. It was designed in the interests of imperialism. Power was transferred not into the hands of the masses of people of South Africa, but into the hands of the White minority alone. The evils of colonialism, insofar as the non-White majority was concerned, were perpetuated and reinforced. A new type of colonialism was developed, in which the oppressing White nation occupied the same territory as the oppressed people themselves and lived side by side with them (SACP, 1962: 27).

South Africa was a 'Colony of a Special Type' because the colonial population was a settled ruling class in the very territory of the colony. But the document did not stop there: it went on to posit an entirely new relation between class and race in South Africa. We have seen that up until then 'national oppression' was deemed functional to capitalism only to the extent that it helped weaken working-class unity. In other words, it bore an external relationship to exploitation proper. In the 1962 programme, however, race was analysed as an economic factor of exploitation itself:

[The] system of race domination and oppression has its origin far back in South African history. However, it has developed into its present, extreme form with the development of capitalism and especially of the great diamond and gold-mining monopolies. … The South African and foreign monopoly capitalists and large-scale landowners, who, together, are the real rulers of this country, have cultivated racial differences and prejudices as their most effective instrument in their insatiable drive for cheap labour and high profits. The colonial status of the African people facilitates the maximum exploitation of their labour. The privileges extended to White businessmen, farmers, professional people and workers are a means of maintaining their support for the ruling capitalist class and for the South African colonialist system (SACP, 1962: 2–3).

'On the one level,' the document later continued,

> that of 'White South Africa', there are all the features of an
> advanced capitalist state in its final stage of imperialism. There
> are highly developed industrial monopolies, and the merging of
> industrial and finance capital. ...
>
> But on another level, that of 'Non-White South Africa' there are
> all the features of a colony. The indigenous population is subjected
> to extreme national oppression, poverty and exploitation, lack
> of all democratic rights and political domination by a group
> that does everything it can to emphasise and perpetuate its alien
> 'European' character (SACP, 1962: 28).

In this analysis the white nation was driven to oppress and exploit the
non-white nation, not simply because it was plagued by racism and
prejudice, but because it was a necessary condition of exploitation.
Politically, this analysis resolved any ambiguity about the revolutionary
nature of 'national liberation'. Indeed, precisely because the oppressing
white nation was equated with an exploiting capitalist class, any
struggle against the former was necessarily a struggle against the latter.
This reading of the South African situation was expressed politically in
the concept of national democratic revolution:

> As its immediate and foremost task, the South African
> Communist Party works for a united front of national
> liberation. It strives to unite all sections and classes of
> oppressed and democratic people for a national democratic
> revolution to destroy White domination. The main content
> of this Revolution will be the national liberation of the
> African people. ... The destruction of colonialism and
> the winning of national freedom is the essential condition
> and the key for future advance to the supreme aim of the

Communist Party: the establishment of a socialist South
Africa, laying the foundations of a classless, communist
society (SACP, 1962: 4).

National democracy was not simply a workers' and peasants' republic.
National revolution – the defeat of the white nation/capitalist class,
that is – was not a synonym for socialism. *The Road to South African
Freedom* – in this respect, profoundly reminiscent of the Freedom
Charter – conceded that 'the people' were composed of diverse
classes and races, not all immediately invested in socialism. They
did not, that is, consist exclusively of the working class and peasants,
but also of a middle stratum of traders and businessmen. National
democracy was, therefore, neither a capitalist state nor a socialist one,
but something on the road between them. *The Road to South African
Freedom* was the beginning of a substantial South African literature
on the relationship between race and class, yet the political effects of
its analysis were, apart from a short period in the 1960s, stalled in
South Africa for at least a decade.

The theory of national democratic revolution
One domain where the effects of this political shift were immediately felt
was in the area of trade unionism. On 5 and 6 March 1955, a few months
before the launch of the Freedom Charter, the South African Congress
of Trade Unions (Sactu) was launched at a conference in Johannesburg.
Its choice of name was not insignificant, referring as it did to its new
partner, the ANC. The union's inaugurating resolution declared:

Only the working class, in alliance with progressive minded
sections of the community, can build a happy life for all South
Africans, a life free from unemployment, insecurity and poverty,
free from racial hatred and oppression, a life of vast opportunities
for all people (Minutes of the inaugural conference of Sactu,
cited in Luckhardt & Wall, 1980: 94).

The chair of the conference, soon to be elected general secretary, Pieter Byleveld, explained this further:

> You cannot separate politics and the way in which people are governed from their bread and butter, or their freedom to move to and from places where they can find the best employment, or the houses they live in, or the type of education their children get. These things are of vital concern to the workers. The Trade Unions would therefore be neglecting the interests of their members if they failed to struggle for their members on all matters which affect them. The Trade Unions must be as active in the political field as they are in the economic sphere because the two hang together and cannot be isolated from each other (cited in Luckhardt & Wall, 1980: 94).

In appearance – but only in appearance – there was nothing new in these formulations. The Council for Non-European Trade Unions had joined the CPSA in the late 1940s. In Port Elizabeth, moreover, there had been a long history of close relations between trade unions and political organisations. Yet the formulations referred to above indicated that from the mid-1950s, political unionism was to be more and more conducted under the banner of 'national revolution'. Sactu, in the words of its official historians, became '[m]ore than just a trade union to protect working class interests, it became an institution of and for *the people*' (Luckhardt & Wall, 1980: 212; emphasis added). This was not simply a discursive shift: the reduction of the working class to an element of 'the people' meant that Sactu participated in – even spearheaded – campaigns with the ANC that did not simply challenge restrictions on black trade unions. Apart from increased strike activities (more than 100 per cent between 1955 and 1957), Sactu was involved in activities against bus fare increases, the 1958 whites-only elections and the pass laws, those regulations restricting the movement of blacks in and into the cities. But the national democratic turn was not so much evident in the nature of the campaigns that Sactu now undertook; it was more evident in the way these activities were organised. For the first time, strikes and other campaigns involving workers were co-ordinated in and through joint councils of the alliance, principally in this case the ANC and the unions. Workers were organised, that is, as national subjects. In the 1958 protest against the whites-only general elections, for example, it was the ANC, and not Sactu, that unilaterally ended the Stay-At-Home Campaign. Despite the fact that Sactu members were the principal agents of mass action, leadership of the protest passed to the ANC (Luckhardt & Wall, 1980: 349–62).

These actions were part of a general climate of protest and insurrection in South Africa from 1954 onwards. In 1960 this process came to a head. On 21 March of that year, police opened fire on a demonstration organised by the Pan-Africanist Congress (PAC) at Sharpeville. Sixty-nine people were killed and one hundred and eighty injured. A few months later the ANC and the PAC were banned, and within a year the ANC and the SACP, now operating underground, embarked on armed struggle against the state. Mkhonto we Sizwe (the Spear of the Nation – MK) was launched in December 1961 to co-ordinate the combined militaries of the two organisations, starting with a campaign of sabotage against selected targets. Within months of its formation, many of Sactu's most militant organisers were recruited into MK. When the police infiltrated MK later in the year, virtually the whole leadership was arrested. By 1965 Sactu, as an internal federation, was effectively dead (Baskin, 1991: 16).

The massive state repression during the 1960s and the flight of the ANC into exile cast dark shadows over the country. As repression intensified and the security police were given almost unlimited powers to arrest and detain, thousands found themselves behind bars. Many faced life imprisonment on the notorious Robben Island: the prison islet off the coast of Cape Town where Nelson Mandela and others were languishing. Others, including Sactu activists, were executed. By the mid-1960s, political, military and trade union resistance to apartheid had been effectively crushed (Baskin, 1991: 16).

Into this brutal environment poured foreign investment – the moment it became clear that the government was not about to collapse. The gross national product grew at an average of 6 per cent per annum during this period. Japan alone could match such rates. A period of affluence and calm came to South Africa – built on violence and starvation wages.

National Democratic Unionism

After a decade of defeat, 'the Giant', as one commentator described black trade unionism, 'began to stir' (Friedman, 1987: 32). Within the first three months of 1973, 61,000 workers went on strike – more, notes Jeremy Baskin, than for the entire preceding eight years (Baskin, 1991: 18). By 1977 there was talk of building a new union federation. Two years later, the government, after the recommendations of the Wiehahn Commission, legalised black trade unions.

What was the nature of the trade unionism that emerged? What lessons did it learn from the Sactu experience? Or, rather, what was the legacy of Sactu deemed to be? Steven Friedman argues that it was precisely in opposition to the nationalist politics that the new unionism emerged. Congress leaders, including those in Sactu, did not value a workers' movement as an end in and of itself. This reached its logical conclusion, Friedman suggests, when scores of officials abandoned union work to take up arms (Friedman, 1987: 32). To this extent, Sactu participated in nationalist campaigns to the neglect of factory organisation. Baskin, however, is unhappy with this conclusion. He argues that Sactu had little choice but to turn to armed struggle and, moreover, that politics did not divert Sactu from its union tasks (Baskin, 1991: 16). Whatever the case, this argument is cast in the wrong terms. It was not so much a question of whether nationalist politics undercut union organisation, but one of the object to which this organisation was attached. In strategic terms, it was a question of political leadership. With whom did ultimate power rest – the ANC or the trade unions? The unionism of Sactu, what the present book describes as national democratic unionism, shifted power to the ANC as the vanguard of NDR. But it was precisely such nationalist leadership that the new unionism refused. It was not so much that after 1973 trade unions forsook politics; it was more the case that they put a premium on their independence. This reflected a strategic concern. Firstly, the memory of the political defeat of Sactu was still fresh. Secondly, the strikes that started in 1973 were usually initiated by migrant Zulu workers witnessing the decline (in absolute terms) of their wages. The majority of these workers were loyal subjects of the Zulu monarchy, and while quickly investing in trade unionism, they were disinclined to accept the nationalist politics of the ANC. This did not mean, however, that they were either disinterested in the fate of white supremacy or, even worse, somehow its (unwitting) allies. These were charges often made during the early 1990s. What it did mean is that they were sceptical about the willingness of revolutionary nationalism to defend the monarchy and the Zulu homestead. Of course, they were right: national democracy had no place for such institutions or practices. We shall see shortly, however, that the unions' turn from NDR was also informed by a new reading of the South African political economy.

The emerging trade unions focused their activities on building strong, factory-based representation. Here they put maximum effort into training and developing local union officials and building democratic and accountable factory councils. Given the hostile environment in which the emerging unionism was operating, a premium was placed on building durable worker committees on a factory-by-factory basis – structures that could survive political repression and management hostility; structures, in other words, that could endure even if economic victories were negligible or few and far between. This meant stressing that the value of the unions lay less in their capacity to win immediate wage increases than in their symbolic function as instruments of opposition, expression and dignity. In short, their immediate value was as vehicles of working-class consciousness-raising – as a route to building strong organisations. This does not mean, however, that the legacy of Sactu was completely erased. Among those involved in the trade union revival during this period were former Sactu activists that had been lying low since the 1960s (Baskin, 1991: 20). They were joined by white academics and students who spurned a campus political life increasingly motivated by Black Consciousness. Many of these were Marxists, formed intellectually in the aftermath of the student revolts in Paris in 1968. Whereas white student protest was traditionally expressed as liberal dismay, the experience from Paris not only radicalised such students, but suggested to them a new avenue of engagement: trade unionism.

For the most part, the unions that emerged after 1973 started their lives as advice centres, essentially to counsel workers about their few remaining rights in law. In Durban, for example, students launched the General Factory Workers' Benefit Fund, ostensibly not a union, but an organisation to offer death benefits and help with factory complaints (Friedman, 1987: 43). In time it would have 60,000 members. In Cape Town, a former Sactu activist started the Western Province Workers' Advice Bureau. Signs that stress on producing a self-conscious cadre of working-class members was yielding rewards came after 1976. In June of that year, the police opened fire on school students in Soweto protesting against the introduction of Afrikaans as the medium of instruction – a language that they associated with the apartheid masters and, more importantly, that they could not speak or understand.

Despite massive state repression and management intransigence – resulting in large-scale union defeats – the emergent unions, nonetheless, survived, precisely because their worth was not measured in economic victories. Indeed, in interviews conducted with workers in 1979, Eddie Webster found that 'in as much as they have a "political consciousness", it is a politics of the factory … a working class factory consciousness.' He adds, '[t]heir commitment to the union arises, not so much from the benefits it offers, but because they believe it will help them in their struggle in the work-place where conflict takes place with management over control of the job' (Webster, 1985: 124). Not only did the emerging unions survive this period, but in 1979 a tightly structured federation was established to further build union muscle in the factories: the Federation of South African Trade Unions (Fosatu). In a move reminiscent of Sactu prior to the Freedom Charter, the new federation stressed non-racialism as a core principle, where this referred once again to worker unity.

Fosatu also pioneered the principle of direct worker control, with workers constituting the majority of delegates in any structure. Unlike previous federations which channelled union resources into national political battles, it would divert resources downwards to strengthen its factory presence (Friedman, 1987: 184). By the 1980s, one commentator could remark that South African unionism had advanced centuries in seven years (Friedman, 1987: 393). Until 1977, noted Alec Erwin, then general secretary of Fosatu (today a minister in the Mbeki cabinet), the new unions had been little more than advice services dealing with complaints and individual grievances. By 1979, they had won the right to formal recognition. The Wiehahn Commission, appointed in 1977 to review the laws administered by the Department of Labour, recommended that black and 'mixed' unions be allowed to participate in factory committees and other wage-bargaining forums.

In the South African literature, Fosatu's unionism is usually discussed as 'workerist' and contrasted to the 'charterist' practice of Sactu. These terms are usually meant to distinguish a trade unionism more interested in political activities from one concerned with the infrastructure of worker and factory committees. Yet this opposition is imprecise. It was not that Fosatu was politically disinterested; it was rather that the political agent that it animated was proletarian rather than popular. Hence, as far as they are useful shorthands, for the purposes of this book, 'workerism' and 'charterism' shall denote different attitudes to the nationalist movement: aligned and non-aligned respectively. What Fosatu refused was national democratic trade unionism, i.e. the subordination of worker unity to the political interests of 'the people'. Simply put, Fosatu, in decisions affecting its members, refused to acknowledge the ANC as the senior partner, or even as a necessary partner at all.

At the 1982 Fosatu congress, the then general secretary, Joe Foster, offered an appraisal of the strengths and weaknesses of the federation. For this purpose, he suggested three critical criteria for measuring Fosatu's position (summarised here):

- the extent to which the unions had established effective organisations based on shop-floor strength;
- the extent to which Fosatu had built national non-racial industrial unions; and
- the extent to which had Fosatu had developed worker leadership that could give guidance and direction to all workers (Foster, 1987: 255).

What the third measure referred to was (a) the degree to which working-class interests were articulated as such, and (b) the extent to which these interests were foregrounded in political campaigns. At stake was the degree to which a popular struggle served working-class interests. Implicit in Foster's address was a critique of *The Road to South African Freedom*, the 1962 programme of the SACP. As we have seen, this programme posited a logically necessary relationship between national oppression and class exploitation. Foster implied otherwise. In the first place, he suggested that the capitalist economy no longer relied on cheap migrant labour – and hence on the attendant system of racially oppressive laws and institutions to maintain it (Foster, 1987: 225). In the second place, he argued that industry and other parts of society were in fact being 'deracialised' (Foster, 1987: 255). South African capitalism, he argued concentrated more and more black workers in large urban townships, and required an increasingly skilled and educated labour force.

In short, as the importance of the mining industry declined as a relative share of the economy, and that of the manufacturing and other industrial sectors increased, so the working class came more and more to resemble an urban, industrial proletariat.[10] In this regard, the nationalist struggle did not in and of itself advance workers' interests. But Foster was in no way disparaging of the nationalist movement. He agreed that such resistance was appropriate to challenge the legitimacy of the apartheid state. However, for him the real question was how workers' organisations related to this wider political struggle. Politically, most unions and their leadership, he suggested, lacked confidence as workers, and instead saw their role as part of a wider struggle. In this regard, they were unclear about their proper political task. As a result, the question of building a proletarian movement was not dealt with, and political energy was spent on establishing unity across a wide front. Such a position was, however, a great strategic error, because it threatened to weaken, if not destroy, any workers' organisation *qua* workers' organisation. All the great and successful popular movements, Foster suggested, had had as their aim the overthrow of oppressive – most often colonial – regimes. But these movements could not and had not in themselves been able to deal with the particular and fundamental problems of workers. It was essential, therefore, that workers strove to build their own powerful and effective organisation, even while part of the wider popular struggle. Such a movement was necessary to protect and further advance their interests and to ensure that the popular movement was not hijacked by elements that would later be driven to turn against them. For this purpose, Foster argued that Fosatu must create the conditions for a working-class movement. The trade union would not itself be such a movement, merely its condition. Strategically, Foster worried about workers' involvement in a wider arena than that of the union struggle. Under conditions where a proletarian identity was weak and worker leadership inexperienced, he was anxious that workers would be 'swamped by the powerful tradition of popular politics' (Foster, 1987: 228–34). Hence, if it was correct that a working-class movement should take up the struggle against racial oppression – precisely because most workers were also oppressed as blacks – in the absence of such an organisation, the time was not yet opportune to join an alliance.

Such political reservations informed Fosatu's attitude to the newly established United Democratic Front (UDF). In 1983 the UDF was formed to co-ordinate and mobilise opposition to the planned reform of influx control – the laws governing and restricting black urbanisation – the reform of the system of local government and the establishment of the Tri-Cameral Parliament. These measures by the state were an attempt to strengthen its authority in the face of a mounting social and economic crisis. The fall of the gold price in 1982 and a balance of payments deficit (caused by the import of capital equipment during the late 1970s) generated a situation of unprecedented indebtedness by the early 1980s. Responding to International Monetary Fund loan conditions, the government froze social spending and increased sales tax – effectively shifting the fiscal burden onto the poor by raising the cost of goods, including foodstuffs. During this period, inflation surpassed all levels hitherto, reaching 16.5 per cent in 1985. In 1982 unemployment mounted steeply, was further exacerbated by negative economic growth in 1983 and an interest rate increase in 1984. By 1985, 25 per cent of the economically active population was unemployed. Over the same period, black secondary school enrolment nearly doubled (from 577,000 to over a million), and the number of graduates entering the job market tripled. Severe drought also crippled rural food production in black reserves already impoverished by overcrowding and overgrazing. Hundreds of thousands left the Bantustans for the cities. To this growing crisis, the government responded with an ambitious plan of institutional and constitutional reform.

Conceding that the government could not 'turn back the tide' of black urbanisation, the Koornhof bills, named after the minister responsible for them, foresaw relaxing influx control and granting blacks political rights in racially segregated local governments. Black Local Authorities, as they were called, were autonomous, elected bodies charged with the provision of urban services to the residents under their jurisdiction. We shall return to this in more detail in a moment. More ambitiously, the government proposed a new constitutional dispensation that would grant Indians and coloureds national political representation in a so-called Tri-Cameral Parliament.[11] Each racial group, excluding blacks, was granted a parliamentary assembly authorised to pass legislation on matters supposedly concerning itself. These measures were designed to temper political resistance by binding opposition into a framework stacked against it. At the same time, the government tried to shift the costs of economic restructuring onto the poor. The UDF organised to oppose these measures. What was Fosatu's attitude to these developments?

In 1983 the *South African Labour Bulletin* (SALB), originally a broadsheet for the newly 'independent' unions, interviewed the secretary of the General Workers' Union (GWU) on his attitude to the UDF. The GWU was one of Fosatu's principal members.

> SALB: Why has the General Workers' Union decided not to affiliate to the United Democratic Front?
>
> GWU: The first point, which we have stated repeatedly, is that we are committed to supporting any organization which opposes the Koornhof Bills, and the UDF would obviously be primary amongst those organizations. We are also committed to the ideal of joint campaigns with the UDF in opposing the bills and the constitution. But we don't see our way to affiliating to the UDF. Our difficulties relate to two broad issues. The first concerns the structures of the other organizations that are affiliated to the UDF relative to the structure of a trade union. Our second major area of difficulty relates to the essentially single class nature, working class nature, of trade unions, relative to the multi-class nature of the UDF and of many of the organizations affiliated to the UDF. ...
>
> SALB: You referred earlier to problems in the relationship between the union as a single class organization, and other organizations affiliated to the UDF which are multi-class organizations. Could you elaborate on that?
>
> GWU: It's not even primarily a question that the union is a single class organization, but that the union is a working class organization, and a working class organization only. ... This means that [our members] identify, quite correctly, as their source of oppression, the bosses and the state. That has a bearing on the question of our affiliation to the UDF. For one thing, unions will inevitably be organizations that incorporate a great diversity of political views and affiliations. We'll have within our ranks members with militant political views, and

we'll have within our ranks members with fairly conservative political views. We'll also have within our ranks a great many members who have few political views at all, people who have joined the organization to fight their bosses. With a certain degree of tension now and again, those diverse views can all be contained within the organization, because they are all held by workers. ...

[S]tudent and community organizations ... tend to identify the state as their source of oppression. This means that they are inevitably more clearly politically defined, and their membership is more clearly a politically based membership. They don't have the bosses to intercede in the struggle in the same way that workers in a trade union do. ... [T]he fact of the matter is that in South Africa, most non-trade union progressive organizations, tend to identify themselves quite strongly with one or another political tendency. ... There was a possibility that affiliation could jeopardise the unity of the ... the unions (*South African Labour Bulletin*, 1983: 48, 53).

Two issues were at stake here. The first was strategic; the second, theoretical. Political affiliation threatened to isolate workers not inclined to the politics of the UDF. More importantly, if the struggle against the state was not also a struggle against the 'bosses', then UDF campaigns did not necessarily address the interests of workers as workers. The GWU supported Foster's position that workers occupied a special position in South African society. They were simultaneously oppressed (by a racial regime) and exploited (by capitalists). What was at stake was the relationship between race and class, i.e. the relationship between nationalism and socialism.

Momentum was building in parts of Fosatu in favour, not simply of linking to the UDF, but of joining so-called 'community campaigns'. In the then Cape Province,[12] a series of fiercely contested strikes saw unions mobilise, not simply their members, but communal support in the form of consumer boycotts. At the Fatti's and Moni's plant in East London, strikers boosted their campaign against management by organising a boycott of the company's products (pasta and bread). The turning point came when the Cape Town black traders decided to support the strike by persuading shopkeepers and merchants not to stock the goods in question. Sales of Fatti's and Moni's products dropped dramatically, and the company's share price fell on the stock exchange. At the Ford motor factory in Port Elizabeth, strikers solicited and won massive support from community organisations. Indeed, the union action had started in response to the firing of a union official who was also leader of the Port Elizabeth Black Civic Organisation. In East London, the South African Allied Workers' Union was formed in 1980. It vigorously participated in campaigns against the pass laws, for universal franchise, against the Group Areas Act[13] and against the independence of the then Ciskei. In his 1982 address, Foster noted that:

> there has emerged into our political debate an empty and misleading political category called 'the community'. All communities are composed of different interest groups and for a worker organization to ally itself with every community group or action would be suicide for worker organization. FOSATU cannot possibly ally itself to all the political groups that are contesting this arena. Neither can it ally itself with particular groups. Both paths will destroy the unity of its own worker organization (Foster, 1987: 234).

Foster added, moreover, that:

> [t]his simple fact ... has nothing to do with wanting or not wanting to be involved in politics. Our whole existence is political and we welcome that. Our concern is with the very essence of politics and that is the relation between the major classes in South Africa, being capital and labour (Foster, 1987: 234).

Why were Foster and the GWU leadership so concerned to stress the strategic error of a united front? Why, in other words, were they opposed to affiliating to the UDF and community organisations? Precisely because they forsook the terms of the theory of NDR; precisely, that is, because they rejected its political and strategic implications. 'The people' were composed of diverse interests, but their component sub-groupings were not reconciled around a common project, one that simultaneously advanced all their interests. That is exactly what the NDR presumed: that the struggle against racial oppression advanced the interests of the black, coloured and Indian bourgeoisie and petit bourgeoisie at the same time as it satisfied workers' interests. The very fact that this was still an issue at all was testament not simply to the durability of the Sactu tradition within the new labour movement, but reflected something else as well: the recent entry into the unions of a younger generation of workers radicalised during the 1976 student revolt. Without wanting to discuss at length the history of the Soweto revolt, it is important to highlight one of its major consequences.

Between 1950 and 1975 the black student population had risen from around 1 million to over 3.5 million. Students found themselves in massively overcrowded classes (in Soweto these averaged 60 students per class and were often as high as 100), in critically under-funded schools staffed by inadequately trained teachers and usually subject to an authoritarian school administration that used violent punishment as a means to control the effects of overcrowding. Opposition to these conditions began to develop a more organised voice from the 1970s with the formation of the South African Students' Movement (SASM).

The SASM was a loose federation of Black Consciousness groups that organised around specifically school issues – it opposed inter-school choir competitions as a distraction from learning, for example, and demanded that student representative councils be established in schools to give voice to 'concerns and grievances'. What is important to note about these actions was their distance from the established conduits of political opposition. The ANC and the SACP had been banned, infiltrated and sufficiently weakened since the 1960s, rendering them merely symbols of resistance. School opposition in the 1970s thus had little or no political contact with these organisations or their strategic and political repertoires. Indeed, the threat represented by the SASM to the apartheid state was that it opposed instruction in Afrikaans.

The massive and violent police response to a march organised by the SASM to Orlando Stadium in Soweto on 16 June 1976, however, would forever change the South African political landscape. The year of revolt following from the sustained massacre that ensued saw the radicalisation of a generation of mostly urban, school-educated youth that would soon enter the work force and the trade unions emerging after the Durban strikes of 1973.

The Black Consciousness Movement was not the principal beneficiary of the new political awakening. Despite the popularity of its message and its images, which continue to inform the South African political imagination, Black Consciousness remained chiefly a literary and intellectual movement, failing to build strong political structures. Thus, when the progeny of the Soweto revolt sought to exercise their newly found political radicalism, there were few well-organised Black Consciousness structures that could accommodate them. They turned, therefore, to the long-established liberation movements, and to the ANC in particular. When thousands fled into exile, they joined the political and military structures of the ANC. The Soweto uprising thus reanimated the political return of the ANC into South Africa.

The revolt would also resolve the workerist–charterist debate for the time being, but not because it brought theoretical clarity to the relationship between race and class. From then on, it was unthinkable to many of the unions' members that they should remain aloof from the nationalist struggle. Many were soon unhappy with Fosatu's strongly workerist tendency and complained that the union federation was invested with a deep 'social conservatism'. The appointment of Chief Mangosuthu Buthelezi, then chief minister of the autonomous region of KwaZulu and leader of Inkatha,[14] to chair the Industrial Information Centre

– a strategy employed to give Fosatu respectability among 'traditional' quarters in KwaZulu and in Natal – seemed merely to confirm this agenda. As a result, there was growing pressure for the unions to link to a host of extra-factory political campaigns. New recruits, in particular, were eager to relate their union activities to wider struggles for national liberation. The strategic success of strikes like those at the Fatti's and Moni's factory and the Ford Cortina plant merely strengthened their hand. Alliances with the 'popular movement' had apparently yielded results for workers as workers. Was this not confirmation of the theory of national democratic revolution?

The formation of the UDF in 1983 and the uprising that started in the Vaal area in 1984 merely accelerated the move away from workerism. In 1985 Fosatu was dissolved, and in its place the Congress of South African Trade Unions (Cosatu) was established. As its name suggests, Cosatu aligned itself with the nationalist movement, entering into a *de facto* alliance with the ANC and the SACP shortly after its launch.[15] Enter the Tripartite Alliance, which exists to this day. We can note that, at the time of writing, this relationship is more strained than at any other time in its history. At stake is, unsurprisingly, the relationship between the NDR and workers' interests. The formation of Cosatu signalled, therefore, that within the labour movement the theory of NDR had regained its pre-eminence. Not only did this authorise trade union alliances with community groups, it actively encouraged them.

Leading on from this discussion, the following chapter will attempt to answer the question posed at the start of this chapter: 'What was nationalist about the discourse of national democratic revolution?'

4

The South African Nation

This chapter will argue that what made the politics of national democratic revolution a nationalist politics was that it posited the citizen as necessarily a member of a nation – as a bearer, in other words, of some or other quality of population. To get sense of our task, let us begin this investigation with a well-known speech of Thabo Mbeki, given on behalf of the African National Congress on the occasion of the adoption of the Constitution in Cape Town in May 1996. In 'I Am an African', Mbeki states:

> I owe my being to the Khoi and the San whose desolate souls haunt the great expanses of the beautiful Cape .... I am formed of the migrants who left Europe to find a new home on our native land. ... In my veins courses the blood of the Malay slaves who came from the East. ... I am the grandchild of the warrior men and women that Hintsa and Sekhukhune led, the patriots Cetshwayo and Mpephu took to battle, the soldiers Moshoeshoe and Ngungunyane taught never to dishonour the cause of freedom. My mind and my knowledge of myself is formed by the victories that are the jewels in our African crown, the victories we earned from Isandhlwana to Khartoum, as Ethiopians and as the Ashanti

of Ghana, as the Berbers of the desert. I am the grandchild that
lays fresh flowers on the Boer graves at St Helena and the Bahamas
… I am the child of Nongqause. … I come from those who were
transported from India and China (Mbeki, 1998: 31–32).

These lines, treating the identity of the African, are punctuated with the
following declaration (and elsewhere, something very similar): 'Being
part of all these people, and in the knowledge that none dare contest the
assertion, I shall claim that I am an African!' (Mbeki, 1998: 32). Here
Mbeki deliberately invokes a term that, in the context, is profoundly
ambiguous. Why does he declare 'I am an African' instead of 'I am a South
African'? Why does his verse slide between allusions to the continent in
general and to South Africa specifically? The South African people, that
is, are also the people of the continent of Africa. These terms are mixed
throughout the speech: 'Today it feels good to stand here as an African.' 'It
feels good that I can stand here as a South African' (p. 35). In this respect,
they are not of any particular language, nor of a particular background.
What is it, therefore, that unites these peoples as Africans?

In the first place, Mbeki says, they belong to a common territory:

I owe my being to the hills and the valleys, the mountains and the
glades, the rivers, the deserts, the trees, the flowers, the seas and
the ever-changing seasons that define the face of our native land. …
The dramatic shapes of the Drakensberg, the soil-coloured waters
of the Lekoa, iGqili no Thukela, and the sands of the Kgalagadi
have all been panels of the set of the natural stage on which we act
out the foolish deeds of the theatre of our day (Mbeki, 1998: 31).

But that is not all. 'Africans', despite their heterogeneity, share a
common history:

I have seen our country torn asunder as these, all of whom are
my people, engaged one another in a titanic battle, the one to

redress a wrong that had been caused by one to another, and the
other to defend the indefensible.

The people are also 'heroes and heroines', those that would not tolerate
oppression, nor allow fear of death, torture, imprisonment, exile or
persecution to result in the perpetuation of injustice (Mbeki, 1998:
34). Africans are people that have seen what happens when those with
superior force deny the divine injunction that all men and women are
created equally in the image of God. Africans know what it means
when race and colour are used to distinguish between humans and 'sub-
humans', and when they are used to enrich some and impoverish others.
An African has seen the effects of the destruction of self-esteem and the
way minds are corrupted when race and colour are used to perpetrate
veritable crimes against humanity. An African has experienced the
concrete expression of the denial of the dignity of a human being resulting
from systemic and deliberate oppression and repression (p. 33).

Mbeki is not simply discussing apartheid, the term is never used.
Instead he insinuates another term, also never used: colonialism. 'I Am an
African' is profoundly ambivalent about the precise identity of 'the people'.
There is a constant shifting between two registers. On the one hand, the
term includes both the *perpetrators* and the *survivors* of the colonial 'crime
against humanity'. On the other hand, it refers exclusively to those who
lived and struggled against this terrible injustice. In the first definition,
those 'migrants who left Europe to find a new home on our native land' are
included in 'the people'. They are not easily 'Africans', however, according
to the second. Or rather, they only become Africans when, in the words
of the Constitution (Chapter 3), they 'recognise the injustices of the past'.
What should we make, though, of the phrase *'our* native land' in the
reference above? Who is the subject there? The *indigenous* inhabitants of
Africa? Does Mbeki imply a hierarchy of 'Africanness'? Or worse, does he
imply that immigrants, especially those from Europe, but including those
from India, Malaysia and China, can never quite become authentically
African? More of this in a moment.

What Mbeki does here is situate 'being African' in the context of the struggle against colonialism. The nation, in other words, is produced in and through the struggle for democracy. This is precise. It is not important if the nation in question is composed exclusively of the people of South Africa or of the people of the continent as a whole. What is important to note is that during the course of the speech the meaning of 'being African' changes. We hear that in the course of the struggle against injustice, 'being African' meant refusing to allow 'a few' to describe one as barbaric. Indeed, it meant refusing to be defined in terms of race, colour, gender or historical origins. Being African under such conditions meant not belonging to a group or class defined by others. With the advent of democracy, however, being African is not simply about refusal: it means being able to define for oneself who one is and who one should be: 'We are assembled here today to mark [our] victory in acquiring and exercising [our] right to formulate [our] own definition of what it means to be African' (Mbeki, 1998: 34).

So who is an African today? The African in a democracy is a new sort of being: an individual, free to belong or not belong to any group he/she sees fit. The democratic nation, therefore, is not simply a nation of multiple identities; it is a nation *composed of individuals*. But we recall that being African was intimately linked to combating racism and refusing apartheid and colonial social taxonomies. What this therefore means is that being African, or being an individual, is contingent on something very special: being able to understand the racist power at work in apartheid and colonial taxonomies. Africans are authentically so when able to 'see' themselves through liberated eyes. This, it appears, is the mark of authenticity.

We will see, in the remainder of this chapter, that 'liberated eyes' come with a certain body, marked with certain physical and social traits.

The politics of national democratic revolution

The theory of NDR has been discussed at some length earlier so as to be able to answer the following question: Who, according to the theory of NDR, are 'the people'? It is to this question that the present chapter now turns. It will be not as concerned with a sociological description of the people as they are – how many languages they speak, where they live etc. as with when they may be considered *free*.

The previous chapter has already established the Marxist pedigree of the theory of NDR. It demonstrated too that as far as 'the people' consisted of the 'nationally oppressed', the majority of them were workers. We know too that, according to Marxist theory, proletarianisation is accompanied by a cultural process: the dissolution of bonds associated with the clan or the lineage group. In other words, the worker is simultaneously an individual.

Now, even if the theory of NDR ultimately identifies the key feature of South African capitalism as the system of migrant labour ('cheap labour') – which entails the reproduction of (in Gellner's terms) 'agrarian' cultural forms – and therefore posits South African society as culturally heterogeneous, the task of the democratic state will be to overcome such differences. After all, the theory of NDR is not simply an analysis of apartheid, it is a vision of a liberated nation (Suttner & Cronin, 1986: ix). Let us note that a free South Africa will not simply be democratic: it will be modern. Indeed, the national democratic state will complete the partial modernisation started under apartheid capitalism. To summarise the Freedom Charter:[1]

- If under apartheid the mineral wealth beneath the soil, the banks and monopoly industry were at the service of a minority, the national democratic state will transfer their ownership to the people.
- If under apartheid not all people had the right to live where they chose, to be decently housed and to raise their families in comfort and

security, the national democratic state will provide preventative health care and free hospitalisation to mothers and young children, demolish slums and build new suburbs. It will provide transport, roads, lighting, playing fields, crèches and social centres. And so on.

What we have here is an account of a free people, where freedom is associated with a determinate cultural form: being an individual in a modern, industrial society. This is what it means to be liberated:

> The South African industrial proletariat, concentrated in the large urban complexes, has emerged as the most organised and powerful mass revolutionary contingent in our country. Its proletariat class consciousness has been developed and deepened by decades of militant trade unionism. This tradition is today embodied in the South African Congress of Trade Unions (SACTU) and in the giant federation, the Congress of South African Trade Union (COSATU). It is a working class that has responded in its millions to calls for national stayaways, shutting down the mines, factories, shops, and bringing the capitalist economy to a grinding halt for days at a time. It is a working class from among whom increasingly large numbers are actively rallying to the Marxist-Leninist positions of the SACP, openly espousing the perspectives of socialism. Within our own country this proletariat is gathering its forces to fulfil the historical role predicted over one hundred years ago by Marx and Engels for the working class movement on a world scale. Assembled in millions within the very heartland of an advanced capitalist economy, and leading the struggle against national oppression, the South African working class is poised to be the gravedigger of capitalist exploitation itself (SACP, 1989).

Let us note too that the references in this 1989 text are to the early Marx; to the Marx of the *Communist Manifesto*. This is important, because it helps us understand better the circumstances of the South African worker for this theory. In particular, they are individuals in a very particular sense: here an industrial worker referred also to one separated from the clan, the tribe and the extended family. This cultural transformation – deemed in Marx's work prior to *Capital* to be an ordinary effect of the shift from handicrafts to manufacture – was an essential condition of being free. What was at stake was the freedom of workers from the hold of the past and the demystification of their relationship to reality. In other words, individualisation was a condition of their being able to apprehend the world as it really was, to refuse to see the world in the false categories of ideology. In contrast, tribalism was a condition of colonial rule precisely because it kept subjects in the dark about their real conditions and therefore prevented them from acting in their own best interests. Refusal to accept the apartheid social taxonomy and resistance to racism and colonial oppression necessarily implied being an individual in an industrial society.[2] Let us summarise, according to the theory of NDR, the argument so far:

- A democratic society is one where its members are free.
- Being free means being an individual in an industrial society.
- Being free means being able to vote in elections.
- Being free means to share in the country's wealth.
- Therefore a democratic society is an industrial society that is composed of individuals and has democratic institutions and public ownership of the means of production.

What we have here is a strange subversion of the democratic project. The measure of democracy is not the public domain: it is the degree to which society is composed of individuals and there is public ownership of a modern industrial economy. In other words, the public domain is deemed contingent on realising the nation. Once we forsake the socialist allusions, then it is a simple step to say that democracy is achieved when the economy is industrial and society is composed of individuals. Let us note here the proper measure of the individual: one's distance from tribal/ethnic associations and practices.

To what extent is this rendition of NDR recognisable in current debates? To what extent has it recently been taken to unforeseen heights that have little or no relation to its original template?[3] Simply put, does what goes for NDR today still invoke industrial individuals (modern humankind) as the authentic bearers of the nation? At stake is the degree to which the measure of freedom is living in an industrial society. Has NDR reconciled itself to feminism and/or other movements that do not predicate freedom on industrialisation? Does NDR today have room for women and/or communal figures (members of clans, tribes, extended families, etc.) as motive forces for revolution?

We can approach these questions in the light of contemporary debates about NDR 'on the terrain of capitalism' (SACP, 2002, secs. 1.3.1, 1.5.2, 5.37). Let us start by returning to an important discussion document, attributed to Thabo Mbeki and prepared for the 1998 Tripartite Alliance summit: 'The state, property relations and social transformation' (ANC, 1998). It brings to the fore many of the shifts, contradictions and continuities that characterise the current situation. What we will notice is that the working class is forsaken as the agent of the NDR in favour of the state and a black bourgeoisie. What we will also notice, however, is that the political-economic objective remains the same: a modern industrial society. Simply put, the working class is no longer deemed the pre-eminent agent of modernisation.

'The strategic challenge of the current phase', the document begins, 'is to transform South African society to become truly non-racial, united, non-sexist and democratic.' In pursuit of these goals 'it should be underlined that a critical element of this process is the active participation of *the people* as the drivers of change' (ANC, 1998: 1; emphasis added). To this end, the document continues, it is necessary to liberate the people from political and economic bondage.

The document adds that the primary beneficiaries of NDR should be the poor, the majority of whom are black and female. Here we have 'the people' seeking to eliminate the 'basic causes of the national grievance' in pursuit of new society that especially benefits the poor. So what is this 'national grievance'? The document continues that the 'state represents class interests and therefore it is part of, and a player in defining, social relations' (p. 2). It then states:

> [A]s a concentrated expression of social relations, as an institution wielding enormous power and resources, the state is for this reason the most critical area of contestation among classes: transfer of state power is thus characterized as the most visible and critical expression of a revolution (p. 2).

Does this help us understand better the nature of the national grievance? Is it primarily a question of class? Indeed, what are the class interests that the apartheid state served? And here there is a curious displacement. Packed into the term 'class' is another concept entirely. If class here refers to a property relation and the state represents a class interest, then it follows that social transformation is predicated on changing the property relation. But this is precisely what the document says will *not* be done. The NDR 'will not eliminate the basic antagonism between capital and labour' (ANC, 1998: 1). Indeed, we are told that 'NDR is not aimed at resolving the central question of property relations: it does not seek to create a classless society' (p. 2).

Class is used here, rather deceptively, as one might use the term 'group', as a colloquial expression that merely denotes a collection of people. It has certainly lost its theoretical and political bearings *vis-à-vis* Marxism. So if the term does not invoke a class in the proper sense, to what does it refer? We are told that the apartheid state was 'illegitimate and structured to serve the interests of the White minority' (p. 3). Class here refers to a racial group:

In the final analysis, one of the objectives of the NDR is to transform property relations: to redefine the relationship that individuals, sectors and groups have to capital. The NDR does not aim to reshape property relations in the most fundamental way of creating a classless society. It does not seek to eliminate capital and capitalism. ... [T]he NDR must see to the *deracialisation* of ownership, accumulation and allocation of capital (p. 5; emphasis added).

As what seems to be an afterthought, the sentence finishes: 'and it should do this in a manner that benefits the poor'.

If 'the people' in general are not the 'motive forces' of change, and neither are certain classes in the sense that the NDR once invoked the term, then who is the agent of NDR? We learn that:

An important element of the task of the state is ensuring the glass ceiling of apartheid is removed from above the aspirations and ambitions of the black middle strata and capitalist class. In a systemic way, the NDR has to ensure that ownership of private capital at all levels ... is not defined in racial terms. Thus the new state – in its procurement policy, its programme of restructuring state assets, utilization of instruments of empowerment, pressure and other measures – *promotes the emergence of a black capitalist class* (ANC, 1998: 6; emphasis added).

In this way, the state promotes the involvement of private capital to expand the economy and it guides the owners of capital towards projects that create jobs and contribute to development. Moreover, we are told, a growing economy assists redistribution by expanding the tax base, through job creation, by improving services and further developing human resources (p. 7).

Let us note a series of fundamental departures from the template theory of NDR. In the first place, capitalism *per se* is acquitted of charges of producing and reproducing poverty. Only a 'skewed' capitalism is said to be at fault. Secondly, the 'motive forces' of the NDR are no longer primarily the working class, but are deemed, rather, the state and the black bourgeoisie. Thirdly, the interests of the poor are, at best, only indirectly satisfied, and then only provided that the economy grows and that the black bourgeoisie can be made to invest in job-creating enterprises. But let us note too a key continuity with the theory of NDR as elaborated from 1962. The objective remains the same: NDR still intends to achieve, not democracy or control of the public domain, but a modern industrial economy and society. What has changed is the identity of the 'motive forces'. Under conditions of globalisation, the collapse of the Soviet Union and so on, the working class is no longer considered to be the best agent of the industrial society: the 'capitalist state' is. It is still 'industrial man' that is the authentic bearer of the NDR, though 'he' is no longer a worker but a bourgeois. There is still no role here for communal figures (clans, tribes, extended families). Despite lip service to gender concerns, women are very much an add-on extra.[4] Women *qua* women are only potentially (indirect) beneficiaries of the revolution – if everything goes according to plan, the economy grows, the black bourgeoisie invest in the appropriate industries, etc. As 'motive forces' of transformation, there is no role here for women except as 'modern men'.

At least here the nation has certain empirical measures: the degree to which people have jobs, houses, transport, and so on. This is not always the case.

Being free in Black Consciousness

For Black consciousness, what does it mean to be free? Let us recall that what is at stake for Mbeki and African nationalism generally is the capacity to apprehend the world, not necessarily as it really is, but at least in terms that do not speak of race, patriarchy or class power.

The political defeat of the ANC and the SACP during the 1960s created opportunities for new discourses of resistance to make themselves felt on the South African scene. The most important of these was the

Black Consciousness Movement which emerged in the early 1970s. And central to this movement was Bantu Steve Biko. He had entered the University of Natal, Durban (non-European section) in 1965. There he became active in student politics through the National Union of South African Students (Nusas). Nusas was a racially mixed student body, and in 1968 he broke away to form the South African Students' Organisation (Saso), which restricted membership exclusively to black students.

What was uppermost in his mind and that of his colleagues in the early 1970s was the 'fragmentation of the black resistance'. He states:

> since the banning and harassment of black political parties – a
> dangerous vacuum has been created .... [P]eople's hearts were
> gripped by some kind of foreboding fear for anything political.
> Not only were politics a closed book, but at every corner one was
> greeted by a slave-like apathy that often bordered on timidity.
> ... After this brief spell of silence during which political activity
> was mainly taken up by liberals, blacks started dabbling with
> the dangerous theory – that of working within the system
> (Biko, 1996c: 34).

Independence was being granted to the then Transkei, and former opponents of apartheid had thrown in their lot with the Bantustans. Most importantly, Chief Mangosuthu Buthelezi, while refusing independence for KwaZulu, accepted political autonomy in the Zulu Territorial Authority. Biko's first interventions thus responded to a double concern: to resist the fragmentation of resistance to apartheid and to wrest control of anti-apartheid activities from white liberals.

Amongst his first articles as chair of Saso publications, Biko contributed 'Black souls in white skins' to the monthly newsletter. It was one of the first major expositions of the 'philosophy of Black Consciousness' (Biko, 1996a). Writing under the pseudonym Frank Talk, Biko analysed the problem in South Africa as that of white racism. The fact that apartheid – 'the arrogant assumption that a clique of foreigners has the right to decide on the lives of a majority' (Biko, 1996b: 27) – has been simultaneously tied up with capitalist exploitation and deliberate oppression merely complicates matters. It does not detract from its central feature. Hence:

> The sooner liberals [a term he used to include Communists and other 'Leftists'] realise this the better for us blacks. Their presence amongst us is irksome and of nuisance value. It removes the focus of attention from essentials and shifts it to ill-defined philosophical concepts that are both irrelevant to the black man and merely a red herring across the track. White liberals must leave blacks to take care of their own business while they concern themselves with the real evil in our society – white racism (Biko, 1996a: 23).

In treating the problem as one of 'segregation' or even of capitalism, white liberals – these 'do-gooders', 'non-conformists' – fail to recognise the nature of the beast. They propose, for example, that integration is the correct step towards the total liberation of blacks. The supposition here is that the problem can be solved by racial reconciliation. 'Nothing could be more irrelevant and therefore misleading':

> The myth of integration ... must be cracked and killed because it makes people believe that something is being done when in actual fact the artificial integrated circles are a soporific on the blacks and provide a vague satisfaction for the guilt-stricken whites (Biko, 1996a: 22).

What for Biko are the real effects of white racism? If they are not principally oppression, segregation and capitalism, what are they? The title of the essay 'Black souls in white skins' is instructive in this regard: this is clearly a reference to Frantz Fanon's *Peau noire, masques blancs* (black skin, white masks) (1952). What might we say about the relationship between them? Was Fanon Biko's major intellectual interlocutor? The relationship between them has important consequences for how Black Consciousness understood the conditions of freedom. Fortunately, we are in a better position to understand the intellectual relation between them since the publication of David Macey's extraordinary biography of Frantz Fanon (Macey, 2000).

In his essay 'We blacks', Biko asks the following question: 'What makes the black man fail to tick?' (Biko, 1996b: 28). For the most part, he replies, it is because he is a 'defeated man'. White domination, this machine that prepares the black man for subservience, produces 'at the output end' a man who is a 'man only in form'. He has lost his manhood. Reduced to an 'obliging shell', the black man can do nothing but look in awe at the 'white power structure' and accept what is given to him as his 'inevitable position'. He yearns for the material comforts of white society, but does not believe himself worthy because he is not sufficiently educated. He hazily understands the scientific achievements of white men, and so resigns himself to the status quo, because he is convinced of the futility of resistance: 'All in all the black man has become a shell, a shadow of a man, completely defeated, drowning in his own misery, a slave, an ox bearing the yoke of oppression with sheepish timidity' (p. 29).

What is at stake for Fanon is the white gaze. 'I arrived in the world', he writes 'anxious to extract a meaning from things, my soul full of the desire to be at the origin of the world, and here I find myself an object in the midst of other objects.' And yet the moment he establishes his own being-in-the world, it collapses under the white gaze into being-for-others:

> 'Look, a negro!' It was an external stimulus that flicked me in passing. I smiled slightly.
>
> 'Look, a negro!' It was true. I laughed.
>
> 'Look, a negro!' The circle was gradually getting smaller. I laughed openly.

'Mommy, look at the negro, I'm frightened!' Frightened!
Frightened! Now they were beginning to be frightened of me. I
wanted to laugh till I burst, but it had become impossible. ...
Having come under attack at several points, the corporeal
schema collapsed, giving way to an epidermal racial schema
(Fanon, 1952: 90).[5]

Like the Jew that is created by the anti-Semite, the 'negro' is produced
through the gaze of the white man. And yet unlike the Jew who is created
as a character, the black is created in and through his *skin*. The character
of the black arises, in other words, because he is *black*. In a colonised
society, the black is not simply black. He is black in the eyes of the white
man. This theme became a recurrent one, not simply for Fanon, but for
the authors associated with the politics of Negritude. Aimé Césaire's
adaptation of *The Tempest (Une tempête)*, for example, explored precisely
this relationship:

Prospero, you are the master of illusion. Lying is your trademark.
And you have lied so much to me (lied about the world, lied
about me) that you have ended by imposing on me an image of
myself. Underdeveloped, you brand me, inferior, that's the way
you have forced me to see myself. I detest that image! What's
more, it's a lie! But now I know you, you old cancer, and I know
myself as well (Césaire, 1969: 88).[6]

The revolt of the colonised, therefore, must be based on the assumption
of his *blackness*. This was the basis of the politics of Negritude, and it
situates *Peau noire, masques blancs* within the tradition of Aimé Césaire
(the Martinican poet and later member of the French Communist Party),
Leopold Sedar Senghor (elected the first president of an independent
Senegal in 1960), Leon-Gontran Damas and Suzanne Lascade (the
writer, born in Guadeloupe, whose novel *Claire Solange: âme Africaine*
scandalised Paris before World War II).

Césaire's *Cahier d'un retour au pays natal* defiantly reclaims

> my original geography [Martinique]; the map of the world
> made for my use, dyed not with the arbitrary colours of the
> scientists, but with the geometry of my spilt blood ... and
> the determination of my biology ... and the nigger every day
> more debased, more cowardly, more spread out of himself,
> more estranged from himself, more cunning with himself, less
> immediate with himself, I accept, I accept all this (Césaire,
> 1983: 55–56).[7]

The relationship between Fanon and Césaire, however, was not an easy
one. David Macey discusses it in terms of a 'fault line' (Macey, 2000)
running through Negritude. At stake were the theoretical implications
of metaphors like 'the nigger ever day ... *more estranged from himself*'
(Césaire, 1983: 56; emphasis added). Underpinning Senghor and
Césaire's politics of Negritude was the celebration of a specifically
'black-African culture and values'. The white gaze, that is, alienated
the black from the 'collective Negro-African personality' that was his
essence (Senghor, cited in Macey, 2000: 185). For Césaire, in particular,
Surrealism was an extension of his search for a new black subjectivity,
which he had sought in Negritude:

> This, for me, was a call to Africa. I said to myself: it's true
> that superficially we are French, we bear the marks of French
> customs; we have been branded by Cartesian philosophy, by
> French rhetoric; but if we break with all that, if we plumb the
> depths, then what we will find is fundamentally black (Césaire,
> cited in Macey, 2000: 184).

The accomplice of Negritude was a resurrection of a noble African past:
Cheikh Anta Diop claimed that the Ancient Egyptians were black. The
Afro-Asiatic roots of Greek culture were said to be obscured by an 'Aryan'

foundation myth (Macey, 2000: 184). Senghor argued that what the black man contributed to world civilization was an innate sense of rhythm.

By 1959 Fanon had become critical of such sentiments, and distanced himself especially from Senghor:

> In no way must I strive to bring back to life a Negro civilization that has been unfairly misrecognised. I will not make myself the man of any past. I do not want to sing the past at the expense of my present and my future …. My black skin is not the repository of specific values (Fanon, cited in Macey, 2000: 184).

What he rejected in *Peau noire, masques blancs* was any form of determinism, insisting that his freedom was both absolute and *self-founding* (Macey, 2000: 186). Fanon asserted the freedom to be what he *willed*, which is what eventually distanced him from the politics of Negritude. He sought freedom not in being black, i.e. in being an African – 'a great black mirage' (Fanon, cited in Macey, 2000: 375). Instead, as he become more and more involved in the Algerian war for independence from 1953, Fanon willed himself to be Algerian. What he took to be Algerian was quite distinctive, and departed from the official thinking of the Front Nationale de Liberation (FLN). Any individual living in Algeria could, for Fanon, become Algerian simply by *deciding* to be one. The FLN, in contrast, was more and more appealing to a measure of population: to be Algerian meant being an Arab Muslim. Macey writes:

> Fanon's 'nation' is the dynamic creation of the action of the people, and his nationalism is a nationalism of the political will to be Algerian, not of ethnicity …. It required the gaze of a white child to teach Fanon that he was a *nègre*; he needed no one to tell him he was Algerian – he was Algérien because he willed himself Algérien (Macey, 2000: 389).

Fanon's idea of nationalism was certainly out of step with those that appealed to Pan-Africanism or Negritude. According to him, the nation was a political and cultural unit, but not one that contained a universal black culture. Freedom was not about inverting the white gaze: making that which whites deemed inferior, worthy. It was not about rediscovering a noble black African past. Pan-Africanism in this regard was to Fanon a chimera. What his nationalism referred to was the dissolution of blackness.

We can now understand why Fanon has received such an ambivalent reception in South Africa. More specifically, despite allusion to his work, Steve Biko does not refer to him by name. He does quote, however, from none other than Aimé Césaire. Even the essay referred to earlier – 'Black souls in white skins' – is more a parody of Fanon than anything else. If in *Peau noire, masques blancs*, Fanon is discussing the 'lived experience' (*'l'expérience vécu'*) of a 'black man' – that he could never be anything but black (according to whites) because he is always betrayed by his skin – Biko is discussing white liberals. Liberals pretend to have black souls, but always act on the basis of their white skins. Now, it is no small thing that Biko chooses to replace the word 'mask' with that of 'soul'. Fanon, let us recall, never spoke of 'black skins, white souls'. But for Biko, and for the politics of Negritude, this is precisely what was at stake. In Césaire's terms, black freedom was contingent on a 'return to self', or in Biko's, 'pumping life into an empty shell'. In short: freedom was contingent on restoring an alienated soul.

For Biko, freedom – Black Consciousness – was unambiguously about a return to 'Nature' (Biko, 1996e: 49). 'I am against', he writes,

> the belief that African culture is time-bound, the notion that
> with the conquest of the African all his culture was obliterated.
> ... Obviously the African culture has had to sustain severe
> blows and may have been battered nearly out of shape by the
> belligerent cultures it collided with, yet in essence even today

one can easily find the fundamental aspects of the *pure African culture* (Biko, 1996d: 41; emphasis added).

What defines this culture, Biko tells us, is the importance it attaches to 'Man'. 'Ours has always been a Man-centred society' (Biko, 1996d: 41). This is evident, for example, in how blacks talk to each other – not, like Westerners, to arrive at a particular conclusion, but simply to enjoy the communication for its own sake. Intimacy for a black, moreover, is not reserved exclusively for friends, but extends to any group that happens to find itself together through work or 'residential requirements' (Biko, 1996d: 41):

> We believe in the inherent goodness of man. We enjoy man for himself. We regard our living together not as an unfortunate mishap warranting endless competition among us but as a deliberate act of God to make us a community of brothers and sisters jointly involved in the quest for a composite answer to the varied problems of life. Hence in all we do we always place Man first and hence all our action is usually joint community oriented action rather than the individualism which is the hallmark of the capitalist approach. We always refrain from using people as stepping stones. Instead we are prepared to have a much slower progress in an effort to make sure that all of us are marching to the same tune (Biko, 1996d: 42).

Africans love song and rhythm (Biko, 1996d: 42), they are not individualistic (p. 43), they have a 'situation-experiencing' approach to life instead of the Westerner's 'problem-solving' one (p. 43). Africans are sentient beings. Biko quotes sympathetically from Kenneth Kaunda (president of Zambia when Biko was writing) to the extent that 'Westerners' have an 'aggressive' mentality, not being able to rest until they have solved a problem. They cannot live with contradiction, vigorously rejecting solutions for which there is no basis in science or logic. In contrast, Africans,

> being a pre-scientific people do not recognise any conceptual
> cleavage between the natural and the supernatural. They
> experience a situation rather than face a problem. They allow both
> the rational and the non-rational elements to make an impact
> upon them, and any action they may take could be described
> more as a response of the total personality to the situation than
> the result of some mental exercise (Biko, 1996d: 44).

This is true, Biko adds, for the 'detribalized' African as well: 'There
remains, in spite of the superficial cultural similarities between the
detribalized and the Westerner, a number of cultural characteristics that
mark out the detribalized as an African.' This is evident, for example,
in the field of music. Jazz is an aspect of a modern African culture that
expresses 'real feelings' (Biko, 1996d: 45).

Who is free according to Black Consciousness? Or: What can we
say about the conditions of freedom? The first step, Biko tells us, is to
'remind the black man of his complicity in the crime of allowing himself
to be misused' (Biko, 1996b: 29). Secondly, Black Consciousness has
to be directed to the past, to 'rewrite the history of the black man and
to produce in it heroes who form the core of the African background.'
This, he tells us, is because a people without a *positive* history is like
a vehicle without an engine. It is necessary to protect the black man's
'sense of belonging to the community', his 'oneness of community' that
is so different to 'whitey's highly impersonal world' (p. 30). In this regard
he must not lose himself by, for example, becoming a 'slave to technology
and the machine' (p. 30). Black people are deeply religious. If the white
God has been talking thus far, however, it is time for the black God to
raise His voice (p. 30). What this means is that black people must find
in the Bible a message that is relevant to them. Instead of preaching
that all authority is divinely instituted, black theologians must teach,
rather, that it is a sin to be oppressed (p. 31). Freedom, finally, for
Black Consciousness involves a return to an essential state of nature: a
fundamental state of *being free*.

Let us conclude: freedom here invokes a determinate being. He is a man; he is black; he is African. As an aid we can note that this is the inherent tension in the politics of President Mbeki. On the one hand, the nation is composed of Fanonian beings: those who are South African merely by choosing to be so; on the other, it is composed of black African men.

Let us note that the frequent masculine injunctive 'men' in Biko's writings, above, is not just stylistic. 'Man' is not a synonym for human being and a 'black man' does not just signify a black human being. When Biko calls the 'black man' to action, that is exactly what he means. In treating black alienation as an affair of white racism, or in Fanon's terms, the 'white gaze', neither Biko nor Fanon take seriously or, for that matter, *can* take seriously the black *woman*. She is not simply produced and reproduced through a white gaze. She is overdetermined through a male gaze too. By making freedom, therefore, contingent on the dissolution of the white gaze, Black Consciousness (and Fanon's 'Third Worldism') forsakes the woman to patriarchy. Indeed, Biko goes one step further. In returning to a 'pure African culture' does he not, indeed, valorise patriarchy as a condition of freedom? In this regard, however, NDR is no less complicit than Black Consciousness. We recall that NDR treats individualisation as a condition of freedom – the condition of seeing the world as it really is. By treating this process as the normal result of the forces of production, NDR, even on its own terms, obscures the ways women are prevented from becoming individuals in patriarchal family settings.

We have seen that, in both the politics of NDR and that of Black Consciousness, freedom is made contingent on determinate states of being: male industrial workers in the case of the first and black African men in the case of the second. At the moment, therefore, when either NDR or Black Consciousness asserts the freedom of the people, they both intend not the democratic public domain, but nations composed of their respective beings. In the name of freedom, therefore, nationalists substitute the goal of a democratic society for that of the nation.

5

The Impossibility of the National Community

This chapter will argue that nationalist politics is driven to exclude and ultimately even repress those that defy its terms. In intending a 'free people', where freedom is incarnate in a specific personality/figure, nationalists must at best ignore, at worst destroy those that do not resemble the national being. Instead of a theoretical proof of this claim, however, the chapter will show how this perspective helps us grasp the logic of a violent conflict that overcame three townships east of Johannesburg between 1990 and 1994. What concerns us will be the conditions or terms of the violence. How did the violence take the form of a conflict between hostel-based, mostly Zulu migrant workers and township youth organised in and through civic structures and youth organisations? What the chapter will suggest is that as the politics of NDR become dominant in the 1980s, two things occurred simultaneously:

- firstly, migrant workers, before then the most active and militant trade unionists, were increasingly alienated by the new unionism; and
- secondly, their estrangement from politics was overdetermined by a crisis in the management of hostels, a taxi war and the unbanning of the ANC that transformed the phenomenon of growing political distance into arguably the most bloody urban war in the history of South Africa.

The chapter will consider this double movement: estrangement and, ultimately, war. The first movement it will situate in the rise of NDR trade unionism on the East Rand. Hostel dwellers, who had until then been among the most militant of the trade unions' members, were increasingly overlooked by Cosatu officials and ultimately alienated by the new style of unionism. We will see how the growing political distance between, in the main, Zulu migrant workers and the new 'social movement' unions began the migrant workers' estrangement from the larger township community. Rather than the product of a long-standing cultural difference or the effect of the particular nature of the hostels, we shall see how this estrangement was brought about by the inability of many Zulus to accept the nationalist politics of NDR. In contrast, we will notice that under the auspices of Fosatu, being a ('traditional') Zulu was not a logical obstacle to behaving as a democrat.

We will not find the trigger for violence in the panoptic cultures of state surveillance and discipline exercised in the hostels. Almost the opposite was true. We will find it in the 'slackening of controls' and the 'unravelling of hostel life' (Bonner & Ndima, 1999: 15). The unbanning of the ANC in 1990 merely exacerbated an already deteriorating situation. It is a mistake, therefore, simply to reduce the fighting in the area known as Katorus (made up of the townships of Katlehong, Tokoza and Vosloorus) to a moment of national political developments, and in particular the escalating constitutional conflict between the ANC and the Inkatha Freedom Party (IFP). Instead, the Katorus war was an accumulation of conflicts that became inscribed in the generic terms ANC–IFP. The chapter will track how certain discursive elements ('youth', 'township resident', 'Zulu', 'hostel dweller') were combined to produce chains of equivalence that eventually posited 'urban youth' and 'hostel dwellers' as antagonists. 'Zuluness' became inextricably linked to the politics of the IFP in the same way that 'youthfulness' became associated with the ANC.

The 'Transvaal War'

During the mid-1980s, the greater Durban area, including Pietermaritzburg, was racked by sometimes episodic, sometimes intense fighting. Pietermaritzburg had been tense since 1985; since, that is, the launch of the UDF (see Chapter 3). After the unbanning of the ANC in 1990, the situation deteriorated further. When Inkatha tried to regain areas lost in earlier fighting, the intensity of the attacks and counter-attacks escalated to unprecedented levels. The death toll was already shocking. In 1988, 691 people were killed in Pietermaritzburg, up from 397 the year before. In just seven days in 1990, 130 people died and hundreds of homes were destroyed. This marked a turning-point. After the 'seven-day war', violence spread from the informal settlements and townships around Durban and Pietermaritzburg to other parts of KwaZulu. It renewed violence, moreover, in other settlements and townships around Durban (Shaw, 1997).

In 1990 violence broke out in the dense urban conurbations to the east and west of Johannesburg. Although it would subside sooner than in KwaZulu-Natal, fighting in the then PWV (Pretoria-Witwatersrand-Vereeniging)[1] area reached an unprecedented ferocity. Pitched battles broke out in Sebokeng in late July 1990, and spread quickly to Katorus. Over 1,500 people were killed in the last half of 1990 alone. On average, the police were collecting eight bodies a day. The scale was truly horrifying. Between June and October 1990, approximately 550 people died in a single township, virtually on or around a single street: the infamous Khumalo Street in Tokoza.[2] On one occasion, in a single day, 143 people were killed.

Violence remained high right up until the first democratic election in April 1994. Around 1,000 people died in 1991, and double that the following year. Violence peaked in 1993, when more than 2,000 people were killed in fighting. A total of 754 died in 1994 (Shaw, 1997: 29). Thousands were injured, fled and were displaced. Thousands of houses were destroyed, and hostels were razed to the ground or severely damaged. Railway lines were uprooted, train stations burnt down and businesses fire-bombed. Massive damage was inflicted on the municipal infrastructure. Entire areas became 'no-go' zones, especially near or around hostels. In Katlehong, the army finally had to build a special road to the hostels at Buyafuthe and Kwesini so that residents could leave the area. The details are gruesome, and the figures given above are unreliable. The army admitted losing count of the bodies it found on morning patrols. Many were unceremoniously and anonymously buried or cremated.[3]

The first incidents of violence in Katorus were those recorded on 12 August 1990. On that day, a Zulu-speaker from Khalanyoni hostel was killed in Tokoza. All that night and the following morning, hostel residents from Khalanyoni and squatters from the neighbouring informal settlement at Phola Park attacked and counter-attacked each other, leaving 20 dead (Minnaar, 1993: 2). The following evening, blanketed assailants from Phola Park entered the hostel and killed at random. Eventually the hostel itself was demolished and removed brick by brick to be used as building material for new shacks. We have an account of these events from interviews conducted by Lauren Segal in 1991:

> It started in Tokoza at Khalanyoni hostel. The people who stay there say that it started in a shebeen [bar]. There was a fight between a Zulu and Xhosa over a woman. She was staying in the hostel with a Xhosa guy but then ended up in a relationship with a Zulu guy. The other Xhosa guys influenced the Xhosa guy who was in love with the woman to demand her back. They asked how they could allow his girlfriend to be taken by 'ichaka' [a Zulu]. The Xhosa guy then fought the Zulu guy but was unlucky as he died. His Xhosa brothers then went to Phola Park to tell them of the incident. They didn't ask, they just went to the hostel and attacked anyone who is Zulu indiscriminately. This all happened in a shebeen then to the whole hostel.
>
> On Tuesday all Zulus were expelled from Phola Park, and all the Xhosas inside the hostel ran away to Phola Park.

The fighting then involved our hostel (Mdala) because every person who survived the Khalanyoni attack came to our hostel for rescue. They came together as a group which divided Xhosas and Zulus and we knew that Xhosas were in Phola Park and Zulus are in the hostel (Segal, 1991: 30).

The violence in Tokoza is not like other places. If you look at Vosloorus, for example, the hostel dwellers were fighting with the ANC in the townships. Just like in Soweto as well. In Tokoza we are fighting with the Xhosas.

The Xhosas and the Zulus started fighting as soon as they heard about Phola Park. The relationship between the Xhosas and Zulus were cordial for a long time. Immediately when people in Phola Park who are Xhosa started fighting the Zulu hostel dwellers, they were then divided along those lines (Segal, 1991: 25).

The ethnic form of the violence generated a lot of commentary at the time. In the 1990s the Nationalist Party spoke of 'black-on-black' violence, implying that a primitive and primordial animus between different tribes was at work (Taylor, 1991). The international media, the state-controlled South African Broadcasting Corporation and the English- and Afrikaans-language press all took their cue from this prejudice. *Time* magazine put the fighting down to 'tribal-based animosities that date back centuries' (cited in Taylor, 1990: 3). The *Star*, the largest daily paper in Johannesburg, headlined leaders with 'Zulus and Xhosas in East Rand battles' (cited in Taylor, 1990: 3). 'Media reports', Rupert Taylor observed at the time, 'linked Zulus with Inkatha, Xhosas with the ANC and identified "victims" not by giving personal names but in terms of ethnic labels, which were taken to determine who lived and died' (Taylor, 1990: 3). When fighting was not attributed to primordial antagonisms, it was commonly treated as the product of either apartheid social engineering or a cultural animosity arising from the hostel as an isolated institution.

This chapter will argue that what is more likely is that the ethnic variable testifies to profound changes in patterns of migrancy. After the lifting of influx control in 1986, Xhosa-speakers from the former Transkei migrated to the Witwatersrand in considerable numbers. In the Transkei, arable land available for agricultural production was massively depleted by apartheid-engineered overpopulation and overgrazing. This was not the same in Zululand and Natal. Whereas Transkeian migrants began leaving their homesteads permanently – many bringing their wives with them to the cities – land in KwaZulu-Natal was not as barren. In particular, it was still productive enough to sustain Zulu households on the land.

At stake in the collapse of the rural economy in the Transkei was the nature of the migrant world in the cities. The effects of this accelerated migration were twofold: it placed further pressure on employment and housing. In interviews conducted by Philip Bonner and Vusi Ndima, Zulu hostel dwellers referred to firms on the East Rand as 'packed with Xhosa'; adding, 'if you are a Zulu you won't get a job' (Bonner & Ndima, 1999: 15). What really aggravated relations was the lack of space. New arrivals crowded into shacks in squatter camps like Phola Park, while many also sought accommodation in the hostels. For the first time there were growing numbers of women in the hostels. Not only did this undermine the migrant ethic,[4] but it also sparked clashes and generally heightened tensions. Let us recall that up till then hostels were single-sex buildings accommodating several hundred men in dormitory accommodation. A hostel dweller's only private space was a single bed in a shared room. Massive overcrowding and little privacy produced a dangerous cocktail. What inflamed deteriorating conditions was the crisis in municipal management. Little maintenance work had been done for some five to six years: the hostels in Vosloorus, for example, were in such a state of disrepair that a local engineering company, several hundred of whose workers were resident there, complained to the council. Security at the gate was almost non-existent: 'all and sundry' could come and go.

Lax control permitted 'a large number of shop and shebeen owners' to ply their trade, further invading people's privacy, 'theft, danger and lack of peace of mind' were widespread, facilities were in state of decay, broken windows were never repaired, and there was seldom hot water (Bonner & Ndima, 1999: 4). These concerns were expressed over and over again by hostel residents:

> There is no more security. In the past everyone who wanted to visit inside the hostel had to ask for permission at the gates: it was safe, we were secured, but now things have changed. We no longer get any security guards at the gate, so it's not safe (Segal, 1991: 18).

The abolition of influx control was thus a double-edged sword. As much as it granted to hostel dwellers unprecedented freedom, it simultaneously undermined the customary instruments of social control and discipline (Segal, 1991: 19). In these deteriorating social conditions, ethnic stereotyping helped transform individual brawls and conflicts into something much worse: proofs of conspiracy, fed by rumours and whispers.

We can stop here. As important as the conflict between Phola Park and the hostels was, we must not equate the Katorus war(s) with it. What is important to understand is the next step: how did a localised fight between hostel residents and those in an informal settlement spread to the rest of the township? How did the violence become a war between, in the main, Zulu hostel dwellers and township youth?

One of the most enduring myths about the East Rand war in particular, and the Reef conflict in general, is the notion of 'isolated' hostel residents (Minnaar, 1993) antagonised by an urban township community. In this regard, fighting between these parties is treated as the consequence of a long-standing animosity. Anthony Minnaar, for example, has argued that influx control and migrant labour generated a cultural antagonism in many South African townships:

> [H]ostel residents ... drawn from the rural poor, largely from
> homeland areas [came] to the cities as unskilled workers
> usually starting off as cleaners and night watchmen or in
> other low-paid menial jobs. Many, despite their years in the
> city, [spoke] little or no English. They tended to be looked
> down upon and scorned by the more sophisticated township
> residents (Minnaar, 1993: 27).

'This has come about', he suggests, 'with increasing urbanisation whereby
the lifestyles of township residents have become more sophisticated and
their links with rural areas ever more tenuous' (Minnaar, 1993: 28).

Minnaar points out that community amenities were often denied to
hostel residents because they were not seen as permanent members of
the community, but as temporary sojourners. They were often accused
by township inhabitants of interfering with local women. In addition,
he suggests, during the 1980s and early 1990s, 'youths' were 'envious' of
hostel dwellers for their jobs. Hostel recreational and sporting activities
tended to remain secluded from wider community involvement. Moreover,
hostel beer halls 'discouraged any social contact between hostel residents
and township inhabitants' (Minnaar, 1993: 36). Hostels also attracted
informal economic activity, including shebeens, prostitution and drug-
dealing, which earned them the stigmas of 'immorality' and 'depravity'.
In this atmosphere, 'hostel residents perceive[d] themselves as being
unloved and despised' (p. 30). They felt that they had 'borne the brunt
of social and political insult of a hostile urban environment for many
years' (p. 36).

Minnaar locates political animosity and the violence itself in
precisely this cultural tension. He remarks: '[S]ince their contact with
surrounding communities was minimal, hostel residents were usually the
last to know about any major community decisions such as stayaways,
consumer boycotts or days of mourning.' As a result, 'hostel residents
bec[ame] the victims of angry groups of township youths trying to
ensure that stayaways or boycotts were observed.' These confrontations

'inevitably' led to violent clashes that would themselves 'escalate into revenge or retaliatory attacks.' 'In this way,' Minnaar concludes, 'the seeds of lasting ill-feeling and violence were sown between the "rurals" and the "urbanites"' (Minnaar, 1993: 40). When various organisations were unbanned in 1990, 'there were persistent public calls by civic and political leaders at rallies that hostel residents should vacate hostels to make way for [political] exiles.' 'Hostel residents resented these calls and organised to resist' (p. 41).

Mahmood Mamdani presents a very similar argument. He argues that hostels were 'military-like' quadrangular compounds – complete with 12-foot fences and a single large gate – containing living quarters. Workers, moreover, were 'communally quartered in prison-like barracks' (Mamdani, 1996: 257). He continues:

> The system of labor control in the hostels was a small version of the indirect rule on the reserves. A hierarchy of mine officials was created to resemble that of chief, headmen, and the heads of homestead in the reserve. In this system, the chief is the white hostel manager, the headman is the native induna, and the heads of homestead are the 'door'-based *isibonda*. ... This reality, a modern barrack-like structure in which the induna (headman) was the chief compound policeman and therefore the chief assistant of the white hostel superintendent, also has to be understood as a fantasy of hostel administration, who hope the hostel would be an extension of the reserve in which migrants would continue to live their lives as in tribal harmony – sleeping in communal quarters at night while submitting to tribal discipline during the daytime (Mamdani, 1996: 261).

While acknowledging that such control did not always have the expected effects – hostels were also springboards for radical organisation – Mamdani reproduces the myth of hostels as isolated institutions. Relative to the township, they were enclaves, enclosed and set apart from their surroundings. 'In the eyes of a township resident,' he writes, 'the migrant was a country bumpkin' (Mamdani, 1996: 263–64), the butt of jokes, and lacking in urban sophistication. In times of conflict, he had to hide his identity in the township. These attitudes, Mamdani continues, were reciprocated by migrants, who disliked the 'rough-and-tumble' of townships.

In this context of isolation, Mamdani's argument continues, two political 'mistakes' further compounded the distance between hostel dwellers and 'communities'. The first was the rise of Cosatu. As unions linked up with township organisations, they withdrew from hostels (Mamdani, 1996: 266). This Mamdani describes as an 'error of inaction' (p. 266). Later and after the unbanning of the ANC, the homecoming exiles proposed emptying the hostels to make way for returning exiles or 'converting' them into exclusively family units. This was the second error (we shall return to this in a moment). Into this deteriorating situation stepped Inkatha. According to Mamdani, in the ensuing violence, the colonial 'structure of indirect rule' collapsed. Indunas became the principle conduit through which weapons were supplied and defensive and offensive actions organised. In this way, the induna, and not the 'white chief', became the channel through which rural indirect rule was strengthened in the hostels (p. 280).

We can disagree with Mamdani on many counts. We can note that even as early as the late 1970s, the 'authoritarian tribal' regime was not as omnipotent as he suggests. Ari Sitas, already in 1984, had this to say:

> The hostel ... conformed with all of Foucault's objective typologies of carceral or disciplinary institutions. The place was an 'administrative formula of domination'. Each individual had his own place and each place its individual; here too 'disciplinary space' tended to be divided into as many sections as there were 'bodies or elements to be distributed'. Yet, if the *de facto* situation contradicts the 'ideal type' of an 'administrative

formula of domination', in principle and *de jure*, the hostels are *supposed* to function as sites of African population control (Sitas, 1984: 253; original emphasis).

If this is how they were *supposed* to function, the distance from this ideal was considerable. Despite increased repression by so-called 'blackjacks' (municipal police), the late 1970s saw a 'dramatic increase' in criminality, intra-hostel aggression and political organisation in the growing Fosatu unions (Sitas, 1984: 256–85). By the 1990s the hold of indunas was negligible, and that of 'white chiefs' even less so. Rather than a 'clenched first', indunas were confined to parochial functions. 'Our duty,' an induna from Kwesini hostel in Katlehong explained, was to 'link community and *amakhosi*. Whatever people complain about we report to the Chief and the Chief [took] it up with His Majesty [the Zulu king].'⁵ In this regard, indunas were responsible for communication between the city and the homestead. They presided over death, organised the conveyance of bodies back to KwaZulu, arranged transport and remittances to homesteads, adjudicated in disputes among hostel residents, and were sometimes the first port of call for job recruitment agents. They did not, however, exercise control over the migrant world in the cities. Mamdani is correct in saying that it was the violence that strengthened the indunas, but not simply at the expense of the white hostel manager. It let them build their power *tout court*.

Let us return, however, to a central empirical question: How did a localised conflict between squatters and hostel dwellers ignite four years of fighting that ultimately set township youths and Zulu hostel dwellers against each other? We cannot be happy with argumentative fiats like 'the violence soon spread'. Let us return to the problem of the strategic errors: Why at the very moment Cosatu embraced the community did it withdraw from the hostels? Why did the ANC urgently pursue the conversion of hostels into family units?

We have seen that after 1986 the idea of the hostel as either a part of the panoptic system of state surveillance or a structure of 'indirect rule' is misplaced. Rather, by 1990 the migrant world in the cities was in profound crisis, partly because the (municipal) disciplinary regime was itself in profound crisis. Indeed, it was simply not in evidence. But if hostel residents were no longer subject to an omniscient municipal regime, nor were they isolated from township residents. Sitas found that 50 per cent of his hostel interviewees in Vosloorus had friendship ties in the adjacent township, 30 per cent claimed to have women friends there and 20 per cent even claimed to have 'lasting friendships'. These figures are surprising for residents supposedly secluded from township life and its inhabitants. Even though many in Sitas's sample found the township an 'alien place' and township people 'morally spoilt', some found that there were 'no moral idiosyncrasies' in the township 'that discriminated against migrants'. Nor did the remainder feel that there was 'dislike emanating from township people' (Sitas, 1984: 277). Ironically enough, these same interviews have been used to argue for the social distance and isolation of the hostels *vis-à-vis* the township.

This is not to suggest that the migrant inhabited the same social world as that of the township resident, or that there were not fundamental differences between them. That would be patently absurd. In the first instance, township residents had Section 10 rights; rights, that is, to live and work in the city. The migrant did not. That already was a world of difference. But to note that there was distance between the hostel and the township is merely a truism; it is not an explanation for why a brutal war would pit the one against the other. Indeed, Mamdani has made a similar point. The fact that there were 'differences in circumstance' between township and hostel, he correctly proposes, did not 'mechanically' translate into a 'point of tension' that produced conflict (Mamdani, 1996: 267). Lauren Segal's interviews, conducted in 1991 when fighting had already started, even led her to suggest that 'hostel dwellers are not totally isolated from township life, and almost all had several points of contact with township residents. Many even perceived themselves as members of the township rather than just the hostel' (Segal, 1991: 7).

Segal was already, however, beginning to detect another register. At the same time that she heard from Zulu migrants that:

> We have lived together with township residents for a long time. There is no problem between us. I have many friends and relatives in the township. If my wife visits me I go to the township to ask for temporary accommodation,

they also told her:

> When we are in the township we have to hide from them that we are hostel dwellers. It is not safe at all. If you are unfortunate to be known that you are a hostel dweller they kill you. They see us as inyamazane (animals). ... They don't even trust you even if you live alongside them. My brothers and relatives cannot come here and spend many days (Segal, 1991: 7).

This was not simply an expression of social distance: suddenly there was a sense of violent threat. Segal remarks correctly that hostel dwellers' impression of themselves as 'members of the community' had developed despite the fact that these feeling were not seen to be reciprocated. She puts this 'contradiction' down to a spatial variable. The township became more hostile the further one was from the hostel. More likely was that this sense of mortal danger, of menace, was something recent. In the interviews conducted by Sitas in 1983, for example, when migrant workers found the township a 'relatively alien environment', it was because it had been morally 'corrupted with wild ideas, bad and urbane influences', and that its residents had been 'physically corrupted': they had become 'weaklings' unable to do 'heavy work' (Sitas, 1984: 277). But township residents were not thought of as hateful and dangerous. The township was, at worst, a place of crookery and dishonesty; it was not treacherous. By 1991, however, something important had changed.

We can get a better idea of what had happened by way of interviews that the present author conducted in 1995. In particular, interviews with Sipho Sithole and Thabane Dlamini are highly suggestive.

Sipho Sithole moved from KwaZulu-Natal to Johannesburg in 1980 to look for work. Here he stayed with his sister until 1985. He married a woman from KwaMashu in 1985, left Soweto and moved his new wife and children to Tokoza. At no stage did he stay in a hostel. This was paralleled by the personal trajectory of Thabane Dlamini. Dlamini was born in Mahlabathini in 1950 and attended school at Mkhiweni Higher Primary School in Ndebele. In 1978 he graduated to the Eikane High School in what he termed 'rural Natal'. Dlamini's parents had in the meantime moved to Johannesburg to look for work. By the time he arrived in Soweto in 1981, his mother and father had already been there for some time. When he failed to find permanent or even long-term employment, he joined the IFP as a full-time office bearer in 1991. At no stage did he seek accommodation in a hostel.

Both men regarded their urban biographies as utterly conventional. Sithole remarked:

> It was very common that people from KwaZulu-Natal ... had family in the townships. Let me tell you something, here in the location ... there is no hot water and no bathroom. In the hostel, because [they] were more advanced than this place [the location], people [came] here [to] wash themselves.

Moreover, he added 'I am telling [a] fact – and you can ask anybody – these people used to go to the hostel and wash themselves and then there was no difference between the hostel and the location.' In this regard, Sithole's and Dlamini's relation to the hostels was typical of many other township men. Indeed, they talked about the hostel like many second- or even third-generation urban youth interviewees – including some of those prominent in offensive activities during the 'war'.

What is important about these particular narratives is the identity of the voices. Dlamini and Sithole were not just random voices in Tokoza. Thabane was chairperson of the IFP Youth Brigade in the township – indeed, he apparently came up with the name for the IFP paramilitaries:

Self-Protection Units. Sithole was also involved in IFP Youth Brigade activities, and at the time of municipal elections in 1995 was nominated to stand as the IFP candidate for Phenduka section – an area with a large hostel population and a housing quarter mainly occupied by refugees from the fighting sympathetic to the IFP.

During the 1980s, therefore, both men had no special or intimate relationship to hostels. Their IFP Youth Brigade activities were confined to sympathetic township youth, and they even experienced hostel residents through a medium common to many township inhabitants: taking hot showers in the hostel (a luxury) and drinking in the shebeens. What had distanced the hostel dweller from the township community by the 1990s was not his lack of sophistication or his backwardness. He was alien and dangerous to those for whom the community had become a community of national democratic subjects. For the rest, they were pretty much the same. What had changed was the rise on the East Rand of the politics of NDR.

Let us note, too, that the schism between the hostel and the township was not just an effect of the ANC–IFP division. In other words, the hostel was not automatically a place of the IFP, and there was no automatic association between Zulu migrant workers and the IFP. This was clearly understood by early Inkatha ye Sizwe[6] organisers on the Rand.

Mrs Zikalala, an Inkatha organiser in the then Transvaal[7] in the late 1970s, remarked in an interview that 'at that time there was Black Consciousness, the ANC was in exile and quiet and Inkatha became the biggest organisation.' What is important about her account is her description of early recruits: 'People who were interested were Zulus,' she commented, i.e. 'teachers, doctors and professionals of both sexes.' Hostel dwellers only entered her talk as an afterthought. Indeed, significant recruitment in this quarter only began in the mid and late-1980s. Before that, she explained, Zulu-speaking hostel residents could not understand the role for an Inkatha-type organisation: they believed themselves to be loyal subjects of the Zulu king, had a direct relationship with their chiefs through resident indunas and could, therefore, see no place for Inkatha. A political entity that wanted to 'fight for their rights' as subjects of the Kingdom of KwaZulu seemed to be superfluous. Indeed, according to Mrs Zikalala, hostel residents worried that Inkatha would 'interfere with His Majesty the King'. Structures therefore already existed for them to 'exercise their rights' as Zulu subjects.

This accords well with Segal's findings. The vast majority of those she interviewed in 1991 (9 out of 13) had joined the IFP in the previous year or so, either because of the deteriorating political situation in KwaZulu – many worried that their families would not be able to access services without a party card – or because they were stigmatised as members of Inkatha, and felt, in the end, that the IFP might be able to protect them in the Reef violence:

> I've seen IFP members starting to organise more strongly with the outbreak of violence.
>
> Inkatha was a very small organisation even last year. It gained more members with the outbreak of violence. It started becoming strong last year.
>
> Ever since the outbreak of violence which isolated all Zulus as IFP members, IFP is much stronger than ever before.
>
> Before the violence there was no recruitment by Inkatha. During the violence, that's when they told people to come and join (Segal, 1991: 23).

What we can say, therefore, is that relations between township residents and hostel dwellers did not deteriorate because the former were supporters of the ANC and the latter members of the IFP. Hostel residents, in the main, joined the IFP because relations had already taken a turn for the worse. Indeed, Bonner and Ndima argue that in the early days of the fighting, 'the hand of the IFP' was 'largely absent' (Bonner & Ndima, 1999: 2).

The coming of the politics of NDR to the East Rand

We saw earlier how, after a long period of dormancy, black trade unionism came dramatically back to life with mass strikes that jolted Durban in late 1972/early 1973. The Metal and Allied Workers' Union (Mawu) was formed at that time, and together with five other industrial unions formed the Trade Union Advisory and Co-ordinating Committee. By the end of the 1970s, Mawu had successfully made and consolidated its transition up to the Rand. When Fosatu was formed in 1979, Mawu became one of its key constituents. The majority of its membership on the Rand were hostel residents and migrant workers. We can pause here to notice how Mawu organised workers in the metal foundries of the East Rand.

Once a majority of workers in a plant had been recruited to the union, elections would take place for a shop steward structure. Shop stewards performed two central functions: they represented workers in negotiations with management, including struggles over the right to be represented. They also participated in all Mawu branch executive meetings, which brought together shop stewards from all over the region. Such meetings, Sitas observes, had 'real executive powers over all trade union decisions.' They ensured 'trade-union accountability to the rank and file' and were the basis for 'grassroots democracy' (Sitas, 1984: 389). The secretary of the union in the Transvaal at the time, himself a hostel resident, explained:

> We believe in democratically controlled organisations and the role of the union is seen as one of promoting democracy in the workplaces. We believe that management shouldn't be left alone to decide on what workers need and we feel their factories should be run democratically so that things will be negotiated before management takes decisions (Sitas, 1984: 390).

What interests Sitas was precisely the effect that worker control had on the 'cultural formations', the 'ideology' and the 'consciousness' of migrant workers. Sitas notes that the presence of Mawu had an unexpected effect: the transfer of the lessons of the factory to the hostels (Sitas, 1984: 415). At stake were the results of a particular way of organising. Firstly, he observed that it created a strict divide between 'us' and 'them': between, that is, workers belonging to Mawu on the one side and cowards and '*impimpis*' (spies) on the other. Secondly, hostel dwellers began to refuse the arbitrary power of indunas and hostel managers and demand elected, accountable committees on the model of the factory. What for our purposes is most important is the transformation that Sitas noticed in what he terms the migrant 'discourse', of which this is an example:

> Morena [the Lord] knows and will forget the white when judgement day comes. The white pretends he is a Christian, he is not. He has taken the land of the ancestors, he has inflicted evil deeds on this land. He makes us work in the factories for nothing and our children are crying. He exploits us. We workers are united. We shall fight the exploiter. It takes a thorn to remove a thorn (Sitas, 1984: 417).

Sitas is looking for the emergence of a working-class consciousness; but we can notice something else as well. Mawu was producing in the factories and also in the hostels a *public domain*; a space, that is, where people were called to articulate *social interests*. Despite the religious metaphors, the romantic populism and the appeals to a Zulu cosmology, the migrant situation was posited as one produced in and through mundane circumstances, and hence changeable through equally mundane activities. What is most important to notice was that the hailing of migrant workers as democrats did not imply a transformation of their souls, of their being: it was not necessary to transform them into secular individuals, removed from their extended families, and they did not have to become modern to behave as democrats. What it required was that they acted as if the mundane had autonomy from the divine. It required, in other words, that they acted *as if* God were dead in the public domain. It was precisely this that was unthinkable to the new social-movement unionism that was about to overtake Mawu. It was unthinkable that a national democratic subject could simultaneously be a traditional Zulu, committed to an extended family.

We have discussed the rise of Fosatu in some detail in Chapter 3. Let us simply recall that the mid-1980s saw an important political shift, as trade unionism after 1976 increasingly eschewed its political non-alignment. After the student revolt, it was less and less easy for unions to remain politically non-aligned. By the mid-1980s, many of the 1976 students and leaders had entered employment. Moreover, many had benefited from the expansion of educational opportunities that occurred after (and partly as a result of) the 1976 uprising. Fosatu thus found a new element among its membership who were young, militant and school-educated. Many were initiated into politics through the radicalism of Black Consciousness and the slogans of NDR. In this atmosphere, there was growing impatience with the federation's strongly workerist tendency. Many complained that the union federation was invested with a deep social conservatism that militated against political interventions outside the factory. As a result, there was growing pressure for union activities to link to a host of extra-factory political currents, and new recruits, in particular were eager to articulate their union activities to wider struggles for national liberation through African nationalism.

We saw that these tensions came to a head after the Fatti's and Moni's strike in the Cape in April 1979. The strike itself was accompanied by a massive consumer boycott that halved factory profits. Within seven months, workers were reinstated and the union recognised. Within Fosatu, the Cape action generated furious debates about the federation's appropriate strategic direction. There was increased criticism of the factory-oriented nature of the organisation and the neglect of wider community and political struggles. By the early 1980s, certain Fosatu affiliates were already beginning to widen their involvement. They collaborated with a host of community struggles, explicitly spoke of NDR and used a host of politically aligned slogans. In particular, many shop stewards either left the unions altogether to help build civic organisations or they donned an additional cap. In Wattville, for example, the Wattville Concerned Residents Committee was established by former Mawu shop stewards. In Tokoza and Katlehong, Sam Ntuli, also a Mawu shop steward, played a critical role in the formation of civics. What effects did this have on the East Rand?

Aggripa Shandu, a one-time Mawu shop steward, who had since left the union and joined the IFP, told a typical story. In the late that 1970s he joined Mawu in the industrial precinct of Alrode in Alberton. In an interview with the author in 1995, he recalled:

> When I joined, I thought that [Mawu] is a union that is going to stand for my rights as a worker. I did not know that [the union] was going to change name and involve politics. Mawu split ... I left in 1985 [to] join Ummawosa [United Metal, Mining and Allied Workers of South Africa]. We did not understand where [the splinter union] stood because it was confusing work and politics. When Cosatu was formed in 1985 I resigned because I was not an ANC trade unionist.

In her interviews, Segal heard similar stories: 'I'm only interested in my rights as a worker, that is all,' one interviewee announced. 'I joined NUMSA [National Union of Metalworkers of South Africa] for their protection at the workplace and not their political alliance' (Segal, 1991: 18).

If labour's new direction accommodated the 'hidden world' of 'African Nationalism' (Webster, 1996), it also alienated others. Speaking of the 1982–83 strikes at the large steel foundry, Scaw Metals, Bonner is quoted as saying: 'You could see their [hostel residents'] interests not being properly represented, eclipsed by other constituencies. We could see migrants retreating into themselves, even when continuing to be union members, e.g. in Zulu ethnic associations' (Bonner, cited in Mamdani, 1986: 247). But what was it about the NDR unions that caused so many migrant workers to become disaffected?

What the new trade unionism antagonised were a complex of traditional sympathies and values. Young men, in particular, played a leading role in township political activities. The youth were highly represented in civic organisations and were the key political actors in the Congress of South African Students and Youth Congresses. The children of 1976 were also radicalised against parental authority (which was judged to be submissive in the face of white power), so that young activists were largely independent of their parents and rebellious in the face of seniority and elders. In Wattville, for example, those civic leaders that did not come from the unions had been petty criminals and/or gang members. Knox Mabuya, a member of the civic executive, remembered fighting under the storm pipes against boys from Galagoon section when he was eight years old. Clive Glaser describes the 'tsotsi cadres' (criminals that become political activists) that foreshadowed the 'com-tsotsis' (comrade-tsotsis) of the 1980s. He is describing here the events after the Sharpeville massacre:

> Thousands responded to the PAC's [Pan-Africanist Congress's] call, particularly the anti-pass campaign. But they were extremely difficult to control. Non-violence, accountability and co-ordinated political action were alien concepts to the tsotsi subculture.
>
> The situation got completely out of hand during the State of Emergency when numerous leaders, whom the tsotsi cadres respected and admired, were detained. The possibility of placing these angry and brutalised street gangs under some kind of political discipline and accountability fell away (Glaser, 1993: 310).

By the 1980s, even if community activists were not simply brutalised com-tsotsis, the values of risk and courage, disobedience and rebellion strongly informed the politics of resistance. In interviews carried out by the author with members of a self-styled self-defence unit in Slovo Section in Tokoza, one of the interviewees, Casca Mokoena, described how they seldom obeyed or even knew about orders from their supposed command structures. Military expeditions were prefaced by heavy drinking and the taking of drugs. For many migrant workers, the youth of the 1980s were an anathema to everything they held sacred. Sipho Sithole remarked:

> Discipline is very important. If you are a child growing up [in a Zulu household] you are not used to speak with your father. You always speak with your mama. If you ask for something you ask your mama and your mama tells your father. If your father feels you mustn't do it, you are not going to do it (author's interview with Sithole, 1995).

Township youth demanding compliance with work stayaways and consumer boycotts was deeply offensive to adult hostel residents – many of whom were also parents. Children ordering parents about: it appeared to many as an inversion of the natural order, as a hostel dweller explained:

> Township residents do not impress me from adults to children. Respect is unknown amongst them. Sometimes you hear that comrades [young political activists] have assaulted the father of the house. That is not human, it's very barbaric. It is an insult to humanity. Nature doesn't allow that a child can beat an elderly person, under no circumstances (Segal, 1991: 9).

If township youth 'indiscipline' seemed to challenge nature, it also placed migrant households further at risk. Hostel workers usually had little or no regular schooling, and were therefore employed to do menial, repetitive tasks that required almost no formal training. They constituted what Eddie Webster calls the 'secondary market'; i.e. a category of casual employment requiring only elementary skills and offering almost no job security. This was aggravated by management policies that saw no threat to productivity by low worker turnover in this market. Regular dismissals were deemed effective for weeding out the slow and the 'cheeky'. Faced with the 'ever-present' possibility of replacement, migrant workers were disinclined to obey orders that put their jobs at risk, issued by a township youth that did not fully appreciate the implications of their dismissal. In this sense, for many migrant workers, instruction to 'reckless' action may have jeopardised their families' often already tenuous subsistence (Webster, 1985). What compounded their disaffection was that the new unions became involved in a host of community struggles that diverted union attention away from wage and safety issues. To workers still deeply implicated in the reproduction of a rural world, community issues were, at best, secondary concerns. In a context, therefore, where trade unionism seemed distracted by issues not arising from the shop floor, the IFP was able to enter a space that had previously not existed. Whereas before the 1990s Zuluness in the city was practised mainly through custom – i.e. through obedience to certain dietary habits, dress codes, and respect for social and gender hierarchies – after 1990 this began to change. There was a growing sense that the very Zulu polity, to which these practices were referenced, was itself under threat: 'If you are a Zulu', an interviewee explained,

> there are customs[to which] you have to adhere. We believe in the ancestors – *amadlozi* – and if things go wrong you have to slaughter a cow to remember those forefathers who passed away. You have to respect them. If I am down in Natal I have to wear the skin of an animal. I have to teach my children where they are coming from and where I am coming from because we are the Zulus and we have hereditary [responsibilities]. I must know that my father's name was a Zulu name and I have to know my father's name (author's interview with Sithole, 1995).

Sithole then juxtaposed this description with the following:

> The Zulu people are a very dangerous people in South Africa.
> We are not conquered even now. That is why the ANC is trying
> to fight us. They extract the King from our nation and by taking
> [him] away [they] take away the past.
>
> If you want to interrupt the system you have to go to the
> strongest point and the strongest point is the King (author's
> interview with Sithole, 1995).

What is important about this discussion was the ease with which the
respondent shifted from a description of Zulu customs to an analysis of
how they were politically threatened. If the 1980s witnessed the deepening
alienation of Zulus from labour and urban political movements, the 1990s
saw this distance expressed as political threat, articulated as a sense of
danger to the very object of Zulu identification itself: the king.

This articulation created a specific and unique opportunity for
Buthelezi and the IFP: 'When he [Buthelezi] became President of
Inkatha [he] didn't move away and forget that he has a tribal authority'
(author's interview with an anonymous Buyafuthe hostel resident, 1995).
Given the perceived capture of Zulu King Goodwill Zwelithini by the
ANC and the apparent assault on the rural homestead, Buthelezi and the
IFP were granted a political role. They were well positioned to defend
the integrity of what they saw as Zulu culture and Zulu institutions.
Several interviewees remarked that Chief Buthelezi is 'very strong, he
is very honest and that is why we are united. He is unifying us' (author's
interview with anonymous Buyafuthe hostel resident, 1995).

Concern during the late 1970s (and even during the 1980s),
therefore, that Inkatha might 'interfere' with the Zulu king had
certainly evaporated by the early 1990s. If Zulu-speaking people had,
in the past, felt comfortable exercising their cultural identity through
the traditional system itself and their urban political interests through
the trade unions, 'interruptions' (see interview with Sithole, above)

to both created the opportunity for another party. In this regard, Buthelezi's role as former leader of KwaZulu and his traditional status as a chief made him best suited to come to their defence. He was ideally placed to reconcile a political intervention with what he would have seen as a 'traditional' one. After all, he bridged both functions himself. The IFP was thus able to define its role as the new interlocutor of social worries and the defender of norms and values. In this way, the conditions for the articulation of what was seen as 'Zuluness' to politicised ethnicity was made possible.

The question becomes: Was there anything peculiar to the politics of NDR *strictu sensu* at play in this growing alienation? The chapter has described a process of withdrawal on the part of Zulu migrant workers. It has described a growing political distance arising from a unionism distracted by community issues. But none of this is enough to explain the rupture that occurred in the mid-1980s between Mawu, later Numsa, and hostel residents. Right up until 1987, Bonner and Ndima found that Zulu migrant workers were still joining the union. Despite the unwelcome UDF and ANC politics, migrant metal workers still found that unions protected them from arbitrary retrenchments (Bonner & Ndima, 1999: 8). By the end of the decade, this was less and less true. Bernie Fanaroff, a leading Mawu and later Numsa organiser, explained:

> Once the unions became easier to join and more fashionable and more successful the urban workers started to join and took the leadership positions and migrant workers were pushed out of the leadership positions because they [didn't] speak English, and how could you elect a shop steward who couldn't speak English to the boss? Then (from 1982) we stopped going to the hostels and stopped having meetings there and hostel workers were members but they were ignored and general meetings were in places that didn't suit them and so on, and then Inkatha got into the hostels (Bonner & Ndima, 1999: 8).

DO SOUTH AFRICANS EXIST?

The effects of the unions' new orientation was felt immediately. In 1991 residents complained:

> [The unions] have never held any meetings in our hostel. They didn't ... see the need and yet most of its members are hostel dwellers. All hostel dwellers are undermined.

> No, they don't come to our hostel. We meet here in the workplace, that's all. It's not because they are afraid to hold meetings in our hostel, it's just because they are not interested. That's why we had a conflict with them because they always went to meetings in the township and make decisions that would affect us without consulting us. That is especially during stayaways so that is what makes us not recognise their calls for stayaways (Segal, 1991: 13).

The systematic exclusion of Zulu migrants from the unions' leadership and the abandonment of the hostels is so much more surprising given that they still formed a considerable section, if not a majority, of the unions' members. What mattered were the figure of a leader and the profile of an authentic member; also at stake was the very future of the union: 'The habit Pedi migrants had of referring to the hostel as a *kgoro* had significant implications for the trade union,' writes Karl von Holdt:

> The *kgoro* was a place of men, where men acted, debated and took decisions according to the modes of discipline, honesty, trust and bravery of men. Township men were different: they would go home and discuss issues with their wives, thus subverting the clarity and discipline of the *kgoro*. Therefore they were not really to be trusted with the leadership of the union (Van Holdt, 2000: 199).

The shift to English (see Fanaroff's statement, above) was not simply a pragmatic move, although certainly in a multilingual workforce it helped to have an acceptable, common medium of communication. Perhaps too, in negotiations with a white management, competence in English was useful. But none of this was new: the management did not suddenly become white in the late 1980s, and metal workers had never been linguistically homogenous. The shift to English, like not holding meetings in the hostel, was symptomatic of something else: the measure of freedom was no longer the degree to which one could think and act as a self-confident worker: it was the degree to which one was modern, urban and urbane; it was the degree to which one was the free individual of NDR. Speaking English was a sign of education, of urbanity: it was the ultimate sign of having exited the world of clans and tribes, of 'superstition'. In short, the Zulu migrant worker did not at all resemble the free figure that could advance the NDR. The combination was deadly. Zulu migrants found the behaviour of township youths deeply provocative; township youths found Zulu migrants backward and counter-revolutionary. We might recall that during this period Zulu hostel dwellers complained of being treated like animals, and that township residents refused to recognise them as humans. By the standards of NDR, it is true, they were still like beasts. In 1990, however, exclusion approached repression.

It was not simply in the area of language, however, that this shift was experienced: it was felt most tragically in the area of housing. In late 1989, then State President F. W. de Klerk released a group of senior ANC prisoners. In February 1990 he announced the unbanning of the ANC, SACP and PAC. As preparations began for the return of exiles, the ANC began to consider plans to accommodate them. One idea that was toyed with seriously was to convert the hostels into family accommodation for returnees. The idea had first been mooted in 1986 by the Nationalist Party, which had suddenly become worried about the spectre of homosexuality in single-sex accommodation. When violence broke out between the hostels in Tokoza and the residents of Phola

Park, the idea was raised again. The ANC argued that the concentration of single men in a single complex made them more readily disposed to violence (Zulu, 1993). It was better, therefore, to remove them to family quarters where the presence of wives and children would have a salutary effect on them. The proposals were a direct and immediate threat to the migrant world in the cities. For those men reluctant or unable to move their families to the city, it meant the potential loss of their accommodation. What made things worse was that rentals in the township were, comparatively, very expensive. A backyard room could cost between R60 and R120 per month; the municipality, in contrast, charged only R15 a month for a hostel bed. Conversion thus seemed to make continued residence in the city unaffordable. This was aggravated further by low wages and tenuous conditions of employment and made even worse by stagnation in the economy generally and in local industries in particular. Given the importance of urban remittances to the reproduction of rural economies, conversion seemed to threaten the very sustainability of the homestead unit. It was hardly surprising, therefore, that the campaign was strongly resisted.

These proposals did not simply threaten the conditions of the migrant world in the cities or endanger the very reproduction of rural households and society. They were the spark that transformed loosely organised hostels into highly militarised camps, presided over for the first time by indunas. For our purposes they were the purest expression that African nationalism had no room for those that did not resemble the national subject.

6

The Production of the Public Domain

Let us move beyond critique here. What this chapter will do is consider the conditions of a democratic public domain that does not, ultimately, conflate the citizen with an authentic national subject. Although the implications of this argument are not confined to South Africa, the chapter will again refer to South African examples. The intention is not so much to consider the theoretical conditions of the public domain as to examine the conditions of its theoretical *practice*. The chapter will suggest that the citizen is such when called upon to *act socially* in the public domain; in other words, the public space is a domain of normative action. As such, the conditions of the public domain are twofold: firstly, a set of institutions and practices that allow for social interests to be expressed politically; and secondly, a political space that captures and holds persons to social, i.e. ethical standards of behaviour. If these are, abstractly speaking, the conditions of the public domain, then the concrete, historical conditions of such a space cannot be stated in advance. They will depend on the peculiar history of the societies in which they are being produced – their particular political traditions, customs and fashions – and their availability to some ideas and practices and not to others. If we are to move beyond a critique of nationalism to posit the conditions of the public domain, then we cannot remain in the abstract. The conditions of the democratic space must be specified in the concrete and contingent.

Measuring the Reconstruction and Development Programme

Much has been written about the Reconstruction and Development Programme (RDP) with regard to its origin, its implementation, the competing political interests that it attempted to reconcile and ultimately its jettison, at least in practice, if not in words. What has not been adequately explored is the gauge of development that it appealed to. Now, in this regard the RDP White Paper was quite explicit. Reconstruction and development were intended to create 'a people-centred society which measures progress by the extent to which it has succeeded in securing for each citizen liberty, prosperity and happiness' (Republic of South Africa, 1994, sec. 1.1.1). In other words, what the business community described sarcastically as a 'wish list' – building a million low-cost homes, providing electricity and water, etc. – were only deemed developmental products to the extent that they contributed to 'liberty, prosperity and happiness'. These last terms have been judged too 'prosaic' (Marais, 1998: 180) to be deserving of serious academic attention – except perhaps for those interested in literature or cultural studies. Or perhaps they are thought to be unrelated to the political economy of the RDP. To avoid their meaning, however, is to misunderstand the significance of development there. It is only once we admit that the RDP was referenced to a certain *political* vision that we can begin to understand its radical import. Indeed, the programme was not simply about 'integrating socio-economic policy' such that its measure was the degree to which it was 'programmatic', as opposed to being merely a 'compendium of poorly coordinated, conventional development projects' (Marais, 1998: 178). What was at stake was the realisation of a certain image of the *good* society.

According to the base document (ANC, 1994), the RDP was informed by six key principles: 'an integrated and sustainable programme', 'a people-driven process', 'peace and security for all', 'nation-building', 'linking reconstruction and development' and 'democratisation'. These were reconciled in the following way: the RDP was an *'integrated programme*, based on the *people*, that *provides peace and security for all* and *builds the nation, links reconstruction and development* and deepens *democracy'* (ANC, 1994, sec. 1.3; emphasis added).

There are a cluster of terms here that require elucidation. Can we say what was meant here by 'the people', by 'the nation' and by 'democracy'? We can agree with Hein Marais that if we search for their meanings in the RDP White Paper itself (Republic of South Africa, 1994), they vacillate between quite different images of the political economy: that of the 'democratic forces' and that of business. Such a binary opposition (business/left) slides too easily into caricature if it is intended to imply that either group were (a) internally unified, and (b) represented a sole position. But the general point is taken. As the RDP 'metamorphosed from being the programme of the "democratic forces" to becoming the policy framework for a government of national unity' it increasingly 'established a "comfort zone" between conflicting forces and interests' (Marais, 1998: 179). What this means is that a close reading of either the White Paper or the base document will only yield vague definitions that are open to a myriad of readings. It was precisely because the *political* measure of the RDP was rendered obscure that (a) the protagonists of the Growth, Employment and Redistribution Strategy (GEAR)[1] could later claim to be pursuing its goals through other means, and that (b) the RDP has come to be associated with a certain 'wish list' of infrastructural products. And yet, as we shall see, neither is true. Firstly, GEAR anticipates quite a different *good* society to the concept of such a society that originally informed the RDP. Secondly, the programme was not simply about the delivery of a host of products deemed in and of themselves developmental. For us to give content to this political vision, we need turn to the political sources on which the document originally drew.

The RDP arose from debates within the National Union of Metalworkers of South Africa about how socialism could be realised within the context of a negotiated transition (Marais, 1998: 185). It had always been an orthodoxy of Marxist thought that profound social change was impossible unless the existing relations of production were transformed through revolution. In post-1994 South Africa, not only was the revolutionary seizure of the state foreclosed by a negotiated political settlement, but the terms of that settlement proscribed the extent to which property relations could be transformed. What is more, the collapse of 'really existing socialism'[2] (i.e. actual socialist states) from 1989 fundamentally discredited the Leninist revolutionary model. In this context, reports Marais, what was mooted was the notion that a host of structural reforms made within a capitalist system could ultimately *tilt* society towards socialism. Here the references were the Russian Marxist Boris Kagarlitsky, Andre Gorz and the Canadian social scientist John Saul.[3] Saul, for example, argued that structural reform must:

> be allowed self-consciously to implicate other 'necessary' reforms that flow from it as part of an emerging project of structural transformation [and] must root itself in popular initiatives in such a way as to leave a residue of empowerment – in terms of enlightenment/class consciousness, in terms of organizational capacity – for the vast mass of the population who thus strengthen themselves for further struggles, for further victories (Saul, cited in Marais, 1998: 186).

For our purposes, what is important to note is that the RDP was conceived as a non-revolutionary path to socialism. Hence its proper measure was the degree to which it empowered the masses – brought them to class consciousness and equipped them with organisational skills – to pursue happiness, freedom and democracy. What we can say too is that community-driven development was not simply intended as a methodology – as an effective means for providing infrastructural products and services. Its utility was attached, rather, to another ambition: producing individuals in a position to act as citizens. A citizen here was not simply a certain bearer of human rights seeking their realisation (the right to a house, to a serviced site, and so on), but an individual in search of liberty, happiness and democracy, where the meaning of these terms was given by the political imaginary to which the figure of the citizen was attached. He/She was someone endowed with a certain (class) consciousness and certain organisational skills to further the struggle for socialism. What is important to note is the *logic* of the problematic here. Development implied the *production*, not simply of houses, etc., but of *certain kinds of individuals*. Who were these individuals, and how were they to be produced?

'People's power': Embryonic state forms

During the early 1980s, the Federation of South African Trade Unions was overtaken by strategic debates arising from differing notions of class and class struggle. So-called charterists suggested that class be treated in relation to the concrete historical processes through which it was was constructed and in which it had to struggle (Norval & Howarth, 1992). Political consciousness was derived not simply from the factory floor or the relations of production, but rather from a much wider discursive field. In contrast, so-called workerists[4] in the federation, following an argument reminiscent of Sidney Bunting, insisted on the specific interests of the working class *vis-à-vis* the national (i.e. multi-class) struggle. The strategic accomplice of the charterist line was the expansion of the political field to include additional areas of struggle. For the first time since the eclipse of the South African Congress of Trade Unions in the 1960s, trade union activists began to organise among township residents, not simply as workers exploited by a racial capitalism, but as urban residents crippled by rising rents and service costs. Mzwanele Mayekiso, formerly of the Alexandra Civic Organisation, observed in this regard that:

> The kind of socialist organizing project discussed in the
> union movement – especially by intellectuals associated with
> the Federation of South African Trade Unions (FOSATU)

– was centred on the shopfloor, and was actually opposed to community struggles. On the other hand, there were other trade unionists … who did reach out to communities, and later FOSATU's successors in COSATU reversed the older animosity to community struggles (Mayekiso, 1996: 51).

For our purposes, what was at stake in the formation of civic organisations was the emergence of a certain kind of *public space*. At stake was the construction of embryonic zones of 'people's power' (a) to displace the authority and reach of the apartheid state and its institutions, (b) to capture residents to the political and ideological campaigns of the democratic movement, and (c) to organise residents in and through structures that instilled among their members certain values and a certain institutional culture, and imbued them with a certain understanding of democracy. Briefly, this involved holding residents to a mode of organisation that emphasised the immediate accountability of elected leaders, public participation in all major decision-making and popular mandates. Let us note too – and the implications of this will be discussed later – that such direct – as opposed to formal or bourgeois – democracy presupposed the production of a certain kind of *ethical* being. Documents and pamphlets from the United Democratic Front and the Mass Democratic Movement at the time are replete with references to 'discipline', to 'commitment', to 'dedication', to 'comradely' behaviour, and so on. In other words, rendering the apartheid state ungovernable hinged, not simply on collapsing its capacity to govern, but on creating counter structures populated by new *democratic subjects*; i.e. disciplined, committed and dedicated *comrades*.

If, during the mid-1980s, the work of these organisations was referenced, in the first place, to the defeat of Black Local Authorities and, in the second, to the overthrow of the apartheid state – their ambitions were referenced strictly to the national state – at the end of the decade, an important shift took place. The precedent was established in Soweto in 1988. Just two years earlier, the Soweto Civic Association had deemed the defeat of the apartheid state *nationally* a sufficient condition for alleviating the burden of rents and service charges, but by 1988 its pamphlets evidenced an appreciation for what Mark Swilling called 'transformational' issues (Swilling, 1992: 6). The Soweto People's Delegation called for the writing-off of arrears, the transfer of houses to residents, the upgrading of services, affordable municapal service charges, and, most significantly, the establishment of a single tax base for Soweto and Johannesburg. Here local issues were accompanied by demands, not simply for the overthrow of apartheid generally, but for what became urban political claims. The conditions of this shift have been discussed at length elsewhere (Chipkin, 1997; see also Swilling, 1998). It is sufficient to say here that what inspired it was a new appreciation of the *structure* of the apartheid city as a reason for the miserable quality of the urban environment in townships, for escalating rents and service charges, and so on. From then on, the defeat of Black Local Authorities was attached to new demands for the transformation of the urban structure.

What emerged from the Soweto experience was an embryonic developmental *concept*. For the first time, the democratic space was conceived, not simply as the mobilisation of residents through civics to protest against apartheid generally, but as the pursuit of political ends through claims to affordable rents, houses, serviced sites, and so on. At stake was the production of the public domain through development work. Put differently, it was now possible to imagine the making of citizens in and through housing and other such projects, instead of through straightforward political resistance. In principle, therefore, two registers informed this thinking: firstly, that houses, lower services charges and serviced sites were good in and of themselves, and secondly – and no less importantly – that engaging the state for services, etc. was another route to establishing organs of people's power and making (interpolating) citizens.

Let us turn now to a recent example of such a practice to see how it implies a radically different kind of community from that of the nation.

The case of Manenberg

Manenberg is a coloured, primarily working-class township, today part of the City of Cape Town. Situated 15 kilometres from Cape Town's city centre, Manenberg is isolated from adjacent black and coloured townships by highways, railway lines and buffer strips. It is home to a population of approximately 80,000 residents living in a combination of formal housing and low-income tenements. Manenberg was established as a coloured township following the forced removal of residents from District Six and other areas declared white residential areas during the 1960s and 1970s.

In Manenberg, the City of Cape Town was faced with a daunting and surprising dilemma. It sought to deliver services and housing in and through forums that provided for high levels of community participation. What it found was an area where residents were more and more dependent for survival on a drugs-based informal economy controlled by violent gangs. Manenberg was prone to violence; rape and attacks on women were frequent; incest was not uncommon; teenage girls were all too commonly pregnant; and there were high levels of alcoholism and drug use. In short, according to officials, many Manenberg residents were 'dysfunctional'.[5] What prospect was there for democratic participation when disputes were resolved violently, when criminal gangs controlled most of the area, when women were under constant threat, when municipal workers feared for their lives, and when development budgets were consumed by the costs of safety and security? If development were to happen democratically, something had to happen to Manenberg residents. They had to become, according to the problematic of the Department of Community Development (Devcom), 'functional'. Let us note too that the New Public Management was not an option.[6] When Manenberg was controlled by gangs and violence was widespread, it made no difference if the workers too afraid to enter the area or do their jobs were from the municipality or not.

This normative conception of the citizen – that he/she was not simply a rights-bearing individual, but someone who behaved according to a certain standard of 'good'/'decent' social conduct – was not peculiar to Devcom officials. Rather, we saw that Devcom's practice brought to the fore an ethical presupposition at the heart of citizenship itself. The citizen is not simply a juridical and political figure: he/she is an ethical one as well. If this were true, then the conditions of the citizen were more than a legal/constitutional dispensation, more than a political system. In posing the question of the citizen, one posed, in addition, the conditions of ethical conduct. What was required so that *de jure* citizens conduct themselves as citizens in fact?

In Devcom's practice there were, hermeneutically speaking, two competing paths to citizenship – one through re-embedding norms within the ideology and practice of the family, and the other in terms of political practice. In the first of these, 'dysfunctionality' was said to be caused by the crisis of the family in Manenberg. High levels of long-term male unemployment, accompanied by the fact of female bread-winners, meant that men struggled to realise their (patriarchal versions of) masculinity in and through normal activities (work; as heads of families). This translated into high levels of pathological male behaviour: alcoholism, wife battery, etc. In turn, the disintegration of the nuclear family saw many Manenberg youths socialised, not in the confines of the home and through parental direction, but on the street in and through the gangs. For Devcom it meant that the measure of development was the degree to which it contributed to rebuilding the coloured nuclear family (Chipkin, 2003). At stake was the idea that in order to become a citizen, one must necessarily belong to a determinate culture: in this case, one composed of nuclear families.

Secondly, within Devcom there was an alternative register, one articulated less in words and policy than in practice. The route to functionality was to be achieved, not so much through social engineering at the level of the family, than social engineering at the level of the political. Residents would become functional by being forced to behave as citizens in and through participatory, democratic forums. This chapter will look at each of these in more detail.

Precisely because these conceptions were not theorised, they were practised simultaneously. Yet they imply *quite distinct conceptions of the citizen*. In the former case, the citizen is deemed necessarily someone belonging to a determinate ethnic formation. This is exactly the form of the nation. But when functionality refers to the capture of residents to democratic institutions, the citizen emerges as a very different creature. Citizenship is indifferent to the social world from which the resident issues. It does not matter what gender he/she is, who he/she has sex with, what religion he/she practises, what race he/she is, the circumstances of his/her family (extended, nuclear, clan, tribe), and so on. What counts is that he/she behaves according to a standard of ethical behaviour in the public domain.

In Manenberg, despite lip service to building the nuclear family, what really consumed time and resources was the establishment of a democratic, participatory forum. In examining Manenberg, therefore, we are reviewing a practice that a) conceived citizenship as much as a political status as a *social* relation and b) pursued the citizen through democratic socialisation rather than ethnocentric engineering.

Manenberg revisited

In March 2000 the Manenberg Area Co-ordinating Team (ACT) was established to be the principal forum through which development in the area was mediated. From the beginning, its meetings were chaired by Dr Ivan Toms, then chief medical officer for Cape Town, today for the Unicity, assisted by another senior official, Russell Dudley. The importance of this will emerge shortly. It was made clear from the outset that the forum was open to any organisation in Manenberg. The purpose of the ACT was to facilitate community involvement in development matters, including drawing up the municipal budget. Lofty ideals aside, the scale of the problem seemed to mitigate against any hope of reversing conditions in Manenberg.

Minutes of the first ACT meeting record the following discussion: 'The Manenberg Clinic explained that it continually had problems with customers verbally abusing staff. Manenberg was the only clinic in the city with the problem. Numerous discussions have been held with the community. Staff are traumatized' (Manenberg ACT, 6 March 2000). Elsewhere, officials complained of shootings in or outside municipal buildings. Indeed, a substantial portion of the budget allocated to upgrading library facilities in Manenberg was spent on fortifying walls against gunshots and giving staff danger pay, as well as on the costs of trauma counselling. By May, the violence and vandalism had become so severe that the city decided to relocate the clinic altogether (Manenberg ACT, 8 May 2000). There seemed little prospect that the forum could sustain itself, never mind initiate a moral and social transformation in Manenberg more widely.

In August of that year, it looked as if the forum itself would collapse. After a tornado destroyed much housing in parts of Manenberg, Devcom used the disaster as an opportunity to fast-track its housing policy. The details need not concern us, other than to note the crisis of legitimacy and representation it provoked for the council and in the ACT. The minutes capture some of the atmosphere:

> The chair [Dr Ivan Toms] indicated that there was no review of formulations around the [terms of reference for the reconstruction of Area 1, the appointment of a Labour Liaison person and the recruitment of local labour]. The report back was interrupted. The MDC [Manenberg Disaster Committee] alleged that what was about to be communicated was known already and that there was disagreement around these issues. The matter at hand was therefore to discuss the objections which had already been tabled at the previous meeting (Manenberg ACT, 10 August 2000).

If the forum was bedevilled by procedural issues, its representivity was also called into question. The minutes note that:

> decision-making is unclear in the ACT. The previous decision to review and rescind was taken in the absence of agreed criteria, what the basis for membership is, whether it is based on credentials. The effect of the review and rescind was to declare the MTC (Manenberg Tornado Committee) not a bona fide organization. Fraud was at play (Manenberg ACT, 10 August 2000).

At stake was one organisation refusing to recognise the rights of another to participate in the forum. From there the meeting simply deteriorated. Somewhat stoically, the minutes record that the 'agenda was not completed and in view of the lateness of the hour, the meeting was closed' (Manenberg ACT, 10 August 2000).

The next meeting proceeded despite the poor attendance (Manenberg ACT, 4 September 2000). The whole mood was depressed. The forum was in crisis, and the area was being overwhelmed by gang violence. Item 6.9 of the minutes notes the following discussion:

> the clinic will be closed for a long time. Can the building not be used by the SAPS [South African Police Service] to set up a satellite station? During the 1997 gang fight this was proposed to the SAPS for the Town Centre but it was not feasible from an operational level (Manenberg ACT, 4 September 2000).

Item 6.10 of the same minutes recommends: 'Manenberg Town Centre – the building should be demolished as it poses a threat to public safety'.

Despite the apparent futility of the exercise, the ACT continued to meet. For the rest of the year there were regular meetings, and throughout 2001. Almost every meeting was chaired by the same two city officials, Toms and Dudley. Whereas similar interventions in the past lacked substance, the ACT was not simply a talk-shop. The sustained presence of the officials involved eventually won them credibility and respect. Over time they were increasingly able to give to proceedings a certain decorum and formality. Moreover, it became evident that it was in the interests of those who participated in the ACT that it continued to function, as there were resources to be had through the forum. In this sense, the forum functioned like a disciplinary institution, capturing and ordering its members according to a standard of democratic behaviour.

Towards the end of 2001, the minutes suggest a very different atmosphere. The meetings are businesslike and purposeful. There are numerous projects on the go, with substantial municipal spending behind them. A Local Area Spatial Development Framework is mooted for Manenberg that anticipates rebuilding the central business district to the tune of R1.5 million over three years. By November 2001, the ACT is debating the reopening of the medical clinic and the return of its staff. The discussion is instructive. It begins by noting the severity of the situation and the risks involved. Although there have been no attacks on municipal staff recently, participants worry that when gang violence starts, clinic staff have to contain the panic. Moreover, in the absence of the police, the community is not in a position to guarantee the safety of staff. The forum suggests that personnel be recruited from Manenberg as a way of dealing with the high levels of staff trauma (Manenberg ACT, 12 November 2001). Apparently, Manenberg residents are habituated to the violence. What is most striking about this meeting is the apparent change in atmosphere. The commitment of the municipality to the forum, the regular presence of senior officials and the willingness to allocate resources through the ACT has seen a new resolve emerge. The minutes record the following excerpt of dialogue: 'We cannot allow this situation to continue where gangsters are given the space to do as they please' (Manenberg ACT, 12 November 2001).

By the beginning of 2002, plans to reopen the clinic are well advanced. In addition, there are moves to upgrade the appearance of Manenberg: to clear dead trees, prevent liquor from being sold from abandoned municipal containers, and generally repair and renovate buildings.

By December 2002 there is a Precinct Development Plan to combat the influence of gangs by 'rejuvenating the physical appearances of neighborhoods' to 'close the window of opportunity for gangs by developing alternative community norms, values and role models' and to provide for 'community safety and law enforcement' (City of Cape Town, n.d.: 5). Together with the Manenberg People Centre, Dudley supports what are described as 'pockets' in the area. Street committees are established to take responsibility for a specific territory: street corners, pavements and so on. These committees create small gardens, remove graffiti and paint murals. At stake is the politics of reclaiming the streets. Street lighting is upgraded, including between blocks of flats. Fences are repaired, drains cleared and gullies unblocked. Staircases are repaired and balustrades replaced. New street signs are installed and parks are improved. All these projects are undertaken with municipal funding (City of Cape Town, n.d.: appendices). NGOs and religious organisations are encouraged to move into the area. Closed circuit television systems are set up in the centre of town as part of the municipality's new emphasis on policing. There is tentative evidence to suggest that the crime rate in Manenberg is decreasing and that the murder rate has peaked (City of Cape Town, n.d.: 18).

What is certain is that the mood in the area has changed. The Manenberg People Centre launches *Manenberg Speaks* in September 2002 – a newsletter to give 'voice' to the residents of the area, to report good news and to lift the morale of Manenberg residents (Manenberg People Centre, 2002). The debut editorial begins:

> For many years the only publicity Manenberg received in the mainstream press has been negative. This negativity has portrayed the community as losers to the outside world. ... The *Manenberg Speaks* is an attempt by the community to voice their issues and concerns. To be their own praise singers and to be a catalyst for economic development in the area. In a nutshell Manenberg has hope and vision for itself.

It ends: 'Manenberg is where it's happening' (Manenberg People Centre, 2002). The publication is in English, not Afrikaans. It is intended to suggest a new mood of connectivity to the rest of the city and the world.

In his draft review of the Manenberg ACT in July 2003, Toms makes the following observations:

- Officials held accountable
- Service delivery has improved
- Communication between council, community and local councillors has improved
- ACT still going strong (50–60 people at every monthly meeting) with a consistent core membership who attend all the time
- Moved from reactive complaints to proactive solutions
- Improving safety: decreased crime stats and gang activity (Toms, 2003).

Generally he notes that the ACT had been meeting every month since 6 March 2000 – more than three years. In that time Manenberg has:

- Seen improved delivery – not just a talk shop
- Building community confidence and capacity building of the community
- Crime stats have dropped because the ACT has helped strengthen civil society and particularly because the role of the pockets where courts have claimed back 'their space'
- Community now reclaiming turf (Toms, 2003).

In their report for the Western Cape Anti-Eviction Campaign, Sophie Oldfield and Kristian Stokke (forthcoming), respectively researchers at the Universities of Cape Town and Oslo, list and describe community-based organisations active in the campaign against housing evictions, water and electricity cut-offs and furniture repossessions. Not one of the 17 organisations discussed is from Manenberg. Given that levels of unemployment there are sometimes more severe than in the areas where the campaign is active, it is impossible to conclude that questions of affordability are not relevant to Manenberg residents. What it does suggest is that there is a responsible forum outside of the campaign where these issues can be addressed. This is surely testimony to the effectiveness of the ACT.

Fardila de Vries, editor of *Manenberg Speaks* and municipal councillor, offers a similar view. The gangs are in retreat as communities, animated by a new civic solidarity, reclaim the streets (author's interview with De Vries, 9 July 2003). She attributes this to the work of NGO initiatives. Given, however, that groups like the Manenberg People's Centre have been active in the area, some since 1986, and that similar initiatives prior to the existence of the ACT yielded little more than brief cosmetic changes, we can certainly wonder if this new mood testifies to the emergence of civil society[7] in Manenberg. It becomes legitimate, that is, to wonder if the sustained and committed presence of a participatory state body has not encouraged (perhaps already latent) solidarities and what is sometimes described as social capital. That is a question for further research. There is much other evidence to suggest, however, that it has.

In her study of social(ising) habits of Manenberg youth, including their consumption of radio, television and the electronic media, Elaine Salo, an anthropologist at the University of Cape Town, observes some significant changes in the way young men and women style themselves (Salo, 2003). Of particular interest is the phenomenon of the *hok* as a physical and symbolic space. Established in the 1980s as sites for unemployed men to meet and create job opportunities, many *hokke* developed into glamorous multi-roomed nightclubs and discotheques. They also served as the headquarters for powerful Manenberg gangs (Salo, 2003). Salo reports of one of the *hokke*:

> A few arcade games machines filled the small *hok*, where
> young men were engrossed in the game flashing on the small
> screens. Other young men stood around in a conversational
> group, sharing a cigarette or taking a swig from an illicit bottle
> of cheap wine. They were discussing the most notorious gang,
> the Hard Livings and their activities intensely, often expressing
> admiration for the gang's defiance and its members' ability
> to avoid arrest. The TV music videos broadcasts of African
> American rap artists such as Tupac Shakur and Dr. D.R.E were
> extremely popular (Salo, 2003: 262).

'The *hok's* dual function, as corner shop and as a male hang-out where gang activities were openly discussed,' Salo reports, 'provided a visible masculine place within the local public space' (p. 262). There, the secret codes, practices and aesthetic of the gang entered the public domain. Together with the new community radio stations that reported on and indeed even valorised gang life, the *hokke* played a crucial role in locating the figure of the gangster at the heart of masculine identities (p.262).

It is important to note that the chapter is drawing here from research done by Salo in 1998. Since then there have been dramatic changes. Many of the *hokke* have been dismantled. Indeed, the most notorious, that which headquartered the Staggie brothers and the Hard Livings gang, is no more. Nothing less than a charismatic church has replaced it. Gone too are the murals and the graffiti. The Reverend Joshua Louw, rector of the Anglican Church (Church of Reconciliation) in Manenberg, reports that there are more than 200 churches in Manenberg, most of them new and most of these charismatic. With the radicalisation of Islam over the last several years, moreover, Islam and Christianity are, in the words of the Anglican minister, in a 'battle for souls' on the Cape Flats (author's interview with Louw, 10 July 2003). What vigorous religious activity in Manenberg has done is unsettle the figure of the gangster as role model. Louw suggests that if you ask a young man in Manenberg today what he wants to be when he is older, there is some ambivalence. This marks an important shift: in the past, the answer would unhesitatingly have been 'a gangster' (author's interview with Louw, 10 July 2003). Indeed, there is circumstantial evidence to suggest that the figure of the pious man, if it has not displaced the figure of the gangster as the masculine ideal, at least competes with it. This is true too of the figure of the graduate. Even among gangsters, the value of education has improved. This may be related to the fact that prisoners detained in Pollsmoor prison now have opportunities to study (author's interview with Salo, 5 July 2002).

Both Salo and Louw caution against any glib celebrations. It is perhaps too early to know whether the docility of the gangs in Manenberg says more about an assertive civil society reclaiming the streets than it does about internal gang politics – regrouping, changes in strategy and tactics, economic cycles, movements to new territories, etc. (author's interview with Salo, 5 July 2002; interview with Louw, 10 July 2003). Yet both give reason for greater optimism that something major is happening. Louw reports that women in Manenberg are more assertive and independent – evidenced by a refusal simply to convert to the man's religion at the time of the wedding, but also by increased female drug use. There are real signs of what he calls 'community accountability' – residents asserting control over and looking after their immediate environments (flat buildings, streets, pavements). What is at stake is the emergence of civil society in Manenberg.

Even if one concludes cautiously – that it might be too soon to attribute the apparent change in Manenberg to anything more than developments in the drug economy and/or the gangs – there is enough evidence, even at this stage, to suggest that something more dramatic is at work. The sustained and dedicated commitment of senior municipal officials to a regular participatory forum has produced, even if tentatively, the *political*. In other words, it has created a space where local residents are called and obliged to be citizens. This is more than simply a question of politics: of providing/demanding forums/institutions where residents can exercise their political rights. What is at stake is a democratic *society*: that residents relate to each other according to values of accountability, solidarity and equality. It is unlikely that the ACT is single-handedly responsible for this ethical renaissance. Manenberg had a long history of political opposition to the apartheid state, and it is likely, therefore, that democratic values were well established in and through UDF organisations. Nonetheless, without state support, they were no match for the violent gang fraternities. What the ACT has done – through its ability to marshal resources and link with other organisations, including the police – is grant to Manenberg residents room to manoeuvre. Making Manenberg 'functional', therefore, has not required ethnocentric social engineering. It has been achieved by consolidating and expanding a democratic ethic through popular political participation. The rewards have been significant.

The case of Manenberg has important consequences for how we theorise democratisation, and how we think about the conditions of democracy. We must stop reducing democracy to a purely political phenomenon, a tendency captured by the critique of 'parliamentarism'. In other words, the measure of democracy is not simply the degree to which there is public participation in public affairs. The measure should rather be the degree to which social relations are governed by ethical constraints and freedoms. In broadening our view of democracy to include the density of ethical relations, for example, we can better understand the threat that capitalism is to the democratic project. This is easily obscured if we reduce democracy to a political system or a set of institutions. Societies structured on the basis of private property seem to have little problem reconciling themselves to formal democratic institutions. If, however, parliaments *et al.* presuppose an ethical norm, then matters change somewhat. What becomes an obstacle to the realisation of democracy are those forces that structure social relations on unethical terms. This is why racism and patriarchy are obstacles to democratic citizenship. So, too, is exploitation. Capitalism is hostile to democracy because it structures society on the basis of relations (exploitation, for example) that are quintessentially unethical.

Let us conclude by noting that we have discussed here a way of thinking about the conditions of the citizen without invoking any *a priori* cultural, racial or political disposition. We do not have to believe, that is, that only 'authentic Africans' can be citizens, for example. What matters is democratic socialisation through, for example, participatory democracy. Are there other paths? Perhaps we should think about schooling with this purpose in mind.

If democratic citizenship does not presuppose a cultural or racial or linguistic trait, then what consequence does this have for how we imagine the limits of democratic society? If a democracy, as opposed to a nation, is not distinguishable from other political communities because it contains a particular cultural, racial or linguistic group, then how does it generate and justify its border or frontier? The following two chapters will take up this question. In the next chapter we will see a failed attempt to generate such a limit in the work of the Truth and Reconciliation Commission. The concluding chapter will try to overcome some of these shortfalls through a theoretical engagement with the work of Ernesto Laclau and Chantal Mouffe.

7

The Truth and Reconciliation Commission and the Identity of 'the People'

> We [the TRC commissioners] were certainly authentic in reflecting the alienations, chasms and suspicions that were part and parcel of our apartheid society. We were a useful paradigm for our nation for if we could eventually be welded into a reasonably coherent, united and reconciled group then there was hope for South Africa.
>
> Archbishop Desmond Tutu, *No Future without Forgiveness* (1999: 70–71)

Underlying the work of the Truth and Reconciliation Commission (TRC) was an ontological imperative. Reconciliation was not simply to be achieved through a process of catharsis through truth telling. More importantly, the TRC sought to provide a principle of commonality that would ground South Africans, despite their differences of culture, religion, language and race, as a *people*. In other words, reconciliation was not simply to be achieved by 'help[ing] the nation both to deal with its painful past and to move on to a more democratic future' (Gibson, 2004); it was to be achieved by determining the basis on which to found South Africans as a nation in the first place. We might recall Immanuel Wallerstein's famous question about India: 'Does India exist?' (Wallerstein, 1991). In a similar vein, we might say that the challenge of the TRC was to overcome the worry that the South African people did not actually exist.

Citizenship and its limits

Shortly after the transition from white minority rule, once the process of working out the constitutional and political arrangements for the new dispensation was completed, and the first democratic election was concluded, there was an urgent drive to define the basis for South Africa's unity as a people. On what grounds, in other words, were South Africans a single people? Nor was this question trifling: it cut to the heart of the political settlement.

Firstly, the idea that South Africans formed *a* people made it sensible to think about the time after apartheid as the time of a single, unitary state. Secondly, it was self-evident that the people of Namibia, say (or a citizen of any other country) were not South Africans. In other words, and inversely, South Africans were their own people seeking self-determination in their own state. South Africa belonged not to everyone, but to South Africans. Therein, however, lay a problem: Why was it reasonable to grant rights to and expect obligations from someone born in South Africa's Limpopo Province, but not, for example, someone born just the other side of the Limpopo River in Zimbabwe? What did someone living in Soweto share with someone in Sandton that they did not have in common with someone born in, say, Bulawayo?

The South African people lacked national marks. It was only really clear who they were not. They were not the South Africans of old: those who had perpetrated and endured the injustices of the past. They did not speak any particular language, nor did they follow any one faith. They had neither a common culture, nor race. Despite this, the first democratic election proceeded as if they had; as if, nonetheless, it made sense to include them in a single demos.

Two things trumped this paradox:[1] a geographical legacy and an intuition. The legacy was of a territory, the land of South Africa, with its *de facto* inhabitants. This made the limit of the *demos* easier to determine – it was given by borders beyond which lay other peoples.[2] More obscure was the internal measure of the people: why these ones and not those? Herein lay the intuition: if South Africans were not a nation, they were, nonetheless, already some kind of people. The issue was therefore: Who was eligible for citizenship and who was not? At stake were the limits of the political community.

Historically speaking, since the great democratic revolutions of the eighteenth century, there has been a single, pre-eminent way of generating this limit. This can be called a national principle. It is a way of simultaneously generating identity and difference that appeals to a *horizontal* relation between persons. We can summarise it as follows:

A is the same as B in respect to X.[3]

It says that A is identical to B to the extent that they share X, where X in this statement refers to some or other feature of population (language, religion, culture, race, and so on). The fact that two citizens are identical to each other except in respect of X is sufficient to disqualify them from the political community. We can state this inversely as follows:

A and B are admissible to C to the extent that they share X.

In this statement, C refers to the political community. The national principle of political community appeals to identity[4] as the basis of the limit. This is not the case with earlier and/or other religiously inspired principles of political community. If we consider briefly the dynastic principle, we see that it has nothing to do with differences or commonalities between individuals and collectivities. At stake, rather, is a vertical relation between subject and the sovereign. We can summarise it as follows:

A and B are admissible to C when subjects of Y.

As in the statement made earlier, C refers to the political community. Y is the sovereign or prince. Identity on the dynastic principle is not relevant: it is precluded by definition, precisely because there can be no similarity between the prince as representative of God on Earth and the subject. What matters is that the territory in which A and B reside falls (through war or treaty) into the domain of the sovereign, and that its residents are subject to him/her. In this way, the domain of the prince could be, and usually was, composed of peoples speaking diverse languages and of different cultures. This is what made dynasties cosmopolitan.[5] On the dynastic principle, the unity of the political community was given by the sovereign who ruled over it. Let us note a contemporary version of this principle. The sovereign is not a prince, but the constitution, such that contours of the people follow the jurisdiction of this supreme law. We will see shortly, however, that modern constitutionalism falls back on national law.

Before continuing, the choice of vocabulary needs to be defined. For the purposes of clarity, it was found to be useful to distinguish between the ontic and the ontological. Here, the former refers to political facts that announce themselves as such. In other words, it refers to practices and institutions that make *general* claims about the way that the demos is organised or governed. Included in this category are republicanism, constitutionalism, liberalism, socialism, and so on. In English, this is the meaning captured by the term politics *(la politique)*. The ontological refers to a category of facts that precede the ontic (not in time, but logically) and that make the latter possible. This is what is meant by the political *(le politique)*. Foremost among them is the way that the demos itself is produced. Hence an analysis at the level of the ontic might discuss the way a people has been governed or governed itself and changes in this regard. A study at the level of the ontological is concerned with how that people came to exist in the first place and the basis of its unity. In short: a new principle of political ontology does not refer to a novel system of government; it signals a new kind of people.

The Principle of Living

In the Preamble to the 1996 South African Constitution there is a line that harks back to the Freedom Charter of 1955. It reads: 'We, the people of South Africa ... [b]elieve that South Africa belongs to all who live in it, united in our diversity' (Republic of South Africa, 1996). The earlier document proclaimed:

> We, the People of South Africa, declare for all our country and the world to know: that South Africa belongs to all who live in it, black and white, and that no government can justly claim authority unless it is based on the will of all the people (Freedom Charter, 1955).

We should notice something peculiar about these statements above: they are unusually self-conscious. Like the US Constitution, both documents adopt the voice of the first person plural: 'We, the people,' they begin. Yet in the South African documents, unlike the American text, there is an immediate self-reflective hesitation. Instead of simply proceeding to state some or other democratic axiom, both the Constitution and the Freedom Charter pause to remind us who is speaking: 'We, the people', they say, are these people who are like such and such .... This might not be strange if the Constitution were intended for an unfamiliar, foreign audience. It is odd when we think that it was not: it was intended for South Africans. Hence, there appears the paradox of a people unsure of what they are, and seeking to remind themselves as they proceed. In 1955 this was not surprising. The Freedom Charter sought to subvert apartheid definitions of 'the people' by including those barred from them. In such a context it was appropriate that the identity of the people be made explicit. The point nonetheless is that the struggle against apartheid was not simply a struggle against a racist political system, its laws and its institutions. At stake was the reconstitution of the South African people. It is worth stating this truism, precisely because it is less obvious than we might believe. Or, rather, it is not self-evident that by redefining the South African people, the Freedom Charter was necessarily referring to nation-building. Rather, the document posits an unusual relationship among three elements: political authority, the territory of South Africa and being South African. The key expression is 'live in it'. The mere fact of living in the territory of South Africa is considered sufficient for entry to the political community. On the Freedom Charter's terms, therefore, it is enough to live in South Africa to qualify for citizenship.

In appearance, this resembles the national principle discussed earlier. It says that A and B are admissible to C to the extent that they share X, where X in this case is the fact of living in South Africa. The grammar is perhaps the same, but in fact we have here a radically new principle of political ontology. Territory is not a quality of population.

Let us assume for a moment that the point is being exaggerated: that the Freedom Charter and the Constitution are quite clear about what they mean by 'the people'. In both cases, they refer to a non-racial society. If the argument *is* overstated, it will not be difficult to define what all these diverse people have in common *qua* a people: it should not be difficult, that is, to define the quality of X that South Africans share beyond the accident of geography.

This is precisely the challenge of nation-building. It is driven to resolve two basic questions: Why should the nation be composed of these people and not others? And: What is the common factor, the X, on which to base a South African identity? We will see that it is impossible to answer these questions. Attempts either beg the very question they set out to answer or they dissolve the specificity of South African people. This difficulty becomes most apparent if we consider briefly the work of the TRC.

The Truth and Reconciliation Commission
The TRC was established by the Promotion of National Unity and Reconciliation Act of 1995 (Republic of South Africa, 1995). Already in the title of the legislation that provided for it, one hears what motivated its creation: the advancement of national unity by reconciling South

Africa's people. In the act itself, one of the introductory clauses refers to the reconstruction of this people. In the main, the TRC was preoccupied with justifying and implementing what was then a controversial model of reconciliation. The peoples of South Africa would be made whole, not by seeking to punish the perpetrators of human rights violations, but by making them speak the truth about their criminal actions. South Africans consisted of perpetrators and victims of human rights abuses arising from the history of apartheid. Already here we have a principle of political ontology. Reconciliation was possible if political crimes were confessed to by those who carried them out, so that they could be forgiven by those against whom they were committed. Reconciliation was this dialectic of confession and forgiveness. The quality of X, therefore, that rendered South Africans common was this shared history.

But could the terms 'victim' and 'perpetrator' do the job they were supposed to? The originators of the TRC understood that this question was capital. The founding act begins by stating that the purpose of the commission is:

> To provide for the investigation and the establishment of as complete a picture as possible of the nature, causes and extent of gross violations of human rights committed during the period from 1 March 1960 to the cut-off date contemplated in the Constitution, within or outside the Republic, emanating from the conflicts of the past, and the fate or whereabouts of the victims of such violations (Republic of South Africa, 1995).

Nothing short of an exhaustive history of the country was expected. The TRC understood this clearly: 'One of the main tasks of the Commission', the final report explained, 'was to uncover as much as possible of the truth about past gross violations of human rights' (TRC, 1998, Vol. I, chap. 4, sec. 3). But this brief is impossibly huge. Indeed, when the final report was submitted by the chair of the commission, Archbishop Desmond Tutu, he was at pains to explain its methodological limits.

'Ultimately,' he warned,

> this report is no more than ... the report of a commission
> appointed by Parliament to complete an enormous task in
> a limited period. ... Inevitably, evidence and information
> about our past will continue to emerge .... The report of the
> Commission will now take its place in the historical landscape
> of which future generations will try to make sense ... searching
> for the clues that will lead, endlessly, to a truth that will, in
> the very nature of things, never fully be revealed' (TRC, 1998,
> Foreword, Vol. I, chap. 1, secs. 15–18).

Given the right resources and time, he implies, such a comprehensive
account might be possible. Was the hopelessness of the task simply
logistical? There was a more serious problem. What would this be a
history of?

It could not simply be a history of human rights violations. This would
render the project unwieldy and arbitrary: where would it end? If it were
a history of apartheid abuses, then there was a further burden of proof.
Apartheid was not a thing in itself. It was, rather, a name for a host of
events, things and processes. What the term did was organise various
facts in a system to give them coherence. Depending on what was named
(racial capitalism, white racism, crimes against humanity), the meaning
of these things changed or shifted in importance. In other words, *an
apartheid abuse was different to a human rights violation in that the meaning
of apartheid was included in the definition of the crime.* What was specific
about an apartheid crime as opposed to a human rights abuse?

If, for example, apartheid was understood as a system of racial
capitalism, then an apartheid abuse included the activities of the capitalist
sector insofar as it produced and reproduced apartheid, precisely because,
on this understanding, it was necessarily involved in crimes against black
people. Such a definition opens up, as abuses, a field of activities that
would not count from the perspective of, say, human rights.

A mere accumulation of endless facts was no more likely to say this than counting grains of sand on the beach. What mattered was the organising concept and this was only available *a priori*. Therein lay the problem: the history of apartheid could not emerge by accumulating endless facts. The appeal to a common history is not a factual claim; it is a theoretical one. It requires that the concept – apartheid – has been defined to everybody's satisfaction in advance.[6] A national history – a history that defines the limits of the people – thus begs the question. It must know, even before it starts, who the people are. How else could it write their story? This is why the project of nation-building is paradoxical. It is driven to suppose that the nation already exists in itself. Indeed, the only sense the term can have is the following: to bring to self-consciousness that which already exists objectively. This becomes clearer if we think about the alternative. If we had to begin with the facts, without any intuition or knowledge of where to start, we would have to start from the point of infinity, from the point of knowing all facts. At least, if one is writing a history of the Germans or the Slavs, or the Arabs, the task is bounded by one or other marker (language, religion, culture, objective social status). What was the equivalent in the South African case? Apart from a geographical marker, there wasn't one.

This becomes even clearer when one considers the terms of the TRC taxonomy: perpetrators and victims. If both sides were 'the people', then apartheid was some kind of civil war, a struggle in the midst of the nation. If that were the case, however, then the people preceded apartheid. Alternatively, the category 'victims' denoted black South Africans. 'Perpetrators' was the group that antagonised them. On this idea, the perpetrators could accede to 'the people' by confessing their crimes and asking their former victims for forgiveness. There is no doubt that this confessional relationship could produce very strong affective relations among people, enough perhaps to form strong social ties. It is what made the TRC, at times, such a harrowing process to watch and at others, such a moving one. Yet, the process was far too restricted to have this effect on anything but a tiny minority of people in South Africa.

A better prospect was if persons who testified at TRC hearings were understood to be representatives of classes of people. Hence 'victims' stood for black people as a whole, and 'perpetrators' stood for a white population seeking forgiveness and entry to the nation. For this to happen, the TRC needed to be seen to function symbolically. This certainly seems to be how the ANC understood the process. The metonymic effect only worked, however, if 'victim' referred exclusively to blacks and 'perpetrator' to whites. In the final report, delivered to President Mandela in 1998, the Commission found that the ANC itself had been responsible for gross human rights violations, i.e. it vitiated any exclusive association between perpetrators and the apartheid state or white South Africans.

It seems that the ANC understood the consequences of this better than the TRC commissioners. The day before handing over the final report at a large ceremony in Pretoria, the organisation applied to the High Court for an interdict stopping the TRC from publishing anything that implicated it in human rights violations. Desmond Tutu was shocked: 'It was so surreal,' he says in his account of the Commission. '[T]he ANC, which had been so supportive of the process – this was totally unexpected and thoroughly out of line with its character and attitude' (Tutu, 1999: 169). It is perhaps less surprising if one understands what was at stake: the affirmation of a principle that could do two things simultaneously. It had to establish relations of identity (sameness) among the inhabitants of the country and identify ties that were specifically South African yet the TRC unwittingly spoilt the effect. The principle of a common history around apartheid was thought to be the only way this could be done.[7] If it failed, a South African people could not be said to exist. If blacks were also 'perpetrators' (and whites also 'victims') then reconciliation simply became a process between human rights abusers and their victims. But what was the difference between a victim of human rights abuse in South Africa and anywhere else in the world? What was lost was the specifically South African character of the story.

Indeed, what the TRC generated was not the South African people, but humanity as a whole. This was not an *ad hominem* failure by the commissioners: it was latent, rather, in the structure of the commission. By casting the effects of apartheid in terms of human rights, the founding legislation prefigured a judgement in these terms. This explains, perhaps, the archbishop's shock at the reaction of the ANC to the final report. Let us consider this for a moment.

The act that established the TRC took its cue from the South African Constitution. At the heart of the latter was the principle of human rights. The legislation declared that the commission was

> to provide for the investigation and the establishment of as complete a picture as possible of the nature, causes and extent of gross violations of *human rights* committed during the period from 1 March 1960 to the cut-off date (Republic of South Africa, 1995: emphasis added).

The language of human rights was the currency of the proceedings and, eventually, of the findings. It was complemented by Christian theology – the two worked hand in hand. At stake was finding that which was common to all South Africans, and this was well understood by Tutu. In *No Future without Forgiveness* he writes:

> We [the newly appointed commissioners] were broadly representative of South African society. We came from diverse backgrounds and we were to discover that apartheid had affected us all in different ways. We learned to our chagrin that we were a microcosm of South African society, more deeply wounded than we had at first imagined. We found that we were often very suspicious of one another and that it was not easy to develop real trust in one another .... Our meetings for the first year or so were hell. It was not easy to arrive at a common mind as each of us tried to stake our claim to the turf and to establish our particular space. You wondered as a black whether your white colleague would have reacted in that way to a fellow white

and vice versa. ... We were certainly authentic in reflecting the
alienations, chasms and suspicions that were part and parcel of
our apartheid society. ... *We were a useful paradigm for our nation
for if we could eventually be welded into a reasonably coherent,
united and reconciled group then there was hope for South Africa*
(Tutu, 1999: 70–71; emphasis added).

We will return to these remarks later. For the moment, let us note that
what counted for Tutu was not a vague atmosphere of good will. At stake
was the ability to work together.

How did the commissioners overcome this manifest inability to work
together? Tutu's answer is important, and it is quoted here at length. It
is important because he does not appeal to a common history, a common
culture or language and so on.

The archbishop begins by noting that four of the ten commissioners of
the TRC were ordained church ministers. Three had been national heads
of their denominations. In selecting these particular people, he remarks:
'The President must have believed that our work would be profoundly
spiritual.' Indeed, instead of appointing a judge to head a quasi-
judicial body, the president selected the head of the Anglican Church
in South Africa. Tutu continues: 'After all, forgiveness, confession and
reconciliation were far more at home in the religious sphere' (Tutu,
1999: 71). It is this intuition, and Tutu's natural proclivity as a minister
of religion, that gave to the TRC its specific character. Tutu explains:

> Despite our diversity, the Commissioners agreed to my proposal
> at the first meeting that we should go on a retreat, where we
> sought to enhance our spiritual resources and sharpen our
> sensitivities. We kept silence for a day, seeking to open ourselves
> to the movement and guidance of the transcendent Spirit .... The
> Commission also accepted my call for prayer at the beginning
> and end of our meetings, and at midday when I asked for a pause
> for recollection and prayer. In the Human Rights Violations

> Committee, we agreed that when victims and survivors came
> to our victim-oriented hearings ... we would have a solemn
> atmosphere with prayers, hymns and ritual candle-lighting ....
> I asked the secretariat of the world-wide Anglican Communion
> to alert the nuns and monks of the religious communities of our
> Church to our desperate need for regular intercession (p. 72).

Unsurprisingly, Tutu describes the TRC as having a 'heavy spiritual, and, indeed, Christian emphasis' (p. 72). '[T]heological and religious insights and perspectives', he admits, 'inform[ed] much of what we did and how we did it' (p. 73).

Not only did this religious atmosphere reconcile the commissioners to each other (Tutu, 1999: 67–68), but, more importantly, it furnished the principle on the basis of which South Africans could be said to be a people. Reconciliation was possible because, despite their awful deeds, perpetrators, like victims, were 'children of God' (p. 74). This is what united them; this was the quality of X in respect of which they were the same. Despite the great diversity of South Africans, what united them, Tutu declared triumphantly, was that they were 'the rainbow people of God' (p. 77).[8] If one were a nationalist, however, the costs to pay for this formulation were high.

In the final report, the archbishop enthuses:

> Ours is a remarkable country. Let us celebrate our diversity, our
> differences. God wants us as we are. South Africa wants and
> needs the Afrikaner, the English, the coloured, the Indian, the
> black. We are sisters and brothers in one family – God's family,
> the human family (TRC, 1998: Vol. 1, chap. 1, sec. 91).

But therein lay the problem. By finding the quality of identity in a divine spark, the TRC did not generate the South African people *per se*: it produced a world people. South Africans are merely instances of humanity, indistinguishable from anyone else.

The notion of human rights has the same effect. Invoked to define the specificity of a people, they must necessarily appeal to all people. This is not in itself a criticism; it does leave, however, the original question unresolved. What is that quality that South Africans share that is unique to them?

We saw the importance of this earlier. If rights refer less to nature than to statuses accorded by the state in the political community, then they can only emerge once the demos is already established. They cannot be principles on the basis of which specific communities come into existence. Rights, that is, are features of the ontic, not the ontological.

Here we come to another paradox. We have discussed two failed attempts to produce the South African people – via an appeal to a common history and via a divine transcendental. Yet we saw in the Constitution and the Freedom Charter a principle that satisfied our test of the people. It was a notion of *living*. The South African people as a unified concept is composed of those individuals *living* in the territory of South Africa. This definition fulfils both the statement:

A is the same as B in respect of X,

and the statement:

A and B are admissible to C to the extent that they share X.

C refers to the demos; X refers to living in the territory of South Africa.

There are several things to note about this formulation. Firstly, it is general enough to apply to everyone in South Africa. Secondly, it specifies a particular people that can be distinguished from other peoples. Thirdly, it has an objective empirical measure that is simple to determine. Fourthly, it defines a political community founded on a principle of territory and not one of population. In other words, the principle of territory provides an intelligible (or conceptual) political limit. But therein lies its own shortcoming. For the political limit designates, above all, an *affective* relation. The measure of population (of race, language, culture, etc.), the basis of the national limit, for example, is a proxy for an affective relation among those enclosed by the limit. In other words, the logic of nationalism says that those who share with their compatriots a common race or culture or language are more likely to find pleasure and friendship with each other than those with whom they do not share these qualities. This is why the principle of territory, despite its conceptual intelligibility, is not a compelling principle of political ontology. Contingent geographical contiguity is not a basis of neighbourliness, i.e. of affective bonds among citizens. Therein lies the challenge of post-national, cosmopolitan citizenship. This is the challenge that the last and concluding chapter will attempt to address.

Conclusion:
Notes Towards a Theory of the Democratic Limit

A meaningful discussion about the democratic limit or boundary is only now beginning. In South Africa, the political transition from apartheid to democracy keeps running up against the substance of 'the people'. In the absence of any traditional unifying principles (of language, culture, religion, race, and so on), the identity of South Africans is elusive. We might note too that much of the cosmopolitan literature on democracy appeals to a shift in scale, from the territorial state to the world, or globe, or even planet.[1] Yet, says John Agnew, such appeals have important consequences for democracy without properly theorising them. He argues that:

> the only way that they [supporters of cosmopolitanism] can conceive of world citizenship without opening up to question the founding condition of democratic theory – the presumption of a territorialized political community – is by 'scaling up' from individual states to the world as a whole (Agnew, 2005: 439).

The merit of Chantal Mouffe's work is that she has recently broached the question of the democratic limit with a view, precisely, to theorising it. She argues that democracy always entails relations of inclusion–

exclusion that speak to a notion of the political frontier (Mouffe, 2000: 43). One of the key problems of democratic theory,[2] she suggests, has been its inability to conceptualise such a limit (p. 43). This has not, until recently, seemed an urgent task. The reason, one can imagine, is largely political. The figure of the citizen has, historically, been deemed either a resident of a nation or of the world, so that nation–world are the two poles that have exhausted the democratic imaginary.

Yet over the last two decades, both identities have become increasingly unsettled. In the first place, the collapse of 'really existing' socialist states and the associated crisis of Marxism have disturbed the prospect of internationalism. In the second, feminist and multicultural critiques of the nation have inspired thinking about new forms of political community. More and more, writers have been drawn together around the notion of cosmopolitanism. It is in this context that there is growing interest in a principle of political demarcation, a principle of the frontier, that can simultaneously discriminate between citizens and non-citizens, but in a way that is not discriminatory. The problem in contemporary terms is of a particular demos that is not constituted on any measure of *population*, be it race, culture, religion, ethnicity, or any combination of these. This chapter will propose a solution to this problem. It will do so by following a major development in the work of Ernesto Laclau – in particular from his collaboration with Chantal Mouffe in their groundbreaking work *Hegemony and Socialist Strategy* (1990) to his most recent book, *On Populist Reason* (2005).

The elusive frontier of radical democracy

We can begin to approach the principle of a democratic limit in relation to the 'democratic revolution'. This is a term that Laclau and Mouffe borrow from de Tocqueville to speak of a decisive mutation that took place in the political imaginary of Western societies about 200 years ago. For these authors, '[t]he key moment in the beginnings of the democratic revolution can be found in the French Revolution since ... its affirmation of the *absolute power of its people* introduced something truly new at the level of the social imaginary' (Laclau & Mouffe, 1990: 155; emphasis added). This new element was that 'the logic of equivalence was transformed into the fundamental instrument of the production of the social' (p. 155). With the Declaration of the Rights of Man on 27 August 1789, it became possible to propose that the different forms of inequality were illegitimate and anti-natural, and hence equivalent as forms of oppression (p. 155).

Laclau and Mouffe's formulation here rests on the distinction they make between a *relation of subordination* and a *relation of oppression*. The first refers to a situation where one agent is subject to the decisions of another – an employee to a boss, a woman to a man, a child to an adult, and so on (Laclau & Mouffe, 1990: 155). In this regard, the relation merely establishes a set of differential positions between social agents; it does not determine the site of an antagonism. A relation of oppression, in contrast, refers to a relation of subordination that has come to be seen as illegitimate, and is, consequently, transformed into a site of antagonism (p. 154). This distinction forms the basis of Laclau and Mouffe's critique of classical Marxism – for failing properly to *theorise* the conditions under which a class relation *qua* differential social position becomes a relation of class *qua* site of class struggle, i.e. a relation of antagonism. When relations of subordination are deemed legitimate and fair, they will not become sites of antagonism. The movement from one to the other requires that the first term is subverted, i.e. is constructed as arbitrary, illegitimate and oppressive: 'This means that there is no relation of oppression without the presence of a discursive exterior from which the discourse of subordination can be interrupted' (p. 154).

This is precisely the importance of the democratic revolution. It grounded political authority in the *free* and *equal* will of the people. 'Here lay', Laclau and Mouffe argue, 'the profound subversive power of the democratic discourse, which would allow the spread of equality and liberty into increasingly wider domains and therefore act as a fermenting agent upon the different forms of struggle against subordination' (p. 155). This was the case with Mary Wollstonecraft's *Vindication of the*

Rights of Women, published in 1792, which gave birth to feminism by applying the logic of the democratic discourse to the relation between the sexes. Laclau and Mouffe trace the origin of many workers' struggles to this moment. From the critique of political inequality, it was not a big step towards a critique of economic inequality. Socialism becomes, in this way, a 'moment internal to the democratic revolution' (p. 154) by expanding the logic of democratic equivalence to the economic domain. On Laclau and Mouffe's terms, therefore, the deepening of the democratic revolution involves the spreading of its imaginary to more and more areas of the social. Writing in the late 1980s, they looked forward to the expansion of the democratic revolution to more and more domains: ecology (the waste of natural resources, the pollution and destruction of the environment) the urban (habitat, consumption, municipal services) and so on (p. 163).

Yet there is a strange elision in *Hegemony and Socialist Strategy* whose consequences for the notion of hegemony are not insignificant. On Laclau and Mouffe's terms, the democratic revolution is a history of two states of being: *egalité* and *liberté*. Yet they omit another term in the series. The break with the *ancien regime*, the origin of the democratic revolution, is achieved, not on the basis of two states of being, but of three: *egalité, liberté* and also *fraternité*. Laclau and Mouffe omit fraternity from the series, which renders their portrayal of the democratic revolution incomplete. For the democratic revolution is simultaneously the origin of the democratic imaginary and the origin of a *new principle of the political limit*, and it is the concept of *fraternité* that is the key to this principle.

Frontier, frontier effect and boundary

We saw that the movement from a relation of subordination to a relation of oppression occurred with a 'general field of discursivity' (Laclau & Mouffe, 1990: 135). The worker–boss couplet, for example, does not designate fixed identities in an *a priori* hostile relationship, but 'elements' whose precise identities are only given through a process of discursive articulation with a third element that is external to the original couplet.

The democratic imaginary *qua* discursive outside constructs such couplets (worker–boss, man–woman, white–black) as antagonistic by transforming the relationship into the site of an injustice. In this way, antagonisms may emerge at multiple sites in the social world. Yet Laclau and Mouffe suggest that there arises a situation, which coincides with the periphery of the capitalist world, where the political struggle is endowed with a centre, i.e. with a 'single and clearly defined enemy' (p. 131). When this relationship is constructed so as to divide the political space into two hostile camps, Laclau and Mouffe describe the subject positions that emerge as 'popular', while the line of division between them they call a 'frontier' (p. 133).

'In the countries of advanced capitalism since the middle of the nineteenth century,' they argue, 'the multiplication and "uneven development" of democratic positions has increasingly diluted their simple and automatic unity around a popular pole. Partly because of their very success, democratic struggles tend less and less to be unified as "popular struggles"' (Laclau & Mouffe, 1990: 133). Under such conditions, democratic struggles are too diverse to constitute a 'people', i.e. to establish chains of equivalence that divide the political space into opposing camps. Laclau and Mouffe argue that it is precisely in such a political arena that the democratic logic comes into its own. We might wonder, therefore, what this implies for the prospects for democracy in the Third World.

The logic of hegemony emerges when there is more than one discourse competing to fix (hegemonise) the meaning of an element. Theoretically speaking, we might imagine alongside a socialist discourse another seeking to naturalise the differential positions of the worker and the boss by appealing to a difference in education or competence, and so on. Hence hegemony only emerges in a field 'criss-crossed by antagonisms' (Laclau & Mouffe, 1990: 135). Every social identity becomes the meeting point for more than one articulatory practice, many of them antagonistic (p. 138). Laclau and Mouffe call a 'hegemonic formation' one that takes place through a confrontation with other articulatory practices and that emerges when a 'social and political space [is] relatively unified through the instituting of nodal points and the constitution of *tendentially* relational identities' (p. 136; original emphasis). A nodal point here refers to an identity whose meaning is more and more fixed in a certain direction. Laclau and Mouffe also call such nodal points, 'moments'. Hence a hegemonic formation may also be described as an 'ensemble of discursive moments' (p. 143). In contrast to a hegemonic formation, an 'organic crisis' corresponds to a 'conjuncture where there is a generalized weakening of the relational system defining the identities of a given social or political space, and where, as a result there is a proliferation of floating elements' (p. 136). The concept of hegemony thus describes a social field where there are multiple antagonisms, and where the frontiers between them are unstable (p. 136). A hegemonic antagonism (as opposed to a popular antagonism) does not, therefore, demarcate an 'evident and given' separation between hostile identities (p. 134): it does not, that is, demarcate a 'frontier' in the sense discussed earlier – as a line separating clearly defined camps. There are only tendential frontiers, which Laclau and Mouffe call 'frontier effects' (p. 134).

Both a *frontier* and a *frontier effect* are internal to the 'political space' or 'general field of discursivity'. Laclau and Mouffe put it this way: the *'place of negation* [the limit] is defined by the internal parameters of the formation' (Laclau & Mouffe, 1990: 139; original emphasis), be it 'hegemonic' or not (a popular political space, for example). This demands the question: Does the political space itself have a limit? Laclau and Mouffe take up this issue towards the end of their third chapter. They warn the reader that they have used the term 'formation' to designate both a 'hegemonic formation' and a 'social formation', though these are 'totally different situations' (p. 143). The first refers to a concept, and the second has an empirical referent. What is the relationship between them? Laclau and Mouffe continue as follows:

> If an ensemble of empirically given agents (in the case of a social
> formation) or an ensemble of discursive moments (in the case of

> a hegemonic formation) are included in the totality implied by
> the notion of formation, it is because through that totality it is
> possible to distinguish them with regard to something that is
> external to the latter (p. 143).

In other words, a hegemonic formation and a social formation are both formations to the extent that they have an *external* boundary. This is why the problem of the limit comes up in a clarification of terms. A formation has two kinds of limit. The first is *internal* and corresponds to two varieties: a frontier and a frontier effect; the second is an *external* boundary. *Boundaries, limits* and *frontiers* designate different concepts. Where a hegemonic formation and a social formation are 'totally different' is in the way that they generate their *external* limits. We might say hegemonic and social formations are identical to the extent that they have boundaries. They are dissimilar to the extent that they generate their boundaries differently. Let us start with the hegemonic formation.

Laclau and Mouffe suggest that we begin from the interior of such a formation, from the perspective, that is, of an identity in a relatively stable system of differences. Under such conditions, the limit of the formation itself cannot be constructed on the basis of difference. In other words, 'what is beyond' the totality cannot be another (positive) identity. If it were, then this identity would merely be another difference in an infinite field of differences. 'If we remain in the field of differences,' they admit, 'we remain in the field of an infinitude which makes it impossible to think any frontier and which, consequently, dissolves the concept of "formation"' (Laclau & Mouffe, 1990: 143). A limit is only intelligible insofar as a set of differences can be 'cut out' as a *totality* with regard to something *beyond*. Hence a formation only emerges through this cutting out process (p. 143). We have already seen, however, that no totality can be cut out if what is beyond the formation is another positivity. It follows, therefore, that the limit is not an effect of the logic of difference. 'This implies', Laclau and Mouffe tell us, 'that a formation manages to signify itself (that is, constitute itself as such) only by transforming the limits into frontiers, by constituting a chain of equivalences which constructs what is beyond the limits as that which it *is not*' (pp. 143–44; original emphasis). Earlier, Laclau and Mouffe tell us that this was the origin of the nation. During the Hundred Years War, the political space was divided into two: on the one side of the antagonism stood the French people (as instantiated in the heroic figure of Jeanne d'Arc) and on the other, a foreign power (p. 133).

Let us recall, however, that a frontier is a phenomenon of a political space that Laclau and Mouffe designated by the term 'popular'; it is not a hegemonic formation. This means that a hegemonic formation generates a boundary to the extent that it becomes something it is not. Surely this is the same as saying that a hegemonic formation *qua* hegemonic formation cannot produce a limit? Or better: the demos *qua* democracy is never particular. Indeed, this is what Laclau and Mouffe do say: the moment we introduce the notion of frontier effect back into the concept of the formation, every frontier is threatened. 'And this is exactly what occurs,' they tell us. 'As the totality is not a datum but a construction, when there is a breaking of its constitutive chains of equivalence, the totality does more than conceal itself: *it dissolves*' (Laclau & Mouffe, 1990: 144; original emphasis). What this means, in effect, is that the territory *qua* democracy (hegemonic formation) is either an infinitude – the whole world (though why stop there?) – or it is impossible.

Let us note that Laclau and Mouffe are using the term 'hegemonic formation' in a double sense: analytic and normative. As an analytical term, every formation, including a popular political space, is a hegemonic formation. Indeed, in Laclau's latest book, *On Populist Reason*, about which we will have a lot to say in a moment, populism is deemed the 'royal road' to understanding the constitution of the political *per se* (Laclau, 2005: 67). To the extent that every social identity is produced through the 'radical construction' (Laclau, 1990: 29) of equivalential chains, every social identity is an effect of a hegemonic practice. Even if identities in a popular field are polarised around a frontier, they are, nonetheless, discursive identities; hence subject to the logic of hegemony.

Yet, as a normative term, not every formation is a hegemonic one. At stake is the very intelligibility of the notion of radical democracy. A hegemonic formation, from this perspective, is one where the logic of hegemony has become an explicit principle of the formation itself. Laclau and Mouffe put it this way:

> Pluralism is radical only to the extent that each term of this plurality of identities finds within itself the principle of its own validity, without this having to be sought in a transcendent or underlying positive ground for the hierarchy of meaning of them all and the source and guarantee of their legitimacy (Laclau & Mouffe, 1990: 167).

What is more, radical pluralism is democratic to the extent that the equivalence of each one of its terms is 'the result of displacements of the *egalitarian* imaginary' (Laclau & Mouffe, 1990: 167; emphasis added). In other words, the basis of commonality (equivalence) among social identities does not refer to some or other transcendental ground (an objective class location, for example) that precedes their interaction. Commonality is a plastic relation in that it emerges through a process – immanent to the political itself – of elaboration. And, what is more, as a democratic formation, the unity of the social is established on the basis of equality. We will see shortly that Laclau has returned to this question in the form of a major revision of his argument. For the moment, let us say that a democrat is somebody who (a) knows that the unity of the social is provisional, and (b) for whom equality is the pre-eminent basis of this unity.

Let us think about the consequences of this analysis for a concrete situation. Take the notion of 'blackness' in South Africa. Before 1994, the term signified someone exploited by South African capitalism, someone oppressed by a system of racial discrimination. These terms were reconciled in the 1980s through the following hegemonic articulation. Raymond Suttner and Jeremy Cronin's political intervention in the mid-1980s reads in part as follows:

> One of the peculiarities of South African society is that written into its structure is this systematic national oppression of all blacks. It is one of the factors that facilitates capitalist exploitation in South Africa. National oppression and capitalist exploitation are inextricably linked (Suttner & Cronin, 1986: 129).

Here the workers' struggle (against capitalism) was reconciled with the struggle against racial discrimination (national oppression) because they were equivalent *vis-à-vis* apartheid. In this regard, the negative of blackness was a whiteness that stood for a system of racial capitalism.

On its own terms, the theory of national democratic revolution divided the political space into two opposing camps. Black and white referred to antagonistic identities, and in this sense they demarcated a frontier. In Laclau and Mouffe's terms, this frontier becomes a boundary when one of these identities is cut out of the formation. What can this mean other than the expulsion of its antagonistic negative from the political arena? In the case of NDR, this happens when a black republic is established, where this expression refers to a non-racial state tending towards socialism. Is such a republic a democracy? The answer must be no.

The native republic (see Chapter 3), a free South Africa, is fixed in relation to a definition of whiteness that is no longer within the discursive field – it has been cut out. In this sense, blackness becomes the essence of the social. Not only must the state constantly ward off any and every (real) resurgence of whiteness (racialism and capitalism) within the demos, but, paradoxically, it must preserve the very whiteness it is driven to negate. Why? The native republic *qua* negative relational term itself dissolves when the term 'white' is negated. More importantly, the demos dissolves if the identity of the term 'black' changes. Yet this is exactly what must be possible in a democracy. The play that is inherent in the logic of the social must be self-consciously alive in the social.

The self-referential border

Chantal Mouffe has recently returned to this problem in an extended essay on what she calls 'the democratic paradox'. She asks how it is possible to envisage a form of commonality that is strong enough to institute a demos, but, nevertheless, permits pluralism in respect of religion, morality, culture and political parties (Mouffe, 2000: 55). At stake for her is the relationship between liberalism and democracy. In order to elucidate better this tension, she draws on Carl Schmitt's rejection of liberal democracy (Schmitt, 1996). As far as a democracy is a particular democracy, and not a world state, it presupposes a substantive equality among its citizens. In other words, citizens necessarily partake of a common substance that distinguishes them from non-citizens.

Schmitt illustrated his argument by referring to the category of aliens and foreigners in modern democratic states. They are excluded from the demos even when citizenship is ostensibly founded on the basis of universal human equality. What they lacked, in other words, was this substantive equality. Schmitt argued that the demos is necessarily founded on a principle of homogeneity as its condition of possibility – on the basis of which these citizens are the same as each other and different from others. He concludes from this that the state was driven to exclude political pluralism and social differences (of language, culture, religion, and so on) among its citizens (Schmitt, 1996).

Mouffe agrees with Schmitt's premise, though she wants to avoid his conclusion. 'What matters', she says,

> is the possibility of tracing a line of demarcation between those
> who belong to the demos – and therefore have equal rights – and
> those who, in the political domain, cannot have the same rights
> because they are not part of the demos (Mouffe, 2000: 40).

This is a key problem for democratic theory. How does a democracy generate a limit that does not simultaneously dissolve its democratic – what Mouffe calls liberal – character? Her solution is to make the limit of the demos, its principle of discrimination, the result of the political process of hegemonic articulation (p. 56). 'The moment of rule', she argues, 'is indissociable from the very struggle about the definition of the people, about the constitution of its identity' (p. 56). It is not clear how Mouffe intends these remarks. Are they strictly analytical, or are they normative? In other words, is she describing how any limit comes into being, i.e. emerges through hegemonic struggle? Or is she saying that a liberal democracy would be one where the very principle of its unity was self-consciously available for contestation? If the latter, then her solution is unintelligible. If the unity of the state derived from the way it was defined, and such a definition was constitutionally available to contestation, then the state risked being *dissolved* every time such a contest was heard in good faith.

Yet Mouffe has not taken up the central challenge of Schmitt's fascism. The limit needs not simply to be intelligible: it must distinguish between friend and enemy. The principle or relative criterion according to which individuals are admitted or refused entry to the political community is a bet against nature. It contains an implicit hypothesis that defines the condition of their *fraternity*.

Fraternity

Let us return to the French Revolution, and think about the consequences of the term 'fraternity' for the political community. Listen to the words of Michelet:

> This nation [France] has two very powerful qualities that I do not find in any other. ... This principle, this idea, which was buried in the Middle Ages under the dogma of grace, is called brotherhood in the language of man .... This nation, considered thus as the asylum of the world, is much more than a nation. *It is a living brotherhood* (cited in Derrida, 1997: 227; emphasis added).

The limit of the French people is given by a special bond, i.e. a fraternal bond. This is what distinguishes the French from other peoples. But let us not forget, Jacques Derrida reminds us, that this fraternity is another name for friendship (Derrida, 1997: 238). It is, moreover, the basis of the French Republic's claim to universalism: France instantiates, close to its ideal form, the principle of friendship among people. Listen to Victor Hugo in 1863 on the events of 1789:

> In the twentieth century, there will be an extraordinary nation. It will be a great nation, but its grandeur will not limit its freedom. It will be famous, wealthy, thinking, poetic, cordial to the rest of humanity. It will be the sweet gravity of an older sibling .... The legislation of this nation will be a facsimile of natural law, as similar to it as possible. Under the influence of this motive nation, the incommensurable fallow lands of America, Asia, Africa and Australia will give themselves up to civilizing emigration .... *It will be more than a nation, it will be a civilization; better than a civilization, it will be a family.* Unity of language, currency, measure, meridian, code, fiduciary circulation to the utmost degree, money bills making anyone with twenty francs in his purse a person of independent means .... The capital of this nation will be Paris, and will not be named France; it will be called Europe. Europe in the twentieth century, and in those following, even more transfigured, will be called Humanity. Humanity, definitive nation .... What a majestic vision. ... *The fraternal continent is the future* (cited in Derrida, 1997: 264–65; emphasis added).

Let us start with the first term, 'nation'. Note the future tense of the sentences above. A movement is implied: from nation to something more than a nation. Derrida distinguishes between a *populace* and a *people* to capture a shift that is too easily missed if we don't read these terms symptomatically. We start with a group of people that is transformed in and through the revolutionary rupture. It is now more than a nation *qua* populace: it is potentially a nation *qua* people. This is what the revolution does: it transforms the very genetic structure of the populace. What is the difference between these concepts? The nation *qua* populace is a group of people with certain things in common: language, currency, measure, law and rules of exchange. The nation *qua* people is a fraternity. The former is merely an embryo, a potential; the latter is an entirely new creature. Revolution, this labour of deliverance, this struggle of blood and sweat, has hatched (germinated) a populace now bonded as a brothers, i.e. a people. Therein lies the extraordinariness of the French nation, according to Hugo: it approaches a perfect brotherhood. Moreover, such a fraternity is nothing less than an instantiation of the natural law itself. Hence this nation is identical with humanity (or, perhaps, Humanity) itself. Therein lies its duty: it has an obligation of tutelage to all other peoples, to lead them to fraternity so that they too may become nations.[3]

Therein lies the specificity of the demos since 1789. For the first time in history, it is imagined as a brotherhood, as a population bonded by special ties of fraternal solidarity. Derrida is adamant on this point: 'Let no one accuse me of unjustly incriminating the figure of fraternity ... with the supplementary accusation of "phallocentrism" or "androcentrism"' (Derrida, 1997: 235). Brotherhood is neither the universal class, nor a spiritual figure that can be instantiated in any concrete determination. A fraternity is precisely a very particular community of friends: it is one that is 'virile'. As proof, Derrida quotes again from Victor Hugo:

> What has befallen Paris? Revolution.
> Paris is the pivotal city around which, on a given day, history has turned ...
> The Commune is rightful; the Convention is right. This is superb. On one side the Populace, but sublimated; on the other, the People, but transfigured.
> And these two animosities have a love, the human race, and

> these two collisions result in *Fraternity*. This is the magnificence
> of our Revolution. ...
> On the fourteenth of July 1789, the hour of the virile age struck
> (cited in Derrida, 1997: 265–66; emphasis added).

It is worth unpacking these passages again. They make explicit how narrow the French Revolution became in *Hegemony and Socialist Strategy* (Laclau & Mouffe, 1990). They also give to the neglected term 'fraternity' its proper place. For Hugo, 1789 dissolved the contradiction – worse, antagonism – between the particular and the universal. The particular nation that is France, its determinate populace, is sublimated in and through the revolution to become a people transfigured – Humanity itself. At least, that is this people's potential – it is in their genes. And the reconciliation between the particular and the universal happens not on the side of liberty or equality, not on the side of law, but *on the side of fraternity*. The novelty of the French nation is not that it is founded on the basis of equality and liberty: it arises because the transformation of the *populace* (the people *qua* datum) into the *people* (the universal/humanity) produces a perfect brotherhood.

Herein lies the basis of a new principle of the political frontier: the demos coincides with the community of brothers. Its unity and its limit are given by the especially strong, 'virile' affective bonds that exist between its members.[4] We can understand why, with the coming of the nation, the border acquires a significance it never had before. Beyond its borders lie, if not enemies, then, at least, not friends. This is where Schmitt deduces the political as such: the friend can only be determined from within the opposition friend–enemy. We shall return to this shortly. This nation, this body of friends, however, is not (yet) the modern nation; the modern demos, that is, is not *logically* the modern nation. There is a space between them: one that is usually passed over as if they are identical. At stake is a concrete response to *the* philosophical question: What is the condition of friendship?

Before we continue, let us note the consequences of what we have been saying for our understanding of democracy. In the series, liberty, equality, fraternity, it is the last term that structures the other two; or rather: the first two derive from the third. In other words, the logic of equivalence that Laclau and Mouffe argue is born of the democratic revolution is, only a *secondary effect* of that revolution. Its primary effect is to establish the demos on the basis of *affective relations*. Put differently, we might say that liberty and equality are *ontic* facts: they belong to the sphere of *politics*. But fraternity is an *ontological* term.

The nation

This corresponds to a real political question: If the demos is a fraternity, what are its proper (historical) conditions of existence? Stated like this, we might say that the question of democracy has been obscured for a very long time: the question of democracy *qua* question of friendship is hardly posed today. From the perspective of such a question, however, we can correctly define the relationship between the demos and the (modern) nation. It was stated earlier that they were not necessarily identical. Rather, the modern nation – the nation *qua* historical community – emerges in the space of a particular reply to the following question of philosophy: What are the conditions of friendship? It is one that invokes a measure of population; in other words, it grounds the conditions of friendship on a cultural, linguistic and ultimately racial identity. This is a *literalist* reply to the question of philosophy. In the terms we discussed earlier, we might say that it simply reads off the nation *qua* people from the nation *qua* populace. A fraternity is literally a brotherhood; hence, family, i.e. kin as traced through culture and language. We have already heard this in Victor Hugo: '[France] will be more than a nation, it will be a civilization; better than a civilization, it will be a family.' Kinship, hence racial identity, becomes on these terms a proxy for fraternity.

This is the history of the national limit. At least since the American and French Revolutions of the eighteenth century, democracy was deemed to lodge in a populace with determinate racial/linguistic/

cultural traits. By the eighteenth century, this view was axiomatic for as diverse a group as Johan Gottfied Herder, John Stuart Mill and the French revolutionaries. The Committee of Public Safety, for example, opposed the cosmopolitan character of monarchical society precisely on these grounds: 'The monarchy', it pronounced in 1794, 'had good reason to resemble the Tower of Babel .... In a free society language must be the same for one and all' (cited in Wimmer, 2002: 60). Herder addressed a similar criticism to the Prussia of Frederick the Great: 'nothing was more manifestly contrary to the purposes of political government than the unnatural enlargement of states, the wild mixing of different human species and nations under one scepter' (cited in Wimmer, 2002: 59). Mill too was sceptical of the prospects of democratic government in anything less than the nation: 'Free institutions are next to impossible in a country made up of different nationalities [because] the boundaries of governments should coincide in the main with those of nationalities' (cited in Wimmer, 2002: 60).[5]

Affect

We have said that the logic of hegemony as described in *Hegemony and Socialist Strategy* (Laclau & Mouffe, 1990) stops short of being able to define a democratic limit. That is, either a hegemonic formation is unlimited, or it subverts its democratic, i.e. hegemonic, character in generating a boundary. Are there conditions, however, when this last statement is not true, i.e. when a hegemonic formation might be both limited and hegemonic? Of concern is a bounded hegemonic formation, i.e. a radical democracy.

According to Laclau and Mouffe, there are two logics at work in the political arena. The *logic of difference* operates by organising the discursive field as a string of positive identities. This produces the series: a, b, c, d, e, and so on. On the basis of this logic, however, there is no way of generating a limit. If, for example, what is beyond a positive identity is another positive identity, then the series is merely extended indefinitely, or, which is the same thing, the 'beyond' of the last term becomes an element *within* the series. Hence, if 'f' is the outside of 'e', it is merely another term *within* the series a, b, c, d, e, f, etc. What the authors of *Hegemony and Socialist Hegemony* thus say is that a border is produced through a process of 'cutting out'. A cluster of positive identities (say b, c, and d) must be cut out from the series (say, a, b, c, d, e, f). Yet this cutting out cannot happen according to the logic of difference. We have just seen why. 'It is only through negativity, division and antagonism', they say, 'that a formation can constitute itself as a totalizing horizon' (Laclau & Mouffe, 1990: 144). This is the *logic of equivalence*. The frontier emerges when the meaning of every identity in a hegemonic formation is fixed as the negative of that which lies beyond it. Let us be careful here. In appearance, Laclau and Mouffe's concept of the political resembles that of Schmitt. Schmitt defined the political as 'the most intense and extreme antagonism' (Schmitt, 1996: 29). On his terms, the more an antagonism resembles a political antagonism, the more it approaches a 'friend–enemy grouping' (Schmitt, 1996: 29). Is this not another way of describing the boundary in Laclau and Mouffe's terms? The demos acquires its identity relative to a negativity. Yet in Schmitt's terms, a negativity has become more than an analytical term: it designates an *affective* relation. This is precisely what is lacking in *Hegemony and Socialist Strategy*: the cathectic aspect of the political. It explains why, subsequent to *Hegemony and Socialist Strategy*, Laclau and Mouffe have both written separately on Schmitt. The stakes are very high for both of them. If the radical democratic project is to be anything more than an abstraction, it must be possible to instantiate itself as a concrete practice. Yet, as a practice, it seems unable to generate a limit without betraying its democratic intentions. This is the spectre of Schmitt: that radical democracy *qua* concrete state is, at best, illiberal, at worst, totalitarian.

On Populist Reason

Laclau has taken up this concern in his latest intervention, *On Populist Reason* (2005). We might say that this book is an exercise in historical recovery. In effect, Laclau returns to the democratic imaginary to salvage the third term in the revolutionary slogan: fraternity. His motives are not simply historical: unless he does this, his theory of the social cannot produce the social itself.

Let us recall that a *totality* emerges through the construction of chains of equivalence between identities. The totality is nothing, in other words, more than this provisional unity. It is provisional, moreover, because there is a permanent tension between the binding of identities in a unity (the logic of equivalence) and the assertion of their own positivity (the logic of difference). In other words, for there to be a totality in the first place, the logic of equivalence must be stronger than the logic of difference. This is the paradox of the totality according to Laclau: it is both impossible and necessary. It is '[i]mpossible', that is, 'because the tension between equivalence and difference is insurmountable; necessary because without some kind of closure, however precarious it might be, there would be no signification and no identity' (Laclau, 2005: 70).

There are two things to note here. Firstly, the unity of the social is not *conceptually* intelligible *a priori*. It is not ultimately grounded in something beyond the social itself: determination in the last instance by the economy, the spirit of the people and so on. Secondly, the totality, the unity of the social, requires a 'radical investment'. This is the site of Laclau's new departure: 'the *affective* dimension plays a central role' (Laclau, 2005: 71; emphasis added).

The chapter has discussed at some length how, according to Laclau and Mouffe, the concept of 'the people' (a popular formation) is produced. It emerges through the construction of equivalential bonds and the demarcation of an internal frontier. Yet for Laclau in his latest work, this is not enough. This is what he says: 'equivalential relations would not go beyond a vague feeling of solidarity if they did not crystallise in a certain discursive identity which no longer represents democratic demands *as* equivalent, but the equivalential link as such' (Laclau, 2005: 93; original emphasis). What is missing, in other words, is an explanation of how a plurality of identities 'becomes a singularity through its condensation around a popular identity' (p. 94). For the totality to be more than a fleeting instant, for it to become a properly hegemonic totality,[6] it must itself become the object of strong feelings and sentiments. This is what Laclau means by an investment. How does this happen? How, in other words, do identities that come together on the basis of their equivalence as unfulfilled demands become affective relations?

Laclau reminds us of two important aspects of popular identities. Firstly, they crystallise around a demand that is internally split: it is both a particular demand (the right of blacks to vote, for example), and it comes to stand for a wider universality (justice, for example). In this way, the right of blacks to vote becomes a horizon against which a multitude of diverse struggles are inscribed (workers' demands, the demands of women for equality, the demands of urban residents for affordable services, and so on). What they have in common *qua* demands is that they are unfulfilled. This is what Laclau means when he says that negativity is inherent to the equivalential chain (Laclau, 2005: 96).

Secondly, the more a particular identity (black, for example) comes to represent a whole series of identities (workers, women, urban residents, etc.), so its particular content (for the right to vote) becomes diluted amongst heterogeneous demands (for workers' rights, for women's rights, for rights in the city). What is important to note is that the identity 'black' becomes the nodal point of a broad front of demands. And if any of these constituent identities (women, workers, urban residents) stop identifying as 'black', the series disintegrates. What gives to the identity 'black', however, its ability to hold the series together? Let us say what does not. There is no *logical* reason for the series to hold together. This could only be the case if 'women' and 'workers' and 'urban residents' were, somehow, destined to come together in a common front – if they shared, that is, a common revolutionary spirit, or they occupied a common class position, etc. Hence there is no conceptual reason for the 'name'[7] 'black' to be the object of strong attachment. Something else must be involved; something, moreover, that Laclau has never before 'brought into the picture'. This is why *On Populist Reason* is such an important contribution.

This is what he says: 'It is clear ... that if an entity becomes the object of an investment – as in being in love, or in hatred – the investment belongs to the order of *affect*' (Laclau, 2005: 110; original emphasis). Moreover, 'the complexes which we call "discursive or hegemonic formations", which articulate differential and equivalential logics, would be unintelligible without the affective component' (p. 111).

If we return to our example, we might say that the name 'black' has the force of a glue because it becomes a 'source of enjoyment' (Laclau, 2005: 115). It does not just represent unfulfilled demands (for the vote, for workers' and women's rights, for affordable municipal services, etc.): it refers to relations of (a) love and friendship among workers and women and people denied the right to vote and those suffering unaffordable charges for water and electricity, etc. and (b) hate or loathing for those that negate these demands.

We can see how Laclau has completed his theory of the political by recovering the fraternal relation from the democratic imaginary. The couplet 'freedom' and 'equality' is structured by a third term: affect. But this is nothing other than the principle of fraternity. In other words, those that are free and equal are also those bonded in fraternity (Laclau's affective investment) – i.e. by love and friendship. Without this investment, 'the people' themselves do not exist. Hence, they cannot be free or equal.

Let us draw out the consequences of this conclusion. We are in a position, finally, to understand the condition of a bounded hegemonic formation, i.e. *a* democracy. We saw earlier how the logics of equivalence and difference could not produce a democratic boundary, merely the effect of a frontier (frontier effect). Every time a popular identity became a popular formation, it required the cutting out – exclusion – of the identity that negated it. Yet such a formation is anomalous in two respects. Firstly, it is not a democracy. Why?

A democratic formation, let us recall, is one where the logic of hegemony has become a self-conscious principle of the demos itself. Social actors understand that their identities, alliances and commonalities are provisional, political and contingent. Yet in a popular formation (a nation), the popular identity is fixed once and for all. At stake is the very intelligibility and unity of 'the people'. In the example we have been using, when 'black' *qua* popular identity (alliance among people without the right to vote, workers, women, urban residents) becomes black *qua* popular formation (a black republic), whites (the system of racial oppression, capitalism, patriarchy) must be cut out of the formation. When this happens, however, the unity of the people (those with a dark pigment, workers, etc.) depends on them still being black in the original sense. The moment they are free to elaborate new identities, the very unity of the demos dissolves. Secondly, a popular formation must constantly preserve that which it is driven to exclude. If it is too successful at eliminating its negative, it will dissolve its own conditions of being as well. Hence the process of cutting out must always be incomplete: more an effect than an absolute exclusion. But this subverts the formation of a boundary and returns us to the logic of a frontier effect.

The introduction of the affective relation allows us to overcome these anomalies. The unity of 'the people' is not simply a discursive effect: it is an affective one. We might say that the demos encloses persons that share a strong bond of solidarity. *This is the basis of its boundary: outside the demos lie, if not enemies, then not friends.* Several things follow from this. If a popular identity becomes an object of love or pleasure, then the social is held together by more than the equivalence of its constituent identities. Indeed, the affective relation, rather than the equivalential one, becomes the basis of its unity. Laclau says as much. But if the unity of the social is achieved on the basis of love or pleasure, and not simply equivalence, then, in principle, the logic of hegemony can be alive in the social formation without threatening its very integrity. In short: the affective bond allows us to think of a hegemonic formation with an external boundary; i.e. a *particular democratic society.*

Democratic love

If the condition of the demos is an affective relation among its citizens, then several questions present themselves. In the first place, will any affective relation do? Or does a democracy require a particular kind of solidarity among its citizens? If so, what are the conditions of democratic love? Laclau does not say anything about the first question, though he hints at an answer to the second.

Let us return to our example of blackness. Let us say that being black becomes an object of love, such that the unity of the social is achieved on the basis of this affective relation. *Workers* and *women* and *urban residents* and *people with a dark pigment* come together as a *people*, even when they no longer share common political or tactical interests. What they have in common is an especially strong bond as black people. Are there conditions when this love is democratic and when it is not?

Let us clarify this difference between democratic and non-democratic solidarity by thinking about their respective conditions. Laclau gives us an important clue about how we might approach this distinction. He suggests that the unity of the social is not something that happens simply at the level of words and images: it is not a question simply of identifying with national symbols, for example. It is 'embedded in material practices which can acquire institutional fixity' (Laclau, 2005: 106). Although Laclau invokes the name of Wittgenstein here, is this not, in fact, an oblique reference to Louis Althusser? Is this not a reference, that is, to the workings of the ideological state apparatus? This is not as far-fetched as it may seem. Laclau invokes Althusser elsewhere in this chapter of his book. Either way it is a useful way forward.

Let us return to the argument in the introduction of the present book. There we said that the citizen was an effect of democratic interpolation: the national subject is interpolated according to a measure of authenticity. The key point to emphasise is that for Althusser individuals are not simply caught in disciplinary apparatuses; they are also interpolated as subjects. What counts is the way that power is subjectivised – internalised as something one believes in for oneself. Let us recall an example of the way that interpolation happens. In the case of Christianity, writes Althusser, Christian religious ideology says:

> I address myself to you, a human individual called Peter (every individual is called by his name, in the passive tense, it is never he who provides his own name), in order to tell you that God exists and that you are answerable to him. It adds: God addresses himself to you through my voice (Scripture having collected the Word of God, Tradition having transmitted it, Papal Infallibility fixing it for ever on 'nice' points). It says: this is who you are: you are Peter! This is your origin, you were created by God for all eternity, although you were born in the 1920th year of Our Lord! This is your place in the world! This is what you must do! By these means, if you observe the 'law of God' you will be saved, you, Peter, and will become part of the Glorious Body of Christ (Althusser, 1997: 113).

This is a banal discourse, Althusser tells us, until something new and remarkable happens. Peter is interpolated as a subject when he replies: '"Yes, it really is me." "I am Peter, a Christian who believes in God and follows His laws and customs"' (Althusser, 1997: 133). The key moment, the moment of interpolation, happens, that is, when the subject (with a small 's') recognises that he or she does occupy the place that ideology designates for him or her; whether as a Christian, or a boss, or a worker (i.e. becomes a Subject with a capital 'S'). The key point to note is that obedience to the law comes when the law itself is internalised; when, that is, the subject of the law obeys the law because he or she believes in it.

Let us extend this logic to the figure of the citizen. Citizens are hailed as Subjects through democratic apparatuses. Democratic ideology says: 'Peter, you are a citizen. Even if you believe in God, here in the demos, the Law arises from the decisions that you and other citizens take collectively. You are free to have your own ideas. You are free to act upon them, but only insofar as you respect the equality of others, who are citizens too.'

A Citizen (with a capital 'C') as such – that is, *qua* Subject – emerges when he or she says: 'Yes, I really am a citizen. I have the same rights and responsibilities as those around me and I will respect them as citizens like me.' What counts is a series of processes (rituals, ceremonies) through which the individual comes to see that he or she really is like those around him or her, that they are all equal in worth, and that despite their differences, they share with each other a deep solidarity. This is how an election functions; even if its effects are short-lived. There in the queue, waiting to cast one's ballot, standing with others also waiting to cast theirs, irrespective of one's politics, background, wealth, culture, religion and so on, so that one comes to see and feel that one really is an individual, equal to those around one. Listen to Desmond Tutu about South Africa's first democratic elections. Writing at the time, he had this to say:

> What an incredible week it has been for us South Africans. We all voted on 27 and 28 April [1994] in the first truly democratic election in this beautiful country. We are still on Cloud Nine and have not yet touched terra firma. I said it was like falling in love. That is why it seems the sun is shining brighter, the flowers seem more beautiful, the birds sing more sweetly and the people – you know, the people are really beautiful. They are smiling, they are walking taller than before 27 April. They have suddenly discovered that they are all South Africans. And they are proud of that fact. ... They stood in the voting queues together – white, black, coloured, Indian – and they discovered that they were compatriots (Tutu, 2006: 257).

We should take Archbishop Tutu seriously here. In those queues, whites, blacks, coloureds and Indians became South Africans. It is there, even if only for a short moment, that they became beautiful to each other, fell in love, and developed a deep horizontal solidarity.

Is this not the challenge of democracy: to regularise such encounters so that they are part of the ordinary lived experience of people? Is this not the proper measure of deliberative or participatory democratic forums? They socialise individuals according to democratic norms and values. There, in the forum, one is called to listen to the other, to accord him or her respect, and, even when one disagrees forcefully with what he or she says, open oneself to his or her thinking. Hence, we might say that the value of multiplying the instances of democratic participation, namely the allocation of state budgets, the development of policy, the delivery of services and so on, is that it will proliferate democratic encounters. Aren't these forums, ultimately, likely to function efficiently and effectively when their members accord each other the respect due to citizens?

We can begin to develop a critique of liberalism from such a perspective. Liberalism asks individuals to treat each other with respect and tolerance in the political arena; it expects them to behave, that is, according to democratic norms. Yet, by valorising the market, and by reducing the (potential) opportunities for democratic participation – through privatisation, for example – it (a) lessens the chances of democratic socialisation, and (b) encourages institutions that interpolate individuals as self-interested (selfish) competitors. Is there not the same problem with certain kinds of post-colonial theory? They look forward to cosmopolitan conviviality while finding the principle of sameness among people of different cultures, geographies, religions and so on in their participation as consumers. In the same way, they value democratic norms while encouraging practices that are at odds with them.

What is important to note is that democratic interpolation opens the individual to the reasoning and demands of those around him or her. The citizen, in other words, is open to a measure of evidence (empirical facts and logical argumentation) upon which his or her beliefs are founded or against which they can be confounded.

Despite appearances, this is not how popular interpolation happens. The nationalist subject is interpolated within a *structure of circularity*.[8] Democratic interpolation is short-circuited so that any opening to the other is closed off.

We have an excellent insight into how this mechanism functions in the 1963 essay of Nat Nakasa, 'Johannesburg, Johannesburg'. It is worth citing at length:

> I remember having dinner with a friend in one of the less prosperous white suburbs. One of the guests that night was a talented Afrikaner painter. … My host had hinted earlier that the painter was a Nationalist [i.e. National Party supporter], a supporter of Dr. Verwoerd's apartheid policy. The same man had spent much of his afternoon trying to keep alive a newborn African baby which had been abandoned on a pavement. … Having talked about his paintings and jazz we gravitated inevitably to the colour question. I wanted to know if he really was a Nationalist, and he said yes. We had by now warmed to each other, lighting cigarettes for one and all, sharing the same concern about the food which seemed to take a long time getting ready.
>
> 'But what kind of a Nationalist are you?' I asked.
>
> 'But why?'
>
> 'How can you vote for apartheid and then come and drink brandy with me?'
>
> 'But there is nothing wrong in drinking brandy with you. I would like to drink with you anywhere. At my place or yours, for that matter.'
>
> 'What if I told you that I have no place?'
>
> 'What do you mean?'

'Just that, I have no place and that's because of the laws you vote for.'

'What? Where are you going to sleep tonight, for instance?'

'I don't know. I may sleep here; wherever I can find a bed tonight.'

The painter was moved. I liked seeing his puzzled face.

'Well, if … you mean what you've said, you can come and live with me. We have a whole empty room in that house.'

Now I stopped being amused. Something was wrong somewhere.

'But the party you vote for has passed the law which says that's illegal, too,' I said.

Now the painter was blushing. He looked the other way and picked up his glass. I became more and more irritated.

'Why are you a Nationalist if you are willing to stay with me? Don't you want the races to be separated?'

Suddenly, the painter took off his glasses and looked at me appealingly: 'You see,' he said, 'I am an Afrikaner. The Nationalist Party is my people's party. That's why I vote for it' (Nakasa, 1975: 21–23).

Let us note that as individuals the painter and Nakasa have much in common: they are both jazz enthusiasts, enjoy painting and are concerned by the delay in the serving of dinner. The painter is even worried that

Nakasa is homeless, and offers him a place to stay. What is important for our purposes is that Nakasa captures precisely the logic that governs the movement from a democratic logic to Nationalism (which we can also write with a lower case 'n' here – nationalism). The moment the painter becomes an Afrikaner, i.e. a nationalist, he ceases to belong to the same society as Nakasa: he ceases to belong to that world where strangers meet as equals and learn to like or dislike each other on the basis of their social qualities (common interests, common values, sense of humour, and so on). There we have a precise description of the nation. It is that domain where people do not meet as equals, but always already as representatives of 'peoples'. Therein lies the nationalist short-circuit.

Nationalist (Party) ideology says: 'You are Nat Nakasa, a black person. You may love jazz and painting and good conversation. You are likeable and friendly and interesting. But as a black, you are essentially unlike me, a white person.' The nationalist subject is rigidly caught in a paradoxical structure where his or her relation to others is defined in advance, before meeting or experiencing them, if you like. Every encounter is always already closed: it can only confirm what one already knows (that blacks have good rhythm, that Jews are miserly, that Arabs are Islamic fundamentalists, that Germans like beer, that the English have a good sense of humour, that Nigerians are corrupt, that the French are arrogant, and so on).

This is the general form of the nation. It is composed of subjects who are marked by a surplus *vis-à-vis* belief. They are indifferent to empirical vicissitudes, because their attitude to other persons and things is always already built into their identity as authentic national subjects. Interpolation does not so much instil within individuals a dominant ideology, in the sense of ideas and beliefs, as organise a *way* of thinking and acting. In other words, the particular content of democratic and/ or nationalist ideas is not necessarily born in either the democratic organisation or the nationalist movement. The point is that popular interpolation organises ideas and concepts in a paradoxical structure such that the relation among terms is always already given in advance.

We are in a position, finally, to give to the demos its proper limit as a democracy. The boundary encloses citizens who share a special solidarity produced in and through democratic encounters. What lies beyond the demos is not another nation, but the nation *tout court*.

Let us conclude with something Alain Badiou has recently written regarding Israel:

> Truly contemporary states or countries are always cosmopolitan, perfectly indistinct in their identitarian configuration. They assume the total contingency of their historical constitution, and regard the latter as valid only on condition that it does not fall under any racialist, religious, or more generally 'cultural', predicate. Anything else is simply archaic (Badiou, 2006: 163).

Yet this is only the ordinary state of affairs in one sense. Every state is *in itself* cosmopolitan, indistinct and contingent because its borders never coincide with any one ethnic or cultural or religious group, and because its particular social character is not the expression of some or other pre-given identity. Yet we must still struggle for this basic fact to become part of the democratic imaginary itself.

Endnotes

Notes to Introduction

1   The term is taken from Mbembe (2001).

2   Discussed in detail in chap. 4.

3   Discussed in detail in chap. 3.

4   I have borrowed this schema from Etiennne Balibar, who describes the 'double conditional proposition' on which universalism rests: 'if men are free (and must be treated as such by political institutions), it is because they are equal, and if they are equal (and must be recognized as such) it is because they are all free' (Balibar, 2004: 59). Hence, exclusions from citizenship are no longer based on what is outside humanity, but rather on what is not free.

5   By a 'mark of population', I mean something similar to what Etienne Balibar has termed a 'fictive ethnicity' (Balibar, 2004: 8). He used the term to refer to the 'nationalization of societies and peoples and thus of cultures, languages, genealogies' (p. 8). This is a process that results in the 'subjective interiorisation of the idea of the border – the way individuals represent their place in the world to themselves ... by tracing in their imaginations impenetrable borders between groups to which they belong or by subjectively appropriating borders assigned to them from on high, peacefully or otherwise. That is, they develop cultural or spiritual nationalism (what is sometimes called "patriotism," the "civic religion")' (p. 8). He continues: 'This is why the democratic composition of people in the form of the nation led inevitably to systems of exclusion: the divide between

"majorities" and "minorities" and, more profoundly still, between populations considered native and those considered foreign, heterogeneous, who are racially or culturally stigmatized' (p. 8). In a similar vein, I understand a mark of population to produce the effect of a frontier between and within populations. It designates those who, in the Greek sense of demos, are properly regarded members of 'the people', i.e. as part of the collective subject of representation, decision-making and rights. I have refrained, however, from referring to an ethnicity, primarily because the term is already strongly associated with other meanings. There is a substantial literature on ethnicity that centres on notions of a genealogical or kinship community. I wanted to avoid confusion with this idea. Even if nations are usually imagined as 'families' in this sense, a mark of population is not reducible to a genealogical relation. In addition, I wanted to convey a practice of belonging that centred on a process of definition, and to stress that this process of defining the limits of the demos involves invoking a quality (being urban-urbane, speaking a particular language, reflecting a culture) or a substance (race). I have called them 'marks of population'. I argue, moreover, that the measure of the nation – these marks – is determined in the nationalist movement. See also Balibar (2002).

6   The expression is that of Bahro (1978).

7   My thanks here to Göran Therborn for his comments.

Notes to Chapter 1

1   Afrikaans term for the Afrikaner people.

2   For example, Aubrey (1991) and Cope (1993).

3   Is Verwoerd protesting too much here? The people had absolutely not remained 'white' in his terms. Indeed, Malherbe's text is a fraud for the racially mixed coupling it simply effaces from the historical record.

4   So important does Chatterjee deem this discourse that it is cited twice in his book.

5   This is the influential typology of African politics used by Allen (1995).

6   Bayart cannot decide whether there is a form of state peculiar to Africa that warrants the designation 'African state', or whether the phenomena he observes are characteristic of something more general.

7   On the state, see Bayart (1993); on governance and politics, see Allen (1995); on corruption, see Szeftel (1998).

8   This term is taken from the title of a recent special edition of the journal *Public Culture*, edited by Achille Mbembe and Sarah Nutall (Mbembe & Nutall, 2004).

9   The title of Mbembe's (2001) book is instructive. The substance of his description is drawn from a case study of Cameroon.

10 I have paraphrased here from Althusser's (1990: 203) description of the Hegelian totality, and, in particular, the way that the Idea functions as an essence of which the social totality merely reflects its phenomena. This seems to me appropriate, especially in light of Mbembe's reading of the master–slave dialectic. For a critique of Mbembe (2001) that makes a similar point to the one above, see Jeremy Weate's review of *On the Postcolony* (Weate, 2003). This is exactly the criticism that Allen applies to these sorts of studies. He describes them as 'blind alleys', locating them within a genus of studies that attempt 'a single characterisation of African politics' (Allen, 1995: 302). He is thinking here of those studies that characterise African politics in terms of 'personal rule' (Jackson & Rosberg, 1982; Sandbrook, 1985); or as a variant of the early modern state (Callaghy, 1992); or as the politics of the belly (Bayart, 1993), or of ethnicity (Ingham, 1990) or of chaos (Kaplan, 1994). Despite the remarkable diversity of African politics, such studies reduce this variety to mere phenomena of *the* African state or *the* postcolony. 'There is too much variation in politics in Africa', however, 'for a single structure or process to be adequate for the analysis of those histories,' Allen objects (Allen, 1995: 302).

Notes to Chapter 2

1   If Zizek is being provocative here, is this not precisely the argument of Jean and John Comaroff? The Southern Tswana, they suggest, had no alternative but to be inculcated into the forms of European discourse. Their text is replete with sentences like: 'They could not avoid internalising the terms through which they were being challenged' (Comaroff & Comaroff, 1991: 213). See also Donham (2001).

2   It is difficult to understand how the post-colonial regime is able to achieve such an absolute hegemony of ideas, cultural repertoires and concepts. Surely, if the state is weakened by the effects of International Monetary Fund-dictated structural adjustment and other measures, it is unable to leverage the kind of total control of society (over families, educational institutions, and so on) that would be required to 'inscrib[e] the dominant and the dominated within the same episteme'?

3   The argument is not rescued, moreover, by way of Durkheimian fiat. Anderson's argument does not permit him to say that the nation idea is premised on a religious epistemology, but that its language and vocabulary are secular. If this were the case, he might argue that the style of the nation resembles that of other religious ideas, but that its substance is new – it employs a novel language to express what are, basically, religious ideas. In this way, he could say that the nation expresses a religious sentiment (the will to immortality) in a new, secular language. But such a strategy would be inconsistent with the basic argument of *Imagined Communities*. The nation, he suggests, is not *superficially* unlike kingdoms and dynasties: it is *radically different*, the product of a new style of thinking. The nation idea is the consequence of a radical breach with the religious epistemology.

4   It is precisely the idea of rights issuing from human nature that has earned the notion suspicion – if not downright derision – in certain quarters. See, for example, Badiou (2002).

5   New Public Management was the broad name of a movement in the 1980s, originating in Britain and the USA, that sought to improve the efficiency of the public sector by making it operate more like private sector businesses.

6   By cosmopolitan, I refer to a political community where racial, cultural, linguistic and/or religious traits are not criteria for membership.

7   See, for example, Chantal Mouffe's engagement with Schmitt (Mouffe, 2000).

Notes to Chapter 3

1 Garveyism is that form of black nationalism that originated from the work of the founder of the Universal Negro Improvement Association (UNIA) and African Communities League, Marcus Garvey. Garvey was born on 17 August 1887 in Jamaica. He went to America in 1916, arriving just in time to witness the bloody riots in East St Louis in 1917, followed by the revolts of 1919. He organised a chapter of the UNIA when he settled in New York City.

2 Sampson, in his Foreword to Bernstein's *Memory against Forgetting*, confesses watching the Bernsteins and other Marxists with a mixture of admiration and apprehension: 'I knew I would never have the courage to commit myself as they did to a programme which was very likely to lead to jail; but I worried about the extent of the commitment to international communism' (Sampson, 1999: x).

3 Rusty Bernstein was arrested at Lilliesleaf Farm, Rivonia, on 11 July 1963. He was tried for sabotage alongside Nelson Mandela, Walter Sisulu, Govan Mbeki and others at what came to be called the Rivonia Trial. Although Bernstein himself was acquitted, he was immediately re-arrested and subsequently left South Africa for exile in the United Kingdom. Mandela and the others were found guilty and sentenced to life imprisonment.

4 See the following footnote.

5 The alliance was composed of the ANC, the South African Indian Congress, the Congress of Democrats (for whites) and the Coloured People's Congress. These four organisations sat together on the Joint Executive.

6 In 1924 the South African elections were won by a pact comprising the National and Labour Parties. Soon afterwards, the new government introduced the 'civilised labour policy' reserving certain categories of work exclusively for whites.

7 We should note that this turmoil was not simply over political-strategic issues. After 1928, Communist Parties outside the Soviet Union were ordered to 'bolshevise' their internal structures, i.e. 'purify' their ranks of those deemed partisan to the 'incorrect' party line. In South Africa, the CPSA went through a period of purges that saw many of its most

accomplished leaders expelled from the organisation (including Bunting). Given, however, that Comintern's line kept changing, the activities of the party were conducted in a poisonous atmosphere of suspicion and political schizophrenia. In particular, following the 'native republic' slogan, the party was divided between what were discussed at the time as 'isolationists' (those not in favour of alliances with 'national' elements) and 'united-fronters' (those that were). Things came to a head in 1935 when the dispute was taken to Moscow for arbitration. The Comintern line had just swung back in favour of 'united-fronters' against fascism. Lazar Bach, representing the so-called 'isolationists', quickly found himself out of favour with the Comintern. He was subsequently arrested, sentenced to death and finally killed in a labour camp. For more about this, see Drew (2000) and Davidson *et al.* (2003). See also Drew (1996).

8   Communism in this statement certainly refers to what Lenin also discussed as socialism, i.e. to a workers' and peasants' republic.

9   The CPSA was relaunched as the SACP, as an underground movement, in 1953.

10 Let us note that the relationship between race and class has, since 1962, been the topic of a rich and furious debate in South Africa. To trace its details and its many turns would take us too far from our present subject matter. But in order to provide some background, it is worth sketching very broadly some of its key terms. In the early 1970s, a number of South African scholars traced essentially functionalist links between the system of racial oppression and the system of capitalist exploitation. Their arguments rested on the notion of 'cheap labour'. Essentially, they argued, the nature of South African gold mining (low-yield ore, high technological costs of production and an externally set gold price) meant that the entire enterprise was unprofitable unless the mines could massively reduce fixed costs by employing cheap labour. In short, not an ounce of gold would have been mined without recourse to cheap labour. The mechanism for recruiting such labour, they argued, was the migrant labour system. The system of racial oppression was designed to keep black families beholden to a rural, agricultural economy that could cover the costs of their biological, but not their social reproduction. For this purpose, black men were forced to enter the capitalist economy to sustain their rural

households. But, because a large portion of the costs of reproducing the family were covered by farming, the wage paid to such workers was effectively subsidised by the agricultural economy.

Apartheid, in this analysis, emerged at the moment of profound crisis in the migrant system; when, that is, a more radical state intervention was required to prevent black urbanisation and maintain the reserve economies in a delicate balance between starvation and poverty. Here, the racial ideology of apartheid was a cover for the class structure that it disguised. See Legassick (1972; 1977), Johnstone (1976) and Wolpe (1974). This is not the place to review the vast literature that these analyses generated. Suffice it to say that they supposed an instrumental 'capitalist state', reduced racism and Afrikaner nationalism to an ideological effect, supposed that apartheid was somehow the product of a preconceived plan and ignored the peculiar historicity of black societies themselves.

These arguments were not simply met by liberal authors who saw a necessary disjuncture between the capitalist economy and apartheid – and looked forward to a day when the normal logic of capitalism would dissolve these 'irrational' racial fetters – but by a younger generation of Marxist scholars who posited an historical – as opposed to a logical – relationship between race and class. What they suggested was that in the period after World War II, state interventions in the economy, as well as private-sector investment in manufacturing, led to the substantial growth of the industrial sector. By the 1970s the manufacturing sector had invested heavily in mechanisation and made technological improvements to its processes. In this regard, its members canvassed more strongly for an urbanised, better-paid, better-educated work force as a means of stabilising and improving productivity. At the same time, the apartheid state invested heavily in decentralisation – going so far in the 1970s as to declare the former reserve areas to be 'independent states' – as a means of shoring up the rural population. This included mass removals of 'surplus' people to the Bantustans. This was necessary to appease the agricultural and mining sectors, which found it difficult to attract labourers capable of earning better wages in manufacturing jobs. What these historians provided, therefore, was a more disaggregated view of capital and a less absolute analysis of the relationship between apartheid and capitalism. See Bonner, Delius & Posel (1993). Moreover, as the secondary and tertiary sectors of the economy grew in importance, and as the struggle against racial oppression intensified, including on the international stage with the imposition of economic sanctions, so that struggle became increasingly disruptive to the economy. Apartheid, that is, came to bear not simply a contingent relation to capitalist production, but a negative relation.

11 The Tri-Cameral Parliament was another oddity of apartheid constitutional planners. It sought to resolve two contradictory political imperatives: safeguard white political control while accommodating (some) non-whites into the political community. This was impossible if one were to accept the principle of universal franchise in a common polity. Non-whites were numerically superior, and granting them citizenship rights, including the right to vote, would see the dissolution of white power. In this regard the new constitutional dispensation appealed to two principles: those of group rights and proportionality. The government held that each racial group (excluding blacks) coincided with a cultural group that had its own specific needs and obligations, which in turn required representation in its 'own' elected assembly. Hence the constitution provided for a House of Assembly (for whites), a House of Delegates (for coloureds) and a House of Representatives (for Indians).

Each of these elected parliaments had autonomous rights to debate and legislate on what were called 'own affairs' – matters supposedly concerning each respective group alone. In the parlance of the day, this was intended to 'prevent race groups interfering in the daily affairs of each other'. What was defined as an 'own affair', however, was at the discretion of the state president – who was elected solely from the members of the white House of Assembly. But this was not the sole mechanism through which white power was preserved. The second was through the principle of proportionality. The constitution accepted that there were certain issues that were 'general affairs' and that should be decided upon in a forum representing whites, coloureds and Indians together. This body was called the President's Council (PC). Representation in the PC was determined according to the principle of proportionality. Excluding the black majority, the white population, on the basis of census figures, was deemed to outnumber the coloured population by 2:1. Coloureds, in turn, outnumbered Indians 2:1. Hence, in the PC, whites were granted 20 seats, coloureds 10 and Indians 5. Moreover, the president directly appointed 25 delegates. The constitution thus secured white political control in two ways. In the first place, any matter could be declared a white 'own affair' and referred solely to the white House of Assembly for decision or it could be referred to the PC, where whites had an automatic advantage. In all of this, blacks were excluded. It was not difficult to see why: they constituted the vast majority of South Africans. The official apartheid excuse was that blacks were said not to be citizens of South Africa, but of their respective 'ethnic' homelands (independent states).

12 The area that today makes up the Western, Eastern and Northern Cape Provinces.

13 The Group Areas Act designated the South African territory according to racial criteria, allocating to racial groups separate and segregated residential areas.

14 While so-called independence was being imposed on the then Transkei and Ciskei, Buthelezi refused to accept such 'independence' for the region of KwaZulu. He did, however, agree to a politically autonomous region governed through an elected parliament.

15 This alliance was only formalised after the unbanning of the ANC and SACP in 1990. Prior to that, formal links between the trade union and illegal parties would have made Cosatu itself liable to banning.

Notes to Chapter 4

1 Classical Marxism could be profoundly ambivalent about colonialism. It may have been brutal and violent, but it was frequently viewed as progressive. Marx, for example, wrote about British colonialism in India that it was the condition of a Western society and the 'annihilation' of the old Asiatic one: 'England, it is true, in causing a social revolution in Hindustan was actuated by the vilest interests, and was stupid in her manner of enforcing them. But that is not the question. The question is, can mankind fulfil its destiny without a fundamental revolution in the social state of Asia? If not,

whatever the crimes of England she was the unconscious tool of history in bringing about that revolution' (cited in Said, 1978: 153). Engels too deemed the French colonisation of Algeria 'favourable to the progress of civilisation'. An industrial society, he argued, was immediately preferable to one composed of Bedouin 'thieves', dominated by feudal lords and characterised by plunder and barbarism (cited in Macey, 2000: 480).

2   We can now understand why traditional authorities are difficult to reconcile to the terms of the national democratic state. It is not simply that such authorities are not democratic; the problem lies with the fact that they produce and reproduce their subjects, not in the image of the nation, but in the image of the lineage group and clan.

3   Thanks to Ulrike Kistner for this formulation.

4   For a fuller discussion of the difficult relation between the women's movement and the nationalist movement, see Hassim (forthcoming).

5   'Tiens, un nègre!' C'était vrai. Je m'amusais.

'Tiens, un nègre!' Le cercle peu à peu se resserrait.

Je m'amusais ouvertement.

'Maman, regarde le nègre, J'ai peur! Peur! Peur!'

Voila qu'on se mettait à me craindre. Je voulus m'amuser jusqu'à m'étouffer, mais cela m'était devenu impossible. Maintenant, ils avaient commencé à avoir peur de moi. Je voulais rire jusqu'à ce que j'éclate, mais c'était devenu impossible. ...

Alors le schéma corporel, attaqué en plusieurs points, s'écroula, cèda la place à un schéma épidermique racial'.

6   'Prospero, tu es un grand illusionniste :

le mensonge, ça te connaît.

Et tu m'as tellement menti,

Menti sur le monde, menti sur moi-même,

Que tu as fini par m'imposer

Une image de moi-même:

Un sous-développé, comme tu dis,

Un sous-capable,

Voilà comment tu m'as obligé à me voir,

Cette image, je la haïs ! Et elle est fausse !

Mais maintenant, je te connais, vieux cancer,

Et je me connais aussi!'

7 'mon originelle géographie [Martinique] ...; la carte du monde faite à mon usage, non pas teinte aux arbitraires couleurs des savants, mais la géométrie de mon sang répandu, j'accepte; et la détermination de ma biologie, non prisonnière d'un angle facial, d'une forme de cheveux, d'un nez suffisamment aplati, d'un teint suffisamment mélanien, et la négritude, non plus indice céphalique, ou un plasma, ou un soma, mais mesurée au compas de la souffrance.'

Notes to Chapter 5

1 This complex more or less corresponds with what today are the boundaries of the province of Gauteng.

2 Images of this fighting were captured by a group of photographers that styled themselves the 'Bang Bang Club'. In April of 1994, only days after one of the group, Kevin Carter, received a Pulitzer Prize, Greg Marinovich and fellow photographer Ken Oosterbroek were shot while covering a firefight in Tokoza.

3 Author's interview with Captain du Toit, commander of South African National Defence Force Group 41, Germiston, 14 June 1995.

4 Migration had long been integrated into the initiation practices of various black polities, constituting an important entry point into manhood. Peter Delius, for example, found among the Pedi that a trip to the mines was incorporated as a stage in the transition to manhood: 'The tendency of Pedi migrants to cluster at particular points of employment ensure that, while entire age grades seldom found work at one place, sections often did and could practice many of the activities – including singing, dancing and fighting – appropriate to mashoboro [initiation]' (Delius, 1993: 129).

5 Author's interview with an induna, 26 July 1995.

6 This was the name of Inkatha before it became the Inkatha Freedom Party in 1990 – indicating, supposedly, its progression from cultural movement to political party.

7   The Transvaal was the name of one of the four provinces of the Republic
    of South Africa as it was from 1910 until 1994. Its area was basically that
    north of the Vaal River, including what are today the provinces of Gauteng
    (including Johannesburg), Limpopo and Mpumalanga, and parts of North-
    West Province.

Notes to Chapter 6

1   GEAR was a macro-economic policy framework introduced by the
    government in 1996 to spur economic growth to 6 per cent per year.

2   This expression comes from Bahro (1978).

3   See, for example, Saul (1991).

4   For an explanation of the terms 'charterist' and 'workerist', see the
    discussion of Fosatu in chap. 3.

5   'According the Department of Community Development, the Manenberg
    community is "dysfunctional" because family units tend towards
    disintegration and are thus incapable of socialising ("interpolating" would
    be theoretically more precise) their youth into adulthood. As a result, young
    men and women are raised in, and through, gang structures that replace
    the function of the nuclear household. These attach little importance to
    education and to the acquisition of the skills necessary to participate in the
    formal economy. This, in turn, compounds the dependency of residents on
    the informal economy, which is increasingly characterised by the drug trade
    and other criminal activities.

    Gangs, moreover, are prone to violence, producing, as a result, high levels
    of stress and violence-induced trauma; are involved in sexual practices that
    encourage teenage pregnancy and HIV/Aids; control the informal economy
    and hence deepen the dependency of families and residents on criminality. It
    follows, therefore, that "treating" dysfunctionality to make possible appropriate
    sustainable development is a question, not simply of trauma counselling, or
    Alcoholics Anonymous, or better policing, but of measures that (a) build and/
    or consolidate the integrity of nuclear families in the face of growing formal
    unemployment and (b) provide youth in unstable families with social outlets

other than gangs' (Chipkin, 2003: 74).

6   See chap. 2, fn 5.

7   The reference here is to civil society in its proper Hegelian sense. The discussion of civil society comes in the third part of *The Philosophy of Right* (Hegel, 2001), in the section on 'Ethical life'. Civil society does not simply refer to that part of society between the family and the state. It refers to an ethical order where the realisation of one's own selfish needs is based on the recognition of the needs, happiness, livelihood and rights of others. At stake for Hegel is an order of interdependence governed by ethical constraints. The emergence of civil society, therefore, refers precisely to the emergence of this ethical order.

Notes to Chapter 7

1   This elementary paradox is not peculiar to South Africa: it is foundational to the political community *per se*. Even in the act of creating itself, the polis must necessarily assume it already exists. Why else should it combine these particular peoples, unless, even prior to their coming together, they already share some or other property, purpose or spirit? At stake is a people *in itself* becoming *for itself*.

2   This refers to the borders of 1910 that set the limits of the Union of South Africa and later, from 1961, the Republic of South Africa. The new territories that emerged from the apartheid-inspired process of Balkanisation in the 1970s were never recognised as legitimate states by anyone other than the apartheid government. It was to the South Africa of the 1910 borders that the ANC and other organisations appealed during the anti-apartheid struggle.

3   I owe this formulation to Teun Dekker, a friend and colleague at St Antony's College, Oxford.

4   By identity, I do not mean a subjective quality: it is not a question of identification. Identity refers here to a quality of sameness, to that in respect of which a person is identical to someone or something else. Despite the risk of confusion, I prefer it to the rather clumsy term 'sameness'.

5   As I write, people from across the world are gathered in St Peter's Square for

the funeral of Pope John-Paul II. It is precisely this dynastic principle that makes the Catholic community a cosmopolitan one: anyone, irrespective of race, language, geography, gender or culture, is potentially a Catholic. This is true precisely because what counts is love for the Christian God as represented on Earth by the figure of the Pope. According to the dynastic principle, if one can accept the divine providence of the sovereign (be he/she prince or pope) one is potentially admissible to the political community. We can thus better understand why Jews were the objects of such extraordinary violence in Christian dynasties. By refusing the divinity of Christ, they challenged the very principle of sovereignty on which authority was based. What they challenged, not purposefully, but just by being Jewish, therefore, was the very principle of the unity of the polis.

6   What the people of South Africa did have in common was that in the past the apartheid state had exercised authority over them, either as citizens or as subjects. In the same way, why was the limit of the new South African people not given by the jurisdiction of the post-apartheid state? Such a fiction is not available to a state that had to derive its legitimacy from the *will of the people*. In other words, for the state to be seen to be legitimate, 'the people' must necessarily precede it. It cannot be seen to be the sole basis of their existence, which would risk rendering its own sovereignty arbitrary.

7   This symbolic principle of reconciliation was fundamentally unstable. It required not simply that black South Africans should accept that those who testified at the commission represented them; it required, in addition, that white South Africans recognised in the testimonies of white perpetrators their own complicity in horrors and crimes. If the first was an uncontroversial expectation, white South Africans, generally, have refused the second. 'It is something of a pity', wrote Tutu in the final report, 'that, by and large, the white community failed to take advantage of the Truth and Reconciliation process. ... Apart from the hurt that it causes to those who suffered, the denial by so many white South Africans even that they benefited from apartheid is a crippling, self-inflicted blow to their capacity to enjoy and appropriate the fruits of change' (TRC, 1998: Foreword, Vol. I, chap. 1, sec. 71). It remains,

however, a coherent model. Forgiveness creates a bond between specific peoples, in respect of which they share a common and particular history.

8　This is the precise formulation of the rainbow nation. God is usually not mentioned, yet without the divine referent there is nothing on which to base the sameness-in-diversity of the people.

Notes to Conclusion

1　See, for example, Gilroy (2004).

2　Although, Mouffe (2000) cites liberalism in particular, her comments are true for any politics that appeals to a universal subject. Indeed, one wonders to what extent she uses the term 'liberal' somewhat playfully, if not provocatively, in her book to refer to democratic theory *tout court*.

3　We can note that Etienne Balibar (2004: 57) argues as follows: 'There is a material correlation between the development of the nation-form ... and the dominant position occupied in the world-economy by the nations in the course of formation.' In this sense, he continues, the 'trajectory of the modern nation is entirely circumscribed by the history of colonization and decolonization.'

4　It is immediately clear in the case of women. If the demos is a fraternity, and fraternity the name for the friendship between brothers – between men – then women are (not yet) admissible to it because not quite brothers, i.e. friends. See Derrida (1997: 238).

5　See Habermas (2001) and Greenfeld (1992). Among historians, there is some disagreement about the origin of the nation. The disagreement hinges on whether nations are 'modern' events or more ancient. At stake is the date 1789 (the French Revolution) or even 1776 (the American Declaration of Independence) as the starting date of the nation. Yet, for already 150 years before the civil wars in England in the seventeenth century, suggests Leah Greenfeld, sovereignty was deemed to lodge in nation states, power and authority thought to derive from the nation-people.

6　Hence, by implication, hegemony is a temporal concept. It refers to a discursive field where the meaning of terms is fixed for more than an instant.

This begs the question: How long is an instant?

7   'Name' is the term that Laclau (2005) uses to designate the term that keeps an assemblage of heterogeneous elements together: 'the unity of the equivalential ensemble, of the irreducibly new collective will in which particular equivalences crystallise, depends entirely on the social productivity of a name' (p. 108).

8   My thanks to Peter Hudson for this expression.

Bibliography

Ackah, William B. *Pan-Africanism: Exploring the Contradictions*. Aldershot: Ashgate, 1997.

Adeeko, Adeleke. 'Bound to violence? Achille Mbembe's *On the Postcolony*.' *West African Review*, 3(2), 2002, pp. 1–15.

Agamben, Giorgio. *State of Exception* (trans. Kevin Attell). Chicago & London: University of Chicago Press, 2005.

Agnew, John. 'Sovereignty regimes: Territoriality and state authority in contemporary world politics.' *Annals of the Association of American Geographers*, 95(2), 2005, pp. 437–61.

Allen, Chris. 'Understanding African politics.' *Review of African Political Economy*, 65, 1995, pp. 301–20.

Althusser, Louis. *For Marx*. London: Verso, 1990.

—. 'Ideology and ideological state apparatuses (notes towards an investigation).' In Slavoj Zizek (ed.). *Mapping Ideology*. London & New York: Verso, 1997.

ANC (African National Congress). 'Africans' Claims in South Africa.' Congress Series No. II. Johannesburgh: ANC, 1943. http://www.anc.org.za/ancdocs/history/claims.html#1

—. *The Reconstruction and Development Programme: A Policy Framework*. Johannesburg: Umanyano, 1994.

—. 'The state, property relations and social transformation.' *Umrabulo*, 5, Third Quarter, 1998.

Anderson, Benedict. *Imagined Communities: Reflections on the Origin and Spread of Nationalism*. London & New York: Verso, 1991.

Appiah, Kwame Anthony. *In My Father's House: A Statement of African Ideology*. Oxford: Oxford University Press, 1992.

Aubrey, Elliot. *Zulu: Heritage of a Nation*. Cape Town: Struik, 1991.

Badiou, Alain. *L'Ethique: Essai sur la conscience du mal*. Paris: Hatier, 2002. (*Ethics*. London: Verso, 2002.)

—. *Polemics*. London & New York: Verso, 2006.

Balibar, Etienne. 'Propositions on Citizenship.' *Ethics*, 98(4), July 1988, pp. 723–730.

—. 'World borders, political borders' (trans. Erin M. Williams). *PMLA*, 117, 2002, pp. 71–78. French text first published in *Transeuropéennes*, 17, 1999–2000, pp. 9–17.

—. *We, the People of Europe? Reflections on Transnational Citizenship* (trans. James Swenson). Princeton & Oxford: Princeton University Press, 2004.

Bascom, W. R. & M. Herskovits (eds). *Continuity and Change in African Cultures*. Chicago: University of Chicago Press, 1959.

Baskin, Jeremy. *Striking Back: A History of Cosatu*. Johannesburg: Ravan Press, 1991.

Bayart, Jean-Francois. *The State in Africa: The Politics of the Belly*. Paris: Fayard, 1993.

Berman, Bruce. 'Nationalism, ethicity and modernity: The paradox of Mau Mau.' *Canadian Journal of African Studies*, 25(2), 1991, pp. 181–206.

Bernstein, Rusty. *Memory against Forgetting: Memoirs from a Life in South African Politics, 1938–1964*. Johannesburg: Penguin, 1999.

Biko, Steven. *Steve Biko: I Write What I Like. A Selection of His Writings*. Randburg: Ravan Press, 1996.

—. 'Black souls in white skins.' 1996a. In Biko (1996), pp. 19–26.

—. 'We blacks.' 1996b. In Biko (1996), pp. 27–32.

—. 'Fragmentation of the black resistance.' 1996c. In Biko (1996), pp. 33–39.

—. 'Some cultural concepts.' 1996d. In Biko (1996), pp. 40–47.

—. 'The definition of Black Consciousness.' 1996e. In Biko (1996), pp. 48–53.

Bharo, Rudolf. *The Alternative in Eastern Europe*. London: Verso, 1978.

Bonner, Philip, P. Delius & D. Posel (eds). *Apartheid's Genesis: 1935–1962*. Johannesburg: Ravan Press & Witwatersrand University Press, 1993.

Bonner, Philip & Vusi Ndima. 'The roots of violence on the East Rand 1980–1990.' Institute for Advanced Social Research seminar paper, University of the Witwatersrand, Johannesburg, 1999.

Brass, Paul R. *Ethnicity and Nationalism: Theory and Comparison.* London: Sage, 1991.

Bunting, Brian. *Moses Kotane: South African Revolutionary.* London: Inkululeko Press, 1975.

Breuilly, John. *Nationalism and the State.* Manchester: Manchester University Press, 1982.

Cabral, Amilcar. *Revolution in Guinea: An African People's Struggle.* New York: Monthly Press Review, 1969.

Callaghy, T. *Politics and Society in Contemporary Africa*, 2nd ed. Basingstoke: Macmillan, 1992.

Césaire, Aimé. *Une tempête.* Paris: Éditions du Seuil, 1969.

—. *Cahier d'un retour au pays natal.* Paris & Dakar: Présence Africaine, 1983.

Chatterjee, Partha. *The Nation and Its Fragments: Colonial and Postcolonial Histories.* Princeton: Princeton University Press, 1993.

Chipkin, Ivor. 'Democracy, Cities and Space: South African Conceptions of Local Government.' Masters dissertation, Department of Political Studies, University of the Witwatersrand, Johannesburg, 1997.

—. '"Functional" and "dysfunctional" communities: The making of national citizens.' *Journal of Southern African Studies*, 29(1), March 2003, pp. 62–83.

City of Cape Town. 'Precinct Development Plan.' n.d.

Cohen, Ronald & John Middleton (eds). *From Tribe to Nation in Africa: Studies in Incorporation Process.* Scranton: Chandler, 1970.

Coleman, James S. 'Nationalism in colonial Africa.' *American Political Science Review*, XLVIII, 1954, pp. 404–26.

—. *Nigeria: Background to Nationalism.* Berkeley: University of California Press, 1958.

—. 'Tradition and nationalism in tropical Africa.' In M. Kilson (ed.). *New States in the Modern World.* Cambridge, Mass.: Harvard University Press, 1975, pp. 3–36.

Comaroff, Jean & John Comaroff. 'Nurturing the nation: Aliens, apocalypse and the postcolonial state.' *Journal of Southern African Studies*, 27(3), 2001, pp. 627–51.

—. *Of Revelation and Revolution*, Vol. 1: *Christianity, Colonialism, and Consciousness in South Africa*. Chicago: University of Chicago Press, 1991.

Commission for Africa. *Our Common Interest: An Argument*. London: Penguin, 2005.

Cope, Nicholas. *To Bind the Nation: Solomon Kadinuzulu and Zulu Nationalism, 1913 –1933*. Pietermaritzburg: University of Natal Press, 1993.

Davidson, Apollon, Irina Filatova, Valentin Gorodnov & Sheridan Johns (eds). *South Africa and the Communist International: A Documentary History*, Vol. I. London & Portland: Frank Cass, 2003.

Davies, Robert, David Kaplan, Mike Morris & Dan O'Meara. 'Class struggle and the periodisation of the state in South Africa.' *Review of African Political Economy*, Special Issue on South Africa, 7, September–December 1976, pp. 4–30.

Delius, Peter. 'Migrant organisation, the Communist Party, the ANC and the Sekhukhuneland Revolt, 1940–1958.' In Bonner, Delius & Posel (eds) (1993), pp. 126–59.

Deng, Francis M. *War of Visions: Conflict of Identities in Sudan*. Washington, DC: Brookings Institution, 1995.

Derrida, Jacques. *Politics of Friendship* (trans. George Collins). London & New York: Verso, 1997.

Diamon, Larry & Marc F. Plattner (eds). *Nationalism, Ethnic Conflict, and Democracy*. Baltimore: Johns Hopkins University Press, 1997.

Diop, Cheikh Anta. *Nations Negres et Culture*. Paris: Presence Africaine, 1960.

Donham, Donald. 'Thinking temporally or modernizing anthropology.' *American Anthropologist*, 103(1), 2001, pp. 134–49.

Drew, Alison. *South Africa's Radical Tradition: A Documentary History* , Vol. I. Cape Town: Buchu Books, 1996.

—. *Discordant Comrades: Identities and Loyalties on the South African Left*. Aldershot & Burlington: Ashgate, 2000.

Dubow, Saul. 'Afrikaner nationalism, apartheid and the conceptualisation of "race".' African Studies seminar paper, University of the Witwatersrand, Johannesburg, 1991.

Emerson, Rupert. *From Empire to Nation: The Rise of Self-Assertion of African and Asian Peoples*. Cambridge, Mass.: Harvard University Press, 1960.

European Union. 'The European consensus on development.' Joint statement, European Council & Parliament, 14282/05, sec. 7, 2005.

Fanon, Frantz. *Peau noire, masques blancs.* Paris: Éditions du Seuil, 1952.

Fernandez, James W. 'The affirmation of things past: Alar Ayong and Bwiti as movements of protest in central and northern Gabon.' In Rotberg & Mazrui (eds) (1970), pp. 427–57.

Foster, Joe. 'The workers' struggle – where does FOSATU stand?' In Johann Maree (ed.). *The Independent Trade Unions, 1974–1984: Ten Years of the* South African Labour Bulletin. Johannesburg: Ravan Press, 1987, pp. 218–38.

Foucault, Michel. *Discipline and Punish.* New York: Vintage, 1979.

—. *The History of Sexuality,* Vol. I: *The Will to Knowledge* (trans. Robert Hurley). Harmondsworth: 1998.

Freedom Charter. As adopted at the Congress of the People, 26 June 1955. http://www.anc.org.za/ancdocs/history/charter.html

Friedman, Steven. *Building Tomorrow Today: African Workers in Trade Unions 1970–1985.* Johannesburg: Ravan Press, 1987.

Fung, A. & Erik Olin Wright. *Deepening Democracy: Institutional Innovations in Empowered Participatory Democracy.* The Real Utopias Project IV. London & New York: Verso.

Gaille, Marie. *Le citoyen.* Paris: Flammarion, 1998.

Gellner, Ernest. 'The coming of nationalism and its interpretation: The myths of nation and class.' In Gopal Balakrishnan (ed.). *Mapping the Nation.* London & New York: Verso, 1999, pp. 98–145.

Gerhart, Gail. *Black Power in South Africa.* Berkeley & London: University of California Press, 1979.

Geschiere, Peter. 'Funerals and belonging: Different patterns in south Cameroon.' *African Studies Review,* 48(2), 2005, pp. 45–64.

Gibson, James. *Overcoming Apartheid: Can Truth Reconcile a Divided Nation?* Cape Town: HSRC Press, 2004.

Gilroy, Paul. *After Empire: Melancholia or Convivial Culture?* Oxford: Routledge, 2004.

Glaser, Clive. '"When are they going to fight?" Tsotsis, youth politics, and the PAC.' In Bonner, Delius & Posel (eds) (1993), pp. 296–315.

Greenfeld, Leah. *Nationalism: Five Roads to Modernity*. Cambridge, Mass. & London: Harvard University Press, 1992.

Habermas, Jurgen. *The Postnational Constellation: Political Essays* (trans. & ed. Max Pensky). Cambridge: Polity Press, 2001.

Hameso, Seyoum Y. *Ethnicity and Nationalism in Africa*. Commack: Nova Science, 1997.

Hassim, Shireen. 'Feminism, nationalism and the politics of the women's movement in South Africa.' In *Identities, Interests and Constituencies: The Politics of the Women's Movement in South Africa, 1980–1999*. Doctoral thesis, University of York, forthcoming.

Hastings, Adrian. *The Construction of Nationhood: Ethnicity, Religion and Nationalism*. Cambridge: Cambridge University Press, 1997.

Hegel, G. W. F. *The Philosophy of Right* (trans. S. W. Dyde). Kitchener: Batoche Books, 2001.

Herbst, Jeffrey. *States and Power in Africa*. Princeton: Princeton University Press, 2000.

Hill, Robert A. & Gregory A. Pirio. '"Africa for the Africans": The Garvey movement in South Africa, 1920–1940.' In Marks & Trapido (eds) (1987), pp. 209–53.

Hobsbawm, Eric. *Nations and Nationalism since 1780: Programme, Myth, Reality*. Cambridge: Cambridge University Press, 1999.

Hodgkin, Thomas. *Nationalism in Colonial Africa*, 6th ed. London: Frederick Muller, 1968.

Hroch, Miroslav. *Social Conditions of National Revival in Europe: A Comparative Analysis of the Social Composition of Patriotic Groups among the Smaller European Nations*. Cambridge: Cambridge University Press, 1985.

Huntington, Samuel. 'The clash of civilizations.' *Foreign Affairs*, 72(31993), 1993, pp. 22–49.

—. *The Clash of Civilizations and the Remaking of the World Order*. New York: Touchstone, 1996.

Ingham, K. *Politics in Modern Africa: The Uneven Tribal Dimension*. London: Routledge, 1990.

Ismagilova, R. & A. Kochin (eds). *Ethnocultural Development of African Countries*. Moscow: Academy of Sciences, 1984.

Jackson, R. H. & C. G. Rosberg. *Personal Rule in Black Africa*. Berkeley: University of California Press, 1982.

James, P. 'The Janus faces of history: Cleaving Marxist theories of nation and nationalism.' *Canadian Review of Studies in Nationalism*, 18(1/2), 1991, pp. 13–24.

Jensen, Stefan. *Claiming Community, Negotiating Crime*. Doctoral thesis, Roskilde University, Denmark, 2001.

Johnstone, F. A. *Class, Race and Gold*. London: Routledge & Kegan Paul, 1976.

Joseph, R. *Radical Nationalism in Cameroun: Social Origins of the UPC Rebellion*. Oxford: Clarendon Press, 1977.

Kaplan, R. 'The coming anarchy.' *Atlantic Monthly*, February 1994, pp. 44–76.

Kenyatta, Jomo. *Facing Mount Kenya*. London: Secker & Warburg, 1938.

Kohn, Hans & Wallace Sokolsky. *African Nationalism in the Twentieth Century*. New York & London: Van Nostrand, 1965.

Kymlicka, Will & Wayne Norman. 'Return of the Citizen: A Survey of Recent Work on Citizenship Theory.' *Ethics*, 104(2), January 1994, pp. 352–381.

Laclau, Ernesto. *New Reflections on the Revolution of Our Time*. London & New York: Verso, 1990.

—. *On Populist Reason*. London & New York: Verso, 2005.

— & Chantal Mouffe. *Hegemony and Socialist Strategy: Towards a Radical Democratic Politics*. London & New York: Verso, 1990.

Laitin, David D. *Language Repertoires and State Construction in Africa*. Cambridge: Cambridge University Press, 1992.

Legassick, M. 'Legislation, ideology and economy in post-1948 South Africa.' *Journal of Southern African Studies*, 1(1), 1972, pp. 5–35.

—. 'Gold, agriculture and secondary industry in South Africa, 1885–1970.' In R. Palmer & N. Parsons (eds). *The Roots of Rural Poverty in Central and Southern Africa*. Berkeley: University of California Press, 1977, pp. 201–20.

Lister, Ruth. *Citizenship: Feminist Perspectives*. Basingstoke: Macmillan, 1997.

—. 'Citizens in action: Citizenship and community in a Northern Ireland context.' *Community Development Journal*, 33(3), 1998, pp. 226–35.

Lodge, Tom. *Black Politics in South Africa since 1945*. Johannesburg: Ravan Press, 1983.

Lonsdale, John. 'The moral economy of Mau Mau: The problem.' In Bruce Berman

& John Lonsdale (eds). *Unhappy Valley: Conflict in Kenya and Africa*, Book Two: *Violence & Ethnicity*. London: James Currey, 1992, pp. 265–504.

Luckhardt, K. & B. Wall. *Organize or Starve: The History of the South African Congress of Trade Unions*. London: Lawrence & Wishart, 1980.

Mabogoane, Ashley *et al.* 'The media vs President T. M. Mbeki.' *Sunday Times*, 6 May 2001.

Macey, David. *Frantz Fanon: A Life*. London: Granta Books, 2000.

Makoe, Abbey. 'We need their views, not their ads.' *Saturday Star*, 12 May 2001.

Malherbe, D. F. du T. *Stamregister van die Suid-Afrikaanse Volk*. Stellenbosch: Tegniek, 1966.

Mamdani, Mahmood. *Citizen and Subject: Contemporary Africa and the Legacy of Late Colonialism*. Kampala: Fountain, Cape Town: David Philip & London: James Currey, 1996.

Manenberg ACT (Area Co-ordinating Team). 'Minutes of meetings.' Various dates, 2000–2001.

Manenberg People Centre. *Manenberg Speaks*. September 2002.

Mangcu, Xolela. 'The thought police ignore our history of moral reasoning.' *Sunday Independent*, 13 May 2001, p. 6.

Maquet, Jacques. 'Societal and cultural incorporation in Rwanda.' In Cohen & Middleton (1970).

Marais, Hein. *South Africa: Limits to Change. The Political Economy of Transition*. London & New York: Zed Books & Cape Town: University of Cape Town Press, 1998.

Marks, Shula & Stanley Trapido, *The Politics of Race, Class and Nationalism in Twentieth Century South Africa*. London & New York: Longman, 1987.

Marshall, T. H. *Citizenship and Social Class*. New York: Anchor Books, 1965.

Marx, Anthony W. *Making Race and Nation: A Comparison of the United States, South Africa, and Brazil*. Cambridge: Cambridge University Press, 1998.

Matshikiza, John. 'The new rules of our politics.' *Mail & Guardian*, 17–24 May 2001.

Mayekiso, Mzwanele. *Township Politics: Civic Struggles for a New South Africa*. New York: Monthly Review Press, 1996.

Mazrui, Ali. *Towards a Pax Africana: A Study of Ideology and Ambition*. Chicago: University of Chicago Press, 1967.

— & Alamin M. Mazrui. *The Power of Babel: Language and Governance in the African Experience*. Oxford: James Currey, 1998.

Mbeki, Thabo. 'I Am an African.' In *Africa: The Time Has Come. Selected Speeches*. Cape Town: Tafelberg & Johannesburg: Mafube, 1998, pp. 31–36.

Mbembe, Achille. *On the Postcolony*. Berkeley: University of California Press, 2001.

— & Sarah Nutall. *Johannesburg: The Elusive Metropolis*. *Public Culture*, 16(3), Fall 2004, pp. 347–72.

Meredith, Martin. *The State of Africa: A History of Fifty Years of Independence*. Johannesburg & Cape Town: Jonathan Ball & London, New York, Sydney & Toronto: Free Press, 2005.

Miles, William F. S. *Hausaland Divided: Colonialism and Independence in Nigeria and Niger*. Ithaca: Cornell University Press, 1994.

— & David Rochefort. 'Nationalism versus ethnic identity in Sub-Saharan Africa.' *American Political Science Review*, LXXXV(2), 1991, pp. 393–404.

Minnaar, Anthony (ed.). *Communities in Isolation: Perspectives on Hostels in South Africa*. Pretoria: Human Sciences Research Council, 1993.

Mouffe, Chantal. *The Democratic Paradox*. London & New York: Verso, 2000.

Nakasa, Nat. 'Johannesburg, Johannesburg.' In E. Patel (ed.). *The World of Nat Nakasa*. Johannesburg: Ravan Press, 1975, pp. 21–23.

Nasser, Gamal A. *Egypt's Liberation: The Philosophy of the Revolution*. Washington, DC: Public Affairs Press, 1955.

Nkrumah, Kwame. *Speak of Freedom: A Statement of African Ideology*. London: Heinemann, 1961.

—. *Neo-colonialism: The Last Stage of Imperialism*. London: Nelson, 1965.

Norval, A. & D. Howarth. 'Subjectivity and strategy in South African resistance politics: Prospects for a new imaginary.' *Essex Papers in Politics and Government*, 85. University of Essex, 1992.

Nyerere, Julius K. *Ujamaa: Essays in Socialism*. Oxford: Oxford University Press, 1968.

Oldfield, Sophie. 'Local state restructuring and urban politics in post-apartheid Cape Town.' Paper presented to the Local Politics and Democratisation in Developing Countries Annual Network Conference, University of Oslo, 2002.

— & Kristian Stokke. 'Building unity in diversity: Social movement activism in the Western Cape Anti-Eviction Campaign.' In A. Habib, I. Valodia & R. Ballard (eds). *Globalisation, Marginalisation and New Social Movements*. Durban: University of KwaZulu-Natal Press, forthcoming.

Opoku, Kofi Asare. 'Freeing the spirit: Religion and liberation in Africa.' Paper presented at a conference of the International Sociological Association, 1986.

Republic of South Africa. Ministry of Reconstruction and Development. White Paper on Reconstruction and Development. Cape Town, 1994.

—. Promotion of National Unity and Reconciliation Act, Act 34 of 1995, 26 July 1995.

—. Constitution of the Republic of South Africa, Act 108 of 1996.

Rodney, Walter. *How Europe Underdeveloped Africa*. Washington, DC: Howard University Press, 1972.

Rotberg, Robert & Ali Mazrui (eds). *Protest and Power in Black Africa*. New York: Oxford University Press, 1970.

Roux, Edward. *Time Longer than Rope: A History of the Black Man's Struggle for Freedom in South Africa*. Madison: University of Wisconsin Press, 1964.

SACP (South African Communist Party). *The Road to South African Freedom: Programme of the South African Communist Party*. London: Inkululeko Press, 1962.

—. *The Path to Power*. London: Inkululeko Press, 1989. <http://www.sacp.org.za/index.php?option=com_content&task=category&sectionid=8&id=64&Itemid=67>

—. 'Socialism is the future, build it now: Strategy and tactics of the SACP in the national democratic revolution.' *Bua Komanisi*, 2(3), June 2002.

Said, Edward. *Orientalism: Western Conceptions of the Orient*. London: Penguin, 1978.

Salo, Elaine. 'Negotiating gender and personhood in the new South Africa: Adolescent women and gangsters in Manenberg Township on the Cape Flats.' *European Journal of Cultural Studies*, 6, August 2003, pp. 345–65.

—. *Respectable Mothers, Tough Men and Good Daughters: Making Persons in Manenberg Township, South Africa*. Doctoral thesis, Department of Anthropology, Emory University, Atlanta, 2004.

Sampson, Anthony. 'Foreword.' In Bernstein (1999), pp. ix–xi.

Sandbrook, R. *The Politics of Africa's Economic Stagnation*. Cambridge: Cambridge University Press, 1985.

Saul, John. 'Between "barbarism" and "structural reform".' *New Left Review*, 188, July–August, 1991, pp. 3–44.

Schmitt, Carl. *The Concept of the Political* (trans. George Schwab). Chicago & London: University of Chicago Press, 1996.

Scruton, Roger. *The West and the Rest: Globalization and the Terrorist Threat.* Wilmington: Intercollegiate Studies Institute, 2002.

Segal, Lauren. 'The human face of violence: Hostel dwellers speak.' *Journal of Southern African Studies*, 18(1), 1991, pp. 190–231.

Senghor, Leopold Sedar. *On African Socialism.* New York: Praeger, 1964.

Shaw, Mark. *South Africa's Other War: Understanding and Resolving Political Violence in KwaZulu-Natal (1985) and the PWV (1990).* Doctoral thesis, University of the Witwatersrand, Johannesburg, 1997.

Simone, Abdou-Maliq. 'People as infrastructure: Intersecting fragments in Johannesburg.' *Public Culture*, 16(3), 2004, pp. 407–29.

Sitas, Ari. *African Worker Responses on the East Rand to Changes in South Africa's Metalworks, c1960s–1980s.* Doctoral thesis, University of the Witwatersrand, Johannesburg, 1984.

Sithole, Ndabaningi. *African Nationalism.* Cape Town: Oxford University Press, 1959.

Smith, Anthony D. *State and Nation in the Third World: The Western State and African Nationalism.* New York: St Martin's Press & Brighton: Wheatsheaf Books, 1983.

—. *The Ethnic Origins of Nations.* Oxford: Blackwell, 1986.

—. *Nations and Nationalism in the Global Era.* Cambridge: Polity Press, 1995.

—. 'Structure and persistence of *ethnie.*' In Montserrat Guibernau & John Rex (eds). *The Ethnicity Reader: Nationalism, Multiculturalism and Migration.* Cambridge: Polity Press, 2003, pp. 27–33.

South African Labour Bulletin. 'Interview with the GWU.' *South African Labour Bulletin*, 9(2), November 1983, pp. 47–62.

Suttner, Raymond & Jeremy Cronin. *30 Years of the Freedom Charter.* Johannesburg: Ravan Press, 1986.

Swilling, Mark. 'Socialism, democracy and civil society: The case for associational socialism.' *Theoria*, 79, 1992, pp. 75–82.

—. 'Rival futures: Struggle visions, post-apartheid choice.' In Hilton Judin & Ivan Vladislavic (eds). *Architecture, Apartheid and After.* Rotterdam: NAi, 1998, pp. 285–97.

Szeftel, M. 'Misunderstanding African politics.' *Review of African Political Economy*, 76, 1998, pp. 221–40.

Taylor, Rupert. 'Ethnic division in South Africa? Township conflict on the Reef.' Unpublished paper, University of the Witwatersrand, Johannesburg, 1990.

—. 'The myth of ethnic division.' *Race and Class*, 33(2), 1991, pp 1–14.

Thomas, George. 'South Africa: A Manenberg miracle! Can other gang areas have this miracle too?' *Christian World News*, 24 June 2005.

Thompson, E. P. *The Poverty of Theory*. London: Merlin Press, 1978.

Thompson, Vincent Bakpetu. *African and Unity: The Evolution of Pan-Africanism*. London: Longman, 1969.

Toms, Ivan. 'Draft review of Manenberg ACT.' July 2003.

Toure, Sekou. *Toward Full Reafricanisation*. Paris: Presence Africaine, 1959.

TRC (Truth and Reconciliation Commission). *TRC Final Report*. Cape Town: TRC, 29 October 1998.

Turner, Bryan. 'Postmodern culture/modern citizens.' In Bart van Steenbergen (ed.). *The Condition of Citizenship*. London & New Delhi: Sage, 1994, pp. 153–68.

Tutu, Desmond. *No Future without Forgiveness*. London, Sydney, Auckland & Johannesburg: Rider, 1999.

—. *The Rainbow People of God: A Spiritual Journey from Apartheid to Freedom* (ed. John Allen). Cape Town: Double Storey Books.

Van Diepen, Maria (ed.). *The National Question in South Africa*. London & New Jersey: Zed Books, 1989.

Van Holdt, Karl. *From Resistance to Reconstruction: A Case Study of Trade Unionism in the Workplace and the Community (1980–1996)*. Doctoral thesis, University of the Witwatersrand, Johannesburg, 2000.

Verwoerd, H. F. 'Preface.' In Malherbe (1966), p. v.

Wallerstein, Immanuel. *Africa: The Politics of Independence*. New York: Vintage Books, 1961.

—. *Unthinking Social Science: The Limits of Nineteenth-Century Paradigms*. New York: Polity Press, 1991.

Walshe, Peter. *Black Nationalism in South Africa*. Johannesburg: Ravan Press, 1973.

Weate, Jeremy. 'Achille Mbembe and the postcolony: Going beyond the text.' *Research of African Literatures*, (34)4, Winter 2003, pp. 27–41.

Webster, Eddie. *Cast in a Racial Mould: Labour Process and Trade Unionism in the Foundries.* Johannesburg: Ravan Press, 1985.

—. 'Cosatu: Old alliances, new strategies.' *Southern Africa Report*, 11(3), April 1996. http://www.africafiles.org/article.asp?ID=3884

Welch, Claude E. *Dreams of Unity: Pan-Africanism and Political Unification in West Africa.* Ithaca: Cornell University Press, 1966.

Willan, Brian. *Sol Plaatje: A Biography.* Johannesburg: Ravan Press, 2001.

Wimmer, Andreas. *Nationalist Exclusion and Ethnic Conflict: Shadows of Modernity.* Cambridge: Cambridge University Press, 2002.

Wolpe, Harold. 'Capitalism and cheap labour power: From segregation to apartheid.' *Economy and Society*, 1(4), 1974, pp. 425–56.

—. *Race, Class and the Apartheid State.* London: James Currey, 1988.

Young, Crawford. 'Nationalism, ethnicity, and class in Africa: A retrospective.' *Cahiers d'etudes africaines*, 103(XXVI-3), 1986, pp. 421–95.

—. *The African Colonial State in Comparative Perspective.* New Haven: Yale University Press, 1994a.

—. 'Evolving modes of consciousness and ideology: Nationalism and ethnicity.' In Carl G. Rosberg & David E. Alter (eds). *Political Development and the New Resistance in Sub-Saharan Africa.* Richmond: University of Virginia Press, 1994b.

— (ed.). *The Rising Tide of Cultural Pluralism: The Nation-State at Bay?* Madison: University of Wisconsin Press, 1998.

—. 'Nationalism and ethnic conflict in Africa.' In John H. M. Guiberney (ed.). *Understanding Nationalism.* Oxford: Oxford University Press, 2001, pp. 164–81.

—. 'The end of the post-colonial state in Africa? Reflections on changing African political dynamics.' *African Affairs*, 103(410), January 2004, pp. 23–49.

— & Thomas Turner. *The Rise and Fall of the Zairian State.* Madison: University of Wisconsin Press, 1985.

Yuval-Davis, Nira. *Gender and Nation.* London & New Delhi: Sage, 1997.

Zizek, Slavoj. *The Sublime Object of Ideology.* London & New York: Verso, 1992.

—. *The Ticklish Subject: The Absent Centre of Political Ontology.* London & New York: Verso, 2000.

Zulu, Paulus. 'Durban hostels and political violence: Case studies in KwaMashu and Umlazi.' *Transformation*, 21, 1993, pp. 1–12.

Index

Printed and bound by CPI Group (UK) Ltd, Croydon, CR0 4YY

09/06/2025

14685804-0001